CHANGE IS POSSIBLE
STORIES OF WOMEN AND MINORITIES
IN MATHEMATICS

PATRICIA CLARK KENSCHAFT

D1119592

AMERICAN MATHEMATICAL SOCIETY

2000 *Mathematics Subject Classification.* Primary 01A80; Secondary 01A70, 01A99.

The cover photos are of Susan Cunningham (pages 33-35) who was one of the original members of the American Mathematical Society in 1891 as a professor of mathematics and astronomy at Swarthmore College. During the author's college years there, a very large portrait of Cunningham, in academic robes, hung in a public area where students passed daily. Seeing a photograph of the young Susan Cunningham in the author's mature years was a startling reminder of how individuals change, a reflection of the potential for further change in society.

Cover photos courtesy of Friends Historical Library of Swarthmore College, Christopher Densmore, archivist.

For additional information and updates on this book, visit
www.ams.org/bookpages/change

Library of Congress Cataloging-in-Publication Data
Kenschaft, Patricia Clark
    Change is possible : stories of women and minorities in mathematics / Patricia Clark Kenschaft.
      p. cm.
    ISBN 0-8218-3748-6 (acid-free paper)
    1. Mathematics–Vocational guidance–United States–History–20th century. 2. Women in mathematics–United States–History–20th century. 3. Minorities in mathematics–United States–History–20th century. 4. Mathematicians–United States–History–20th century. 5. Mathematicians–United States–Biography. 6. Kenschaft, Patricia C. I. Title.

QA10.5.K46   2005
510′.82–dc22
                                        2005048105

CHANGE IS POSSIBLE
STORIES OF WOMEN AND MINORITIES
IN MATHEMATICS

Contents

Acknowledgments

Every book owes its existence to a variety of people, but it is dizzying to contemplate the many people who have contributed significantly to this one. A logical place start might be to express my gratitude to Donald Saari. At the Association for Women in Mathematics party in August 2003 in Boulder, Colorado, Don told me how much he had enjoyed reading my articles. Then he brightened. Why not write an entire book about "stories" of women and minorities in mathematics? I liked the idea, but wondered at its practicality.

At that time Donald Saari was one of two nominees for president of the American Mathematical Society, and before long I received a phone call from Sergei Gelfand, an editor at the American Mathematical Society, asking if I would be interested in writing such a book. Interested?!! I interrupted some other projects, and have enjoyed working with Sergei ever since. His patience, vision, and good humor as a mathematics editor suddenly finding himself shepherding a history-sociology book has been remarkable and delightful.

An equally logical beginning would be to thank my parents, the late John Randolph Clark and Bertha Francis Clark. Both had been chemistry majors, and they encouraged my interest in science and mathematics at a very young age. They shared with me stories of people, especially scientists, and my mother read me the *Child's History of the World* when I was seven. My late uncle George Clark, professor of philosophy at Lafayette College, gave me math books at every opportunity during my adolescence. The second most memorable (second to George Polya's *How to Solve It*) was Edna Kramer's *The Main Stream of Mathematics* with its silent message that a woman could write about mathematics and mathematicians — even about women mathematicians. More recently, my younger brother Roger Clark, professor of sociology at Rhode Island College, has mentored me in sociological research and writing. My husband, Fred Chichester, has been a remarkable companion not only in exploring mathematical, sociological and activist ideas together, but also in the more practical matters of doing all the shopping and laundry and in providing transportation and protection as my body became less reliable. (See pages 165–167.)

My creative writing teacher at Nutley High School, the late Maxine Hoffer, graded a 250-word essay every evening for the first semester (for 80 days!) and a 2000-word composition every week during the second semester. Although she was also teaching five other classes, she returned the essays routinely on the next day with thoughtful comments. How could a teacher care so much that students learn to write? I have also had many excellent mathematics teachers and professors, too many to name.

When I attended my first national mathematics meeting in the summer of 1977, Lee Lorch adopted me as his protégé. For years his conversations, letters, and telephone calls entertained and informed me. Our times together were always delightful and inspiring. In recent years our email relationship has been animated, never more so than when I was writing this book. His touch is in almost every chapter, and I am grateful.

Scott Williams came to one of my early talks about black mathematicians, and afterward pleasantly informed me of some omissions, pointing me in new directions. Since then we have stayed in touch, and his guiding wisdom has been continual in the evolution of this book. His website about Mathematicians of the African Diaspora (http://www.math.buffalo.edu/mad) is an abundant source of further information for those intrigued by the stories of this book.

Many Latino mathematicians have helped my exploration into their group, especially Luis Ortiz-Franco and William Vélez. Most of the living subjects of the book have been generous in sharing their time and wisdom. Along with Lee, Scott, Luis, and Bill, these include David Blackwell, Gloria Conyers Hewitt, Lida Kettrell Barrett, Abdulalim Shabazz, Cleopatria Martinez, Richard Tapia, Manuel Barriobázal, Mary Gray, Alice Schafer, Bettye Anne Case, Anne Leggett McDonald, Sue Geller, David Sadker, Barbara Keyfitz, Carolyn Gordon, Catherine Roberts, Helen Moore, William Massey, Trachette Jackson, and Fern Hunt. Cathleen Morawetz, Mary Ellen Rudin, and Jonathan Farley have helped by checking facts and providing photos. Cecil McAfee told me much about his mother and sent a photo. David C. Gilbreth sent a photo of his grandmother. I hereby thank the following archivists: Christopher Denmore at Swarthmore College, Barbara Ward Grubb and Gertrude Reed at Bryn Mawr College, Sydney Roby at Goucher College, Dean M. Rogers at Vassar College, Patrick Collum and Heather Morgan at the American Catholic University, Joellen Elbashir at Howard University, Helena Vargas at Rice University, Debora Pfeiffer at the University of Illinois, and Christopher Prossel at the Mathematical Association of America.

And then the lists! I appreciate the email correspondence with all nine founders of the Association for Women in Mathematics and the various mathematicians who acted in the skits performed at the national Mathematics Meetings. Making a list of current Latino mathematicians in the Southwest would have been impossible without the cooperation of many people, including those on the list and many others, both Latino and not.

Judy Green and Jeanne LaDuke provided not only their abundant research, but answers to specific questions. Ronald Mickens gave insight into Bouchet and raised other interesting ideas. Sally Anderson's professional editorial expertise during the final stages has not only corrected the minor errors and inconsistencies of punctuation and similar items, but has also greatly improved my writing. I have accepted a majority of her rewrites, and most of the others have inspired me to find an even better way of expressing the idea than my first try or her suggested revision. It has been great fun to work with Sally again, thirty years after our collaboration on two mathematics texts.

I have drawn extensively from Betsey Whitman's research about nineteenth century women mathematicians, and also from her ongoing encouragement and suggestions. She recently retired from serving as chair of the mathematics department of Framingham State, Massachusetts, and now enjoys teaching occasionally in Taipei, Taiwan, and Malawi, Africa as well as at Framingham State. She is working on a book on Mary Winston Newson, and her contacts with the family enabled me to acquire a photograph.

Lori Kenschaft, who has taught courses on equity issues in education and the history of higher education at the Harvard Graduate School of Education, has been a great resource for her mother. Her own books are about outstanding nineteenth century women: *Lydia Maria Child: the Quest for Racial Justice*, published in 2002 by Oxford University Press and *Reinventing Marriage: the Love and Work of Alice Freeman Palmer and George Herbert Palmer*, who married in 1887, published in 2005 by the University of Illinois Press. It was a mind-boggling experience to be tutored in historical research and writing by one whose first cry I remember so clearly. But it is symbolic of the theme that change is indeed possible — and also of the generosity of so many people who contributed to this book.

Finally, Claudia Zaslavsky has read the entire manuscript from beginning to end twice, and many parts more than that. Her editing is truly incredible. She not only catches typos and more serious goofs, but she has an amazing knack for rewriting sentences so that they say what I mean instead of what I originally wrote. A retired high school mathematics teacher, Claudia has written thirteen books, eight of which are still in print. A complete list can be obtained by googling her name. Her first was *Africa Counts*, based on her first-hand research in Africa about the mathematics used there. Its third edition was published by Lawrence Hill Books, Chicago, in 1999. Three children's math activity books were published by Chicago Review Press in 1998, 2001, and 2003, respectively. Claudia, like Lee Lorch, is almost the age of my parents, and, like him, she reached out to nurture me from my early adulthood. I have been incredibly fortunate to have someone with her talent and dedication to edit my work.

I am grateful to and awed by these people who have given me so much. I am humbled by their trust, and I hope that readers will forgive the remaining mistakes of commission, which are always the responsibility of the author. Personally, I am even more concerned about the omissions, especially the worthy people whose stories I have omitted. May they forgive me. However, I hope others will continue to add to my themes and stories, so that this endeavor is only one piece of a much-needed discussion.

CHAPTER 1

Introduction

"We hired a woman in our department fifty years ago, but her students had trouble getting jobs. I don't see why we should make that mistake again!" So said a leading retired mathematician at the business meeting of the American Mathematical Society in January 1990.[1] By then, it was shocking to hear such sentiments expressed publicly, but apparently he felt he could say it — and he clearly believed it.

"Have things changed? No, I mean *really* changed?" We hear these question repeatedly, prompted by such incidents. When stories from the past seem ancient and quaint, we realize that others' efforts *have* made change. From this we gather hope for the future both in our own and other cultures.

Change is difficult. Changing oneself, by adapting to a challenging job, a new home or a restricted diet are all acknowledged to be difficult. Changing society might well be even more difficult. Little wonder that we hear so often, "But I am only one person!" Kevin Danaher[2] responds to that, "Pleased to meet you. I'm Siamese twins." Change will happen only if some people believe it can. Changing a culture is not a quick process, but it can happen if such people find ways to make their own individual contributions. Knowing the past helps. This book is dedicated to those in the present and future who will strive to change our society toward one that provides a satisfying life for all.

This book contains *stories* of mathematicians who have bucked the social climate of their time. It tells about women and men, both whites and people of color who believing that society could change, struggled for a better life for themselves and for others. None of us lives alone, and we do affect others.

This account does not pretend to be a traditional history. The writer is a professor of mathematics with a doctoral dissertation in "C^*-algebras over S^n" from the University of Pennsylvania. However, I am writing about mathematicians — about the people, not about the mathematics they did.

Admittedly, one of my minors at Swarthmore College was English and I like to spin yarns. The stories in this book are true as far as I can tell, but I

---

[1] Patricia Clark Kenschaft, "Chronicle of the Committee on Participation of Women," in *Winning Women into Mathematics*, Kenschaft and Keith, editors, MAA, Washington, DC, 1991, p. 9.

[2] Co-founder of Global Exchange, a change-making organization that promotes international communication.

cannot vouch for their statistical validity. Nor can I guess how different they would be from stories in another intellectual endeavor. It's a platitude that history is written by the victors, and I would add that it also tends to be *about* the victors. We can only guess at the innumerable unnamed women and men who yearned to delve deeper into mathematics and were not able to hurdle the economic, social, and structural obstacles they encountered.

Unlike mathematics, there are no proofs in history or sociology. I write as a mathematician with no pretense of being an "outside observer." I am involved in these stories, and my own stories will occasionally surface. The stories primarily reflect life in the United States, with only an occasional glimpse beyond its borders.

As a woman, my interest in these topics grew out of an eagerness to know my own roots. However, just as my own interests soon expanded, stories of "minority" mathematicians appear in almost every chapter of this book, because minorities pervade the history of mathematics. In some sense, of course, we are all minorities; nowhere is this more true than in the United States. As we welcome new waves of immigrants, each previous wave retains less of its "majority" status.

In the spirit of full disclosure, I admit to some known biases at the beginning. It is my impression that over the past 150 years it has become easier for women and minorities to study mathematics. The trend has not been monotonic, and it is likely to be only asymptotic to equity. We still have a long way to go. However, there are many variables in any life — or any society — and it is hard to isolate one, such as the role of gender or ethnicity. While it is my impression that sexism and racism have gradually decreased, I can speak with more conviction about the former than the latter.

One story from my own youth influences my impression of "progress." When I was four months pregnant with my first child, my husband took a job in a state that was new to us. That summer when my mother was visiting, she suggested we go for a ride. Casually, she then found herself nearing the campus of a nice liberal arts college. "Let's see if we can find the math department and see if they have a job for you next fall." I gulped, but couldn't deny that I had no more pressing plans for the near future. Deftly, she found the math department and suggested I go in and see if the chair were there. He was. I explained that my baby wasn't due until the end of January.

"Yes, I do need someone to teach Calculus 1. I think it's good to have a woman in the department and Helen is on sabbatical this year. Yes, you're hired." My triumphant mother, waiting in the car, smiled as mothers do when they know they've done a good deed.

Two days later my phone rang. It was the aforementioned department chair. "A young man just stopped in my office. He really *needs* a job, so I gave him yours. I'm sure you understand." Would that story have happened in the twenty-first century? I believe there have been changes.

Another bias I bring is my belief that there have always been many good men in mathematics, a higher proportion than in the general public. I myself never had a woman math teacher in high school, college, or graduate school, and I can't *remember* any discrimination on the basis of my sex. Since human memory is admittedly shaky, this does not imply I was never the victim of *any* sex discrimination during my mathematical studies, but it suggests that gender wasn't a major factor in my own math classroom experiences.

Surely there was nothing in my own education as memorable as the admonition of one of my daughter's middle school teachers in 1978 to a boy who insisted he needed help with a particular math problem. "If you can't do a problem as easy as that, you should be sitting on the girls' side of the room!" My daughter and I conferred at length, and decided to give her teacher an anonymous membership in the Association for Women in Mathematics. After a few copies of the AWM newsletter had arrived in his school mailbox, his behavior changed remarkably, and he even began giving speeches in math classes about the need to be fair to girls! This reflects another bias I bring to this writing: I believe many people do what they do because they don't *understand*, but they are educable. Some people are more educable than others.

An unwilling, almost unwitting bias may arise from the fact that I am a married woman with two (adult) children. A pre-publication reviewer claimed that the book suggests that marriage with children is the only good lifestyle; if this is so, I am very sorry in both the "regret" and the "apology" senses of the word. However, for centuries marriage and family life have been used as an excuse to discriminate against women. That they are merely an excuse needs to be emphasized — over and over — until most people believe that both women and men can be both domestically comfortable and professionally successful. Alas, the expectation has been that women must sacrifice marriage, parenthood, and even a dating life if they were to be worthy of the professional opportunities routinely allowed to men with similar aspirations and talents. I believe that both women and men, both straight and gay, should be able to choose the family style she or he prefers without feeling pressured to sacrifice family for vocation or vice versa. It has been my privilege to show how many mathematicians, of both sexes, have put their energies into both family and profession satisfactorily.

An undeniable bias I bring to this writing is my conviction that a wider knowledge of mathematics by many people at many levels is crucial for the survival of the human race — and I desperately want my species to continue for a long time. When I was young, I spent much of my non-mathematical time working for gender and racial equity. During the past decade, that time has been largely spent on environmental issues. When the ship is sinking, it depends little what deck you are on.

However, in the Conversations on the Environment that I led at the Summer 2003 MathFest it became clear that all roads to human survival involve reducing the human population on this planet. The correlation between education for women and lower birth rates is beginning to be noted even in the popular press. What more effective way to preserve the habitability of our planet than to encourage girls and women to enjoy mathematics? Math takes few resources and provides great pleasure.

There is nothing more damaging to the environment than war. What better way to promote peace than to foster mathematical pursuits and camaraderie among all ethnicities? The bonding of the mathematics research community worldwide is truly inspiring. Perhaps it can serve as a model for people to build relationships across many divides, based on common interests and goals.

Furthermore, the more I study a variety of environmental issues, the more I am convinced that knowing and using many fields of mathematics by many people may be a necessary condition for human survival — although it is clearly not a sufficient condition.[3]

The person who suggested I write this account wanted a record of women and minorities who were not at the Emmy Noether level, but had credible careers in mathematics. (Emmy Noether (1882–1935) developed modern algebra. Albert Einstein said in his obituary of her in the *New York Times* that she was the greatest mathematician her sex had produced.) Emmy Noether and Olga Tausky Todd (1906–1996), a student of Noether's who was a leading American mathematician, for example, are completely missing from this book; I do not pretend to have a rationale for choosing those I did include. All mathematicians are considered "successful" by the general public. Even those at the bottom of the mathematical pecking order have jumped through formidable hoops, and most have enviable careers and at least adequate personal lives. Thus I confess to another bias: mathematicians as a group are a fine lot, and I wish there were more of us! Let's reflect upon a fascinating heritage.

---

[3]For examples, see *Mathematics for Human Survival* by Patricia C. Kenschaft, Whittier Publications, Inc., Island Park, NY, 2002 and *Environmental Mathematics*, edited by Ben Fusaro, Mathematical Association of America, Washington, DC, 2003.

CHAPTER 2

With the Help of Good White Men

One of the best-kept secrets about the mathematical communities is the remarkable number of fair, kind men among those who love mathematics. It is one of the ironies of our culture that mathematics has a reputation for being inhospitable to women. Quite the opposite is true! As we shall see the first doctorate granted to a woman in the nineteenth century was in mathematics. This woman, Sofia Kovalevskaia later became the first woman in the nineteenth century to become a university professor. The first doctorate earned by an American woman, Christine Ladd-Franklin, was in mathematics — with the help of a fellowship from her department! David Blackwell, the first black to be inducted into the National Academy of Sciences, was a mathematician (after earlier well-qualified black scientists in other fields had been bypassed). He was also the first black ever to be allowed as a student or professional on the Princeton campus, with the mathematicians at the Institute for Advanced Study fighting the senior administration for Blackwell's right to participate in the Institute on that campus.

I suspect the myth that math is especially hostile to women arises from the challenge that math poses to anyone. To do mathematics, you *must* have some protected time to think alone, and you are much better off if you have someone to talk with. Both alone time and quiet conversation have been in short supply for the sex that has traditionally been expected to prepare the food, clean the house, and raise the children — and for most other people as well. Even in the late twentieth century a research mathematician is fortunate if a hundred people read his or her papers. Earlier, companionship was even harder to come by. The joys of email, commercial airlines, and inexpensive telephones were not available in the youth of many of those still alive today. Too many people have not had a community of mathematical joy in which to be nurtured — but this has been especially true of women and minorities.

Let's look briefly at the lives of the three people already mentioned in the first paragraph, namely, those of Sofia Kovalevskaia, Christine Ladd-Franklin, and David Blackwell, and then at Julia Robinson, the first woman mathematician to be elected to the National Academy of Sciences and to the presidency of the American Mathematical Society. This chapter concludes with the remarkable story of the fifth American black woman to receive a doctorate in mathematics, Gloria Conyers Hewitt.

Sofia Kovalevskaia (1850-1891) was born into the rural gentry in Russia in 1850, and was much impressed with the freeing of the serfs when she was thirteen. Her bedroom was papered with mathematical formulas that she tried to figure out, and her uncles tutored her in mathematics. Hardly a typical girlhood! When she was eighteen, she entered into a "fictitious marriage." Rebellious young Russians of that time would pretend to fall in love, get married, but not consummate the marriage so that they could pursue their educations and social activism free from parental supervision. (Under Czarist law, the woman then ceased to be the property of her parents and became the property of her husband.) Following their wedding, Vladimir Kovalevskii took his bride to western Europe, where they separated. Sofia Kovalevskaia convinced Karl Weierstrauss (1815-1897) to tutor her in mathematics, after he was unsuccessful in persuading the faculty senate of the University of Berlin to admit her to the regular program.[1] Her letters to her husband began, " Dearest Brother."

After seven years of this lifestyle both Sofia and Vladimir had earned doctorates. Hers, from the University of Göttingen *summa cum laude* in 1874,[2] was the first granted to a woman in the nineteenth century. She wrote three papers, any one of which might have been a dissertation. According to Charles Hermite in 1889, one paper "is now regarded as the first significant result in the general theory of partial differential equations."[3] The couple decided to return to Russia and please their parents by having a "real" marriage and a family. Their daughter was born in 1878, ten years after their wedding. However, Vladimir Kovalevskii was too non-conformist to fit into nineteenth century Russian society. After several business failures, he committed suicide.

Sofia Kovalevskaia was now in the most employable condition for a nineteenth century woman: a widow. Male mathematicians began searching on her behalf, and Gosta Mittag-Leffler (1846-1927), another Weierstrauss student acting on Weierstrauss' advice, obtained a job for her at the four-year-old Stockholm University. She thereby became in 1883 the first woman university professor in nineteenth century Europe. The first year there she received no salary, but merely payments from students. Twelve students signed up for her course, but for her first lecture the hall was full — with students, professors, and ordinary citizens. At the end there was applause. Quite remarkable for someone who had learned Swedish a few months earlier and who had never been allowed to attend classes herself![4]

The following year Kovalevskaia became the equivalent of an assistant professor with a small salary, after considerable politicking by Mittag-Leffler.

---

[1]Koblitz, Ann Hibner, *A Convergence of Lives, Sofia Kovalevskaia: Scientist, Writer, Revolutionary*, Birkhäuser, Boston, 1983, p. 101.

[2]ibid, p. 123.

[3]ibid, p. 122.

[4]ibid, p. 182.

Sofia Kovalevskaia and her friend Anna Carlotta Leffler. During her lifetime, Leffler's writings were compared to those of Ibsen and Strindberg. The two women in this photo had a strong influence on each other and wrote two plays together. Photo courtesy of Ann Hibner Koblitz.

In 1888 she won the cherished Prix Bordin of the French Academy of Sciences, whose winner was chosen from essays written without accompanying names, which meant the judges did not know they were choosing a woman. Its financial reward was increased because of the outstanding quality of her paper. She was, naturally, ecstatic about the prize. She became involved in even more exciting research, and also serious writing. Alas, she died suddenly and perhaps needlessly three years later, less than a month after her 41st birthday. She had developed a cold in "late January" while traveling home from her Christmas holiday in southern France. Ignoring her health, she worked intensely on mathematics with leading mathematicians in Paris and Berlin, and then switched trains in the middle of the night while crossing Denmark. Despite feeling seriously ill, she worked non-stop on Thursday, her first day back in Stockholm, and gave her scheduled lecture on Friday, February 6. By Saturday she was bedridden, and early on

Tuesday morning, February 10, 1891, she died, apparently of pneumonia or pleurisy.[5] Her daughter, who was twelve at the time she was orphaned, later became a physician; as an adult in the U.S.S.R. she lectured widely about her mother's life. Several complete biographies have been written about Sofia Kovalevskaia's dramatic life. My favorite is that of Ann Hibner Koblitz, who read her letters in the original Russian but whose native language is English.[6]

The United States did not have many research mathematicians in 1876, when Johns Hopkins University opened. The mathematics department convinced James J. Sylvester (1814-1897), a published British mathematician who had had serious career difficulties in England because he was Jewish, to cross the Atlantic. Hiring a Jew, even one as mathematically accomplished as Sylvester, was an unusual statement on behalf of equity. Accepting a woman among their first graduate students was downright daring.

Christine Ladd-Franklin (1847-1930) was already 31 years old in 1878, but as a graduate of Vassar and a teacher, she had contributed to the Mathematical Questions section of the London-based *Educational Times* and to a new American journal, *The Analyst*. When she applied to Johns Hopkins in 1878, Sylvester, who knew some of her mathematical work, urged that she be admitted and that she be granted a fellowship. The all-male mathematics faculty agreed.[7]

In the next four years Christine Ladd made further contributions to the *Educational Times* and *The Analyst* and contributed three papers to the *American Journal of Mathematics*, which Sylvester had started at about the time of her arrival at Hopkins. She also wrote a dissertation on "The Algebra of Logic" under C. S. Peirce. In 1882 the mathematics department determined that she had completed the requirements for the Ph.D. degree. That wasn't good enough for the Board of Trustees; *solely* on the grounds of her sex, they refused to grant her the degree she had earned. In 1926 she was finally granted the Ph.D. by Johns Hopkins.

Not having the doctorate did not ruin Christine Ladd-Franklin's life. She married one of the members of the Hopkins mathematics department, Fabian Franklin, had a daughter who later became an active suffragette, did research in the mathematics of color perception, and taught occasionally at Columbia University.

---

[5] ibid, p. 232-236.

[6] Two others that should be mentioned are *Love and Mathematics: Sofya Kovalevskaya*, by Pelageya Kochina, translated by Michael Burov, Mir Publishers, Moscow, 1985, and Kovalevskaia's own autobiography, *Sofya Kovalevskaya: A Russian Childhood*, translated and introduced by Beatrice Stillman, Springer-Verlag, New York, 1978.

[7] Judy Green and Jeanne LaDuke, "Women in the American Mathematical Community: The Pre-1940 Ph.D.'s," *The Mathematical Intelligencer*, 9:1, 1987, p. 13.

Christine Ladd-Franklin c. 1909. Photo courtesy of the Ferdinand Hamburger Archives of The Johns Hopkins University, James Stimpert, archivist.

James Joseph Sylvester (1814-1897) was a Jew whose entry into the most prestigious mathematical circles was thwarted by his religion. Although he placed second in Cambridge University's prestigious Tripos examinations in 1837, he was unable to receive a degree because he would not sign an oath of allegiance to the Church of England. After two years teaching science at the University of London, he went to Trinity College in Dublin, where he was awarded both the B.A. and M.A. degrees that Cambridge would not grant to Jews.

He then crossed the Atlantic Ocean in 1841 to accept an appointment at the University of Virginia. The Richmond newspapers opposed the hiring of a Jewish foreigner and made their opinions clear and widespread. The students, however, lighted the arches of the campus with flares to greet him, and he responded with an address that was apparently well received. "He entered into his duties with enthusiasm, directing the work of about four dozen students in arithmetic, geometry, and the calculus."[8]

He was quickly disillusioned, however, with the insolence of the prevailing student culture. Earlier in the century there had been appalling violence on campuses including arson, and beating up of tutors and faculty members, especially by Southern students. In one case a faculty member at the University of Virginia had been murdered by a group of students. Student rebellion from authority was rampant. By the 1830s they had "won" in the sense of establishing fraternities and sports programs on campuses as a structured outlet for their belligerent tendencies.[9]

At least one student, W. H. Ballard from Louisiana, did not welcome Sylvester. Sylvester's first-person account of their culminating confrontation, carefully preserved in the minutes of a faculty meeting on February 23, 1842, raises issues still alive a century and a half later. Was this more than a personality conflict?

> "He engaged (to all appearance) in reading some book, held beneath the desk during the lecture, at all events paying no attention....
>
> "On being called up after the lecture and privately recommended to pay more attention in the future, he answered (still with increased violence of demeanor and tone) that he understood the subject — could follow the lecture without looking at me and had not his spectacles.
>
> "On this as he was leaving it occurred to me to recommend him to bring them with him in the future. Hereupon he answered in a very violent tone, manner and language, but the exact words I do not remember. It is proper to observe that Mr. Ballard's mode of addressing me has been almost uniformly marked with insolence and defiance.
>
> "I then felt it right to state that such conduct must not be persisted in and that if Mr. Ballard could not alter his conduct he must cease to attend my lecture room.
>
> "On this he answered with increased insolence and violence — but I cannot recall the terms employed. I answered that I had been in different parts of the world, but

---

[8]R. C. Yates, "Sylvester at the University of Virginia," *The American Mathematical Monthly*, 44:4, April 1937, pp. 194-201, p. 197.

[9]Lori Kenschaft, personal telephone conversation, July 15, 2004. She suggests "The Rights of Man and the Rites of Youth: Fraternity and Riot at Eighteenth Century Harvard," by Leon Jackson in *The American College in the Nineteenth Century*, Roger L. Geiger, Ed., Nashville, Vanderbilt University Press, 2000, and *The Rights of Youth: American Colleges and Student Revolt*, 1798-1815 by Steven J. Novak, Cambridge, Harvard University Press, 1977.

had never witnessed similar conduct in persons brought up amongst gentlemen.

"To this he replied that 'I was not to prate to him, to hold my jaw, that I might go to hell' — and other abusive terms which I cannot recall.

"I declined altercation with him and ordered him to leave the room, which he declared he would not do.... Before my leaving Mr. Ballard was guilty of additional abusive language."

The account continues with other incidents, reported in less detail. There were ten men on the faculty at that time, and the group decided to take no action. One of them, a Catholic who had received similar negative comments from the press, asked not to be included in the vote. The situation was revisited several times in the next month, but without satisfaction for Sylvester. In March of 1842, after only four months on the campus, he submitted his resignation. It was promptly accepted, and he left.

He spent the next year in New York living with a brother and "trying desperately to find work either as a teacher or an actuary." Columbia University did not accept his application. According to one archived letter, his strong desire to stay in this country was motivated by romance.[10]

Finally, he did return to England and became an actuary there. At this time he also tutored **Florence Nightingale** (1820-1910) in mathematics. She had written, "A British home is like a prison," but she managed to break out, as is well known, during the Crimean War from 1854 to 1856. Less well known are the records she kept at that time and the imaginative graphs that she made. She used her mathematical understanding, developed partially under Sylvester, to make graphs that convinced the British Parliament that military deaths from non-combatant causes such as hunger, cold, and disease were vastly greater than from actual battle, and she succeeded in persuading them to provide for the men's welfare in ways that preserved many lives. Later in life she used similar techniques to address cholera and other massive outbreaks.[11] Her use of quantitative methods and graphs to make convincing social arguments was similar to the "women's work" of nascent United States sociology described in the following chapter.

During this time J. J. Sylvester also studied law, and in 1850 he met another lawyer with a passionate interest in mathematics, Arthur Cayley (1821-1895). Together they did ground-breaking research in linear transformations. In 1863 Cayley became the Sadlerian professor of pure mathematics at Cambridge University, but Jews could not join Cambridge faculty. Sylvester was able to become a professor of mathematics at the Royal Academy in Wolwich in 1856, but he was forced to retire in 1870, ostensibly because of his age, which was 56. Then the Academy tried to deny him part

---

[10]Yates, p. 201.

[11]Edwin W. Kopek, *Journal of the American Statistical Association*, 1916.

of his pension, but letters to the editor in the *London Times* and a lead article there helped him obtain his full pension.[12]

James Joseph Sylvester c. 1880. Photo courtesy of the Ferdinand Hamburger Archives of The Johns Hopkins University Archives, James Stimpert, archivist.

In 1876, at the age of sixty-two, he came to the United States again, this time for a much better experience than his youthful sojourn, as part of the initial faculty at Johns Hopkins University. He soon established the *American Journal of Mathematics* and served as its editor for its first five years. In 1904 AMS founder Thomas Fiske said in a speech honoring the Society's tenth anniversary, "With the arrival of Professor Sylvester at Baltimore and the establishment of the *American Journal of Mathematics* began the systematic encouragement of mathematical research in America."[13] As

[12]Kaila Katz and Patricia Kenschaft, "Sylvester and Scott," *The Mathematics Teacher*, 75:6, September, 1982, pp. 490-494, p. 491.
[13]ibid, 491.

mentioned earlier, Sylvester played a crucial role in the acceptance of Christine Ladd-Franklin into the Hopkins mathematics department in 1878, with a fellowship. He left Hopkins in 1883 to become the Savilian Professor of Geometry at Oxford University, finally at the age of 69 to receive a British appointment appropriate to his gifts. He continued his mathematical research for another fourteen years until his death, but ill health forced him to retire when he was 79.

Julia Robinson (1919-1985) is warmly remembered by women and men mathematicians of my generation. She was friendly and kind and we were delighted to have her elected to be the first woman president of the American Mathematical Society. Much has been written about her; the book *Julia: A Life in Mathematics* by her sister Constance Reid is charming.[14] However, talented and diligent as she was, her success could not have been accomplished without several good men. Two major mentors of Julia Robinson were the logician Alfred Tarski (1902-1983), her thesis advisor, and the statistician Jerzy Neyman (1894-1981), who provided her employment and encouragement. Her outstanding mentor, however, was one of her freshman-year instructors, Raphael Robinson, who became her husband in 1941. She wrote, "I doubt I would have become a mathematician if it hadn't been for Raphael. He taught me and has continued to teach me, has encouraged me, and has supported me in many ways, including financially."[15]

When her physician told her she could not have children, Raphael did not believe she had become a wifely failure. "For a long time I was deeply depressed by the fact that we could not have children. Finally, Raphael reminded me that there was still mathematics."[16] He pulled her out of her doldrums by giving her a fascinating and difficult math problem, and suggesting she lose herself in it. She solved (almost!) one of Hilbert's famous problems (the Tenth) posed at the 1900 International Congress of Mathematicians.

True, she was not able to get a permanent professional position for many years because of the "nepotism rules" of the mid-twentieth century. These said that close relatives could not have the same academic employer. The justification was to keep family favoritism at bay, but the primary consequence was to keep highly qualified wives from obtaining employment near their (also highly qualified) husbands. However, Raphael Robinson was a fair and kind husband, and his wife's life was a good one. She did some adjunct teaching at the University of California at Berkeley, was deeply involved in the movement for racial equity, and did amazing mathematical research. It is said that the nearby faculty were surprised when she was elected to the National Academy of Sciences in 1976. Shortly thereafter

---

[14]Constance Reid, *Julia, A Life in Mathematics*, Mathematical Association of America, 1996.

[15]ibid, p. 39.

[16]ibid, p. 45.

the Berkeley department chair John L. Kelley insisted successfully that she be given a regular job at the university. (Kelley had been restored to his own position there several years after being dismissed for refusing to sign a loyalty oath.[17])

Julia Robinson some time after the heart surgery in 1961 that enabled her to enjoy, for the first time, hiking, canoeing, and biking. She said in her "autobiography," written by her sister Constance Reid, "One month after the operation I bought my first bicycle. It has been followed by a half a dozen increasingly better bikes and many cycling trips in this country and in Holland. Raphael sometimes complains that while other men's wives buy fur coats and diamond bracelets, his wife buys bicycles." (Page 69 of *Julia, A Life in Mathematics*, by Constance Reid.) Photo courtesy of Constance Reid.

Meanwhile, every year when she blew out the candles of her birthday cake, she wished that Hilbert's Tenth problem would be completely solved

---

[17]Lee Lorch, personal email July 22, 2004.

before she died. Finally, a 22-year-old Russian, Yuri Marijasevich, provided the final step. She wrote to him, "I am especially pleased to think that when I first made the conjecture you were a baby and I just had to wait for you to grow up!" Later she marveled, "That year when I went to blow out the candles on my cake, I stopped in mid-breath, suddenly realizing that the wish I had made for so many years had actually come true."[18]

David Blackwell was born in 1919 (the same year as Julia Robinson) in Illinois, the son of a hostler for the Illinois Central Railroad who loved his job. A "hostler is a kind of innkeeper for steam locomotives; he takes them from the engineer and drives them to the roundhouse (their hotel). Then he drives them out of the roundhouse and delivers them to the next engineer. All jobs at the IC railroad were rigidly classified by race: all hostlers were black, all engineers, white."[19]

A friend of his father, a member of the Pulaski County School Board, promised David a job when he finished college, so he planned and expected to become an elementary school teacher. "In those depression days, a job was a JOB."[20] However, three of his high school teachers went out of their way to encourage him in his education and remained in contact with him for years after he left high school. "All three were white; a black teacher was unheardof, maybe even unthoughtof, at Centralia High School in the early 1930s."[21]

He received a remarkable education in mathematics from the all-white predominantly male faculty at the University of Illinois. (There were at least three women in the mathematics department that he can still name.[22]) By the age of 22 he had received three degrees in mathematics, culminating in the doctorate. The white males who ran the Institute of Advanced Study in Princeton recognized the talent of this young man, and in 1941 the mathematicians determined to invite him into their midst. This was not as straightforward as it might seem now. The Institute was on the Princeton University campus, and the University had a rigid "white male only" code. It had rejected Paul Robeson's application for admission solely on the grounds of race, although his father was a leading Princeton minister. When the Institute invited Blackwell to join its group for a year, the president of the university wrote to the director of the Institute that it was "abusing the university's hospitality" by welcoming a black professional onto the campus.[23]

[18]Constance Reid, *Julia, A Life in Mathematics*, Mathematical Association of America, 1996, p. 73.

[19]David Blackwell, personal email on October 22, 2003.

[20]David Blackwell, personal email on October 20, 2003.

[21]David Blackwell, personal email on October 22, 2003.

[22]David Blackwell, personal email on October 4, 2004.

[23]Dean Montgomery, personal conversation, March 25, 1982, reported in "Black Men and Women in Mathematical Research," Patricia Clark Kenschaft, *Journal of Black Studies*, 18:2, December, 1987, pp. 170-190, p. 179.

David Blackwell in the Mathematics Club of Centralia High School, as pictured
in its 1935 yearbook. He is sixteen and the others are either seventeen or
eighteen. The caption says that the club's purpose was "to foster, encourage,
and develop abilities along mathematical lines." Its twenty members met once
a month. The caption continues, "At one of the meetings David Blackwell,
a member of the club, demonstrated his solution of a problem that he had
published in a mathematical magazine. The publication of this solution was a
credit to our school as well as an honor to David." Photo courtesy of David
Blackwell.

After his year at the Princeton Institute, Blackwell taught first at Southern University and then at Clark University in Atlanta.[24] Then he spent
seven years as department chair at Howard University, where he had a
great impact on many young black mathematicians. During this time Jerzy
Neyman in the mathematics department at the University of California at
Berkeley recommended that Blackwell be offered an appointment, but the
department chair objected.[25] However, in 1954 the Department of Statistics separated from the Department of Mathematics, and Jerzy Neyman
became chair. Blackwell was promptly hired, first as a "visitor," and then
full-time.[26]

He spent most of his career on the faculty at the University of California
at Berkeley. Blackwell later became the first black inducted into the National Academy of Sciences, a vice president of the American Mathematical
Society and president of the Institute of Mathematical Statistics. He and his

---

[24]David Blackwell, personal email on October 12, 2004.
[25]David Blackwell, personal email on October 4, 2004.
[26]David Blackwell, personal email on October 12, 2004.

wife Annlizabeth Madison Blackwell celebrated their sixtieth wedding anniversary in December 2004, having produced eight children. In 2004 they had 13 grandchildren and 14 great-grandchildren.[27]

Meanwhile, the mathematicians at the Institute of Advanced Study at Princeton were not deterred in their quest for excellence. In 1942 they invited J. Ernest Wilkins, Jr. (who had received his doctorate at the age of nineteen from the University of Chicago) and in 1944 Clarence Stephens, two more African Americans who have had successful, although difficult, careers and have made an enormous impact on the mathematical community.

Gloria Conyers Hewitt (b. 1935) is not as famous as these previous four, but her life — as she is the first to claim — is a witness to the good will of a remarkable series of white men. She grew up in Sumter, South Carolina, the youngest of four children and the only daughter of Crenella and Emmett Conyers, Sr. Her three older brothers, all of whom went to the public high school, became a physician, sociology professor, and data analyst, respectively. She was sent to Mather Academy, a boarding school for black boys and girls in Camden, South Carolina. Her mother worked hard as a teacher to pay the private school bills; her father was a printer. She liked Mather and did well, so that in 1952 she was able to enter Fisk University at the age of seventeen. There she studied with Lee Lorch.

Lee Lorch (b. 1915) is a white Jewish man who had already lost two academic jobs in the North because of his support of racial equity.[28] After losing two jobs in the South for similar reasons, he would be forced to spend the remainder of his career in Canada. Lorch now has four honorary doctorates, two from universities — Fisk and the City University of New York (CUNY) — that fired him in his youth. More accurately, he was "dumped" for his anti-racist activities (trying to integrate his apartment building) from City College in 1949, which was later included in CUNY when the university was established years later.

Lee Lorch was born and grew up in New York City and was graduated from Cornell University in 1935. He then began his graduate work at the University of Cincinnati. During his last year there he helped organize what may have been the first racially integrated Southern union of public school teachers. To do so he traveled to Louisville, a hundred miles from his home. He had two white friends in the local community college, and they decided to strengthen their proposed union by including K–12 teachers. They soon discovered that the public teachers of Louisville had seven pay scales. The high school teachers earned more than the elementary school teachers. White men were paid more than white women, who were paid more than black men, who were paid more than black women. Black women were paid thirty percent less than white men for exactly the same work. The three

---

[27]David Blackwell, personal email on October 13, 2004.

[28]Patricia C. Kenschaft, "Black Women in Mathematics in the United States," *American Mathematical Monthly*, 88:8, October, 1981, pp. 63-83, p.76.

white men met, by careful pre-arrangement, with six African Americans in a lawyer's office with the shades drawn, each coming separately. After months of careful planning, they had their first public meeting of the integrated union. Hundreds of teachers came, both black and white. A Howard University professor was the keynote speaker and it was the first time many of the blacks had heard a black intellectual speak.

The group elected a white president. He asked to speak before the board of education, and did so in front of a large group of teachers. When he said they wanted an equalized pay scale, the board thought he meant only gender equality. When he said he wanted also racial equality, it was obvious that the group supported him. The board voted for it on the spot. Lorch believes this may be the only time racial equality was attained in the South without a court order.[29]

In 1941, back in New York City with his new doctorate, he was the target of anti-Semitism at City College. He went to the office of the chair of the Department of Mathematics to inquire about a possible job, and wasn't even asked to sit down. "When did you change your name?" was the first question. When Lorch denied having changed his name, he was immediately asked, "When did your father change his name?" When he replied that his father had also not changed his name, the interview ended. Lorch provided his unrequested resume and left the office.[30]

After some odd jobs, in 1942 he became an "assistant mathematician" at the National Advisory Committee for Aeronautics, which later evolved into NASA. He resigned this draft-exempt post to join the army and served in India and the Pacific during World War II.

Shortly before going overseas he married Grace Lonergan, a Boston school teacher. At that time the Boston School Committee had a regulation that "a female teacher will resign on marriage." Grace Lonergan Lorch became the first to refuse to do so, generating considerable local publicity from the hearings about her insistence that she should be allowed to continue in her job. But the Committee refused to make exceptions to its policy, even for service wives who had no other means of support. In 2003 the Boston Historical Society affixed a marker in her memory for her courageous resistance and her post-war civil rights activities; she was the first teacher to challenge the regulation, which remained in effect until 1953. Meanwhile, she lived in terrible conditions with another woman and their two babies.

When Lee returned, he was promptly offered several jobs and accepted the one at City College, which now had a different chair of the mathematics department. There was a pressing shortage of faculty to teach the huge number of returning veterans who were enrolling in colleges and universities, and

---

[29]Lee Lorch, personal conversation at the Joint Mathematics Meetings in Louisville on January 16, 1990.

[30]Lee Lorch, personal conversation at the Joint Mathematics Meetings in Atlanta on January 7, 2005 and personal email on January 12, 2005.

he hypothesizes that the general horror at Nazi policies had softened American attitude toward Jews. At first he lived with his wife and young daughter in a small hut, but then they felt fortunate to be able to move into the new apartment complex called Stuyvesant Town in New York City. However, African Americans were excluded, and soon Lorch was vice president of an organization of tenants and neighbors trying to integrate the building. This came to the attention of the City College administration, which is why his contract was not renewed in 1949 despite a recommendation for promotion by his peers.

Fortunately, he promptly obtained a job at Penn State in University Park, Pennsylvania. When he moved, he invited an African American family to live in his vacated apartment in New York City, on which the lease had two more years to run. Later in the year, the acting president of Penn State called him in and said that the trustees had instructed him to do so. He wanted to know when Lorch would give up the New York anti-segregation struggle, now or when the lease expired. Lorch would give no commitment. He was then asked if he were a Communist. He pointed out that if he answered that question, it might legitimize the question, a matter that was being seriously resisted elsewhere, and asked the president to withdraw the question. The interview was immediately terminated and very soon thereafter he received a one-sentence letter announcing that his appointment would not be renewed. No reasons were given.

He next joined the faculty of Fisk University in Nashville, Tennessee. Four of the first five graduates of Fisk University with doctorates in mathematics (and the only one with a doctorate in mathematics education) studied with Lorch in the five years that he was there; there appear to have been fewer than four in the half century since. He lost the job at Fisk University after trying to enroll his ten-year-old daughter in the neighborhood (black) school after the 1954 United States Supreme Court decision declaring segregation in public education to be unconstitutional. Alice wrote recently, "My memory of it was that it was entirely my idea to register and I was convinced I would be able to go to the Pearl Elementary School, which is where my friends went."[31] Following this "suspicious" act, Lee was promptly summoned before the House Un-American Activities Committee and indicted for "Contempt of Congress." At his trial, the vice chair of HUAC "couldn't remember" why he had been summoned, or even how the committee knew where he lived so he could be subpoenaed.[32] He was promptly acquitted of the charges.

He then joined the faculty at Philander Smith University in Little Rock, Arkansas, a small black college operated by the Methodist Church. There a group of nine African American students attempted to integrate Little Rock High School, pursuant to a court order. One girl became separated from the

---

[31] Personal email from Alice Lorch Bartels, February 21, 2005.
[32] Personal email from Lee Lorch, March 1, 2005.

Lee Lorch with his wife Grace Lonergan Lorch and their seven-year-old daughter Alice in front of their home on the Fisk University campus in Nashville, Tennessee, in early 1952. Photo courtesy of Alice Lorch Bartels.

others, and Lee's wife rescued her from an angry mob. The name of Grace Lonergan Lorch appeared on the first page of the *New York Times*, and she was then summoned before the United States Senate Internal Security Subcommittee of the Senate Judiciary Commission led by Senator James O. Eastland of Mississippi. The rescue and resulting publicity led to serious physical and financial threats against the already poorly financed college. Back in Little Rock, dynamite was placed under the Lorch family's garage door, and their daughter was beaten while at her (white) school.[33] Lorch was let go from Philander Smith by an administration fearing for the future of the college, and he then moved to Canada. The only graduate of Philander Smith College with a doctorate in mathematics studied under Lorch in the two years he taught there.

---

[33]"York Professor honoured for civil rights activism," *York University Gazette*, 26:32, May 8, 1996, p. 7.

Three of the fourteen African American women who earned doctorates in mathematics before 1970 studied under Lorch at Fisk. One of them, Vivienne Malone Mayes, wrote, "In the early Fifties, the idea of encouraging Blacks, and especially females, to prepare for academic careers was unheard of.... Not even Lorch himself in 1950 could have guessed that students of all colors and ethnic groups in the Sixties and Seventies would benefit so much from his efforts at Fisk in the Fifties.... His perspicacity in recognizing talent in its early stages enabled him to help students whom he had taught for only short periods of time."[34]

When Lorch was forced to leave in 1954, Gloria Conyers Hewitt, who was introduced on page 17, was only a sophomore. Meanwhile, she had married at the end of her freshman year. She returned to her parents' home for the December birth of her son part way through her junior year. She remained there and devoted herself to mothering during the spring semester, but took summer courses in education at South Carolina State in Sumter so that she would be able to graduate on time and become a teacher. Her parents persuaded her to return to Fisk while they cared for their grandson. However, her senior year was greatly marred by the dissolution of her marriage. She returned to her parents' home after her graduation in 1956 to become reacquainted with her child and to consider what the future might hold for her.

She was not in a receptive mood when letters arrived from both the University of Washington and the University of Oregon. Carl Allendoerfor and David Moursund, respectively, were the white male chairs of the mathematics departments at these institutions. They both urged her to apply for doctoral studies, offered a teaching fellowship, and enclosed application forms. In her confused state, she didn't realize the implications of such letters and put them aside. Her mother, however, found them and realized their import. She and one of the brothers insisted that Gloria fill out the forms and send them back.

Later she discovered that these invitations were at the prompting of Lee Lorch, although she hadn't seen him for two years until he returned to Fisk for her graduation. They talked then about her uncertain future. He asked if she had considered graduate school, and she responded that, no, she didn't even know what that meant. She believes she didn't tell him about the existence of her son at that time. She suspects that Robert Rempfer, who was also at Fisk during Lorch's last year, may have spoken to Allendoerfer and Moursund at national meetings.

When she was accepted at both Washington and Oregon, she had to make a decision between them. Her brother John had traveled through Seattle during his military service, and that gave her a small feeling of

---

[34]Vivienne Mayes, "Lee Lorch at Fisk: A Tribute," *The American Mathematical Monthly*, November, 1976, pp. 708-711.

familiarity. Her parents offered to take care of their grandson again. She decided to go to the far-away University of Washington.

Soon after she arrived, she discovered that her mathematics education had essentially stopped when Lorch left two years previously. Not to worry. Her all-white-male colleagues took over where Lorch had left. They would come to her office and say, "Isn't this an interesting problem? Let me show you how interesting it is!" She remembers that Carl Stromberg was often in her office when she first arrived in the morning, ready to show her the problem of the day. She also feels especially grateful to Kenneth Ross and Robert Phelps. One day the latter said to her, "The trouble with you is that you don't know trigonometry. I am going to teach it to you." She listened for two hours and then she understood trigonometry. Yes, super-achievers in mathematics are fast learners, but they are also the beneficiaries of many good deeds. There were at least eight students who helped her significantly, all of them white males. Eventually, she felt free to approach them with questions herself. When they went to a tavern or the best restaurant in Seattle, she went too. She also appreciates her thesis advisor, Richard Pierce, "whose faith in me remained even when my own faltered."

Cross-country travel was expensive in the 1950s, and it was common for students who were a continent from home not to return for the holidays. (I remember a teacher telling our class in 1957 that she had been on an airplane that was so smooth that you could actually drink a cup of coffee while flying.) Gloria Hewitt finally accumulated the necessary resources to visit Sumter in the Christmas vacation of her second year of graduate school. As she approached her childhood home, "I well remember that little boy running out the door calling 'Bang, bang!'" She thought he was accustomed to thinking of her mother as his own mother, so she asked him where his mother was.

"In Seattle Washington," was the reply.

"What!"

"She's in school." Her parents had been scrupulous in telling him they were his grandparents and that some day his mother would come and take him to live with her. She visited once again during her graduate school years, and that time he recognized her. When she received her Ph.D. in 1962, Hewitt obtained a job at the University of Montana. Her mother traveled across the country to bring the six-year-old Ronnie to join his mother in Missoula. "Then I did lots of little boy things," she said. "Fishing, hiking and skiing. We did a lot of camping."[35]

For many years she was the only black and the only woman in the mathematics department of the University of Montana. "They were so busy loving me, they forgot they didn't respect me," she told me in 1991 about her relationships with her colleagues in the 1970s. However, by the 1990s

---

[35]Gloria Hewitt in a telephone interview on November 4, 2003.

they successfully pressured her to became department chair. (By then there was another woman in the department.) She was a visiting lecturer for the Mathematical Association of America from 1965 to 1972, giving lectures and colloquia in many institutions. From 1976 to 1986 she was a member of the Educational Testing Service committee that made up questions for the Graduate Record Examination in mathematics, chairing that committee from 1984 to 1986. She has supervised a doctoral dissertation in homological algebra at the University of Montana and co-authored a publication with a student, a copy of which she saw at the mathematical institute in Beijing when she visited with the Women in Mathematics tour of China in 1990.[36]

Gloria Conyers Hewitt teaching in 1986. Photo Courtesy of the University Information Office of the University of Montana and Gloria Conyers Hewitt.

She retired in 1999, but took a post-retirement three-year contract afterward. She has worked in the EDGE (Enhancing Diversity in Graduate Education) Project with women who have been accepted into doctoral programs in mathematics during their summer between college and graduate school. Her son is a Morehouse College graduate, has been married for 27 years, and "messes with computers and photography." In October 2003, she gave herself a gala 68th birthday party with a jazz band. She invited 43 friends and all 43 came. Her life is — and has been — exciting and active.

---

[36] Patricia C. Kenschaft, "Hewitt, Gloria Conyers (1935-)," *Black Women in America: An Historical Encyclopedia*, Carlson Publishing, Inc., Brooklyn, NY, 1993, pp. 557-558.

Not all stories of aspiring mathematicians are as cheery as these five. Many have not been as fortunate in their interactions with more established mathematicians. In the next chapter we shall see how the lack of $25 prevented Kelly Miller from completing his doctorate and how the perfidy of examiners kept Susie Johnson (McAfee) from fulfilling her mathematical promise. The victims, however, are not just women or minorities. Elsewhere one can read how the delay of Augustin-Louis Cauchy (1789–1857), a leader in the French Academy of Sciences, in considering a paper submitted by the teenage wonder Évariste Galois (1811–1832), whose research is now included in the standard undergraduate curriculum for mathematics majors, prevented Galois from receiving recognition in his lifetime and may have contributed to his becoming involved in activities that resulted in his death in a duel at the age of 21. It is sobering to think of all the forgotten names of people who wanted to be mathematicians and received no outstretched hand.

Still, as many of us who have attained mathematical careers look back to our own youth, we can remember someone who were there for us at a crucial time. When I surveyed what I thought was the first 21 (actually it was 21 of the first 25) African American women to earn a doctorate in mathematics, *every* one could name both an older family member who had sacrificed for her *and* a secondary-school teacher who had encouraged and helped her.[37] This is not as universal among whites and males, but when they scratch their heads, most can name several people in the previous generation who deserve some of the credit for their success.

Whether or not the reader enjoys mathematics, it behooves us all to reach out to younger people when they show enthusiasm for mathematics. Our support is not enough for them to attain their dream, but it may be the breath of wind over the Rocky Mountains that sends them toward the Pacific instead of the Atlantic. The remainder of this book tells some happy stories and some that we wish we could rewrite.

---

[37]Patricia C. Kenschaft, "Black Women in Mathematics in the United States," *American Mathematical Monthly*, 88:8, October, 1981, pp. 63-83, p. 80.

CHAPTER 3

Women and Mathematics in the Nineteenth Century

Throughout human history a few women have pursued and enjoyed mathematical endeavors. Theano, wife of Pythagorus, and their daughters carried on his work after his death.[1] About 2500 years ago they attached his name to a theorem that had been known millenia earlier, thereby giving him mathematical immortality. Another woman, Hypatia (370–415) was a leading mathematician and philosopher at the University of Alexandria at the beginning of the fifth century A.D. Laura Bassi and other women earned doctorates in seventeenth century Italy. Maria Agnesi, whose life spanned the eighteenth century, wrote a calculus text that was translated into many languages and was standard for decades; she also did some mathematical research herself. However, throughout most of history the vast majority of women, like the vast majority of men, were illiterate.

The nineteenth century saw a burgeoning of artistic and intellectual activities, including mathematics. There were more people and, in particular, more people with leisure time. The population of the United States grew from only five million in 1800 (less than the population of New York City today) to 76 million in 1900. By then people lived in much larger cities, and there were far more effective means of transportation and communication. Railroads not only moved people unthinkably fast, but also facilitated quick and reliable mail delivery. People who were far apart could write to each other; letters explored ideas and kept people connected.

Since mathematics thrives where people are connected and exchanging ideas, there was an explosion of mathematical research in the nineteenth century. At the beginning of the century, the center of mathematical activity was almost entirely in Europe; Gauss, Cauchy, and Lagrange are a few of these early nineteenth century Europeans whose names still dominate our college math texts. Americans were pursuing more practical mathematics, such as that needed to guide ships and plan cities. Benjamin Franklin's and Benjamin Banneker's almanacs were masterpieces of computation, but Thomas Jefferson, after five years in France (1784-1789) as the resident United States minister to the French government, felt mathematically excommunicated when he returned to the United States. Not until decades

---

[1]Lynn Osen, *Women in Mathematics*, MIT Press, Cambridge, MA, 1974, p. 17.

after the death of Franklin, Banneker, and Jefferson, did the United States mathematical research community begin to thrive.

In the earlier part of the century, the Jacksonian belief in total equality among men produced deep distrust of elitism; all men should be able to do all things. Education, most people believed, was needed only to provide practical skills. In the South that meant that most laborers — white and black, male and female — did not need any education at all. They were easier to control if they were illiterate. In the North, the focus on practicality led to disputes about what should be taught in the common schools, which provided a few years of basic education.[2]

Some people thought it was more practical for girls to learn sewing than arithmetic. Husbands took care of the meager commerce of the family, so boys needed to learn basic arithmetic. Women, however, had to sew the entire family's wardrobe without modern machines or commercial patterns, an endeavor that required considerable skill. Some argued, therefore, that the schools should not waste girls' time with unnecessary subjects such as arithmetic, but should instead teach them the various arts needed to make clothing.

However, there was already a lively defense of girls and women studying mathematics as well as attacks on such practices. David Novak quotes writings in the early nineteenth century urging that girls be taught the basics of arithmetic so they could perform their womanly duties of managing the home and raising the next generation. He has even located two stories for popular consumption, one written in 1798 and the other in the 1830s, telling how a firstborn daughter in her mid-teens saved the family business when her father fell on hard times because she knew enough arithmetic to maintain a business. In both cases, the father eventually resumes control, so the daughter was not too threatening to male leadership. These stories, written for girls and their parents, illustrated the value of teaching daughters arithmetic. In the later nineteenth century, ardent polemics against teaching girls any mathematics at all appeared.[3]

In the eighteenth and early nineteenth centuries, most science was done at home, so the ability to pursue it depended more on an individual's family than on other institutions. Therefore, any person who pursued science or mathematics was merely eccentric, and such pursuits were not as gender-linked as they became later. According to Abir-Am and Outram, "... for the majority of scientific practitioners — especially in Britain and America, where the tradition of the gentleman/woman amateur [scientist] remained intact well into the nineteenth century — the experience of involvement in

---

[2]Lori Kenschaft, telephone conversation July 16, 2004. She tells me that the classic reference for these issues is *Pillars of the Republic: Common Schools and American Society*, 1790-1860 by Carl F. Kaestle, Hill and Wang, New York, 1983, pp. 62-103, 136-181, 192-217.

[3]David Novak, Simmons College, "The American History of the Fear of Math in Women," unpublished manuscript.

science was not as radically demarcated between the sexes as it became later in the century. Although actual scientific posts were wholly monopolized by men, such posts were few in number; not all men producing science held such posts; and most amateurs, male or female, worked from a domestic base. Often other family members greatly affected the actual resources of time, energy, and assistance available for scientific work of any kind."[4]

These researchers continued, "The gradual transition from domestic to institutionalized production of science also explains why... Maria Mitchell [(1818-1889), whose biography is outlined below] should have emerged at precisely that junction in history of science when a relative fluidity was still possible."[5] In her early adulthood, Maria Mitchell pursued science at home, as did most eighteenth century scientists. But later, as an employed professional, Maria Mitchell was crossing from the "women's sphere" to the "men's sphere," an increasing problem as these spheres became more rigid. "It is no accident that Mitchell's difficulties increased with the growing institutionization of science."[6]

After the Civil War, people realized that a broader range of skills was useful in an increasingly industrial society. In addition, there emerged a critical mass of people who cared about the life of the mind for its own sake. Specialization became more common and valued after the Civil War, and institutions of higher education began to flourish.

Two types of ambivalence emerged concerning this intellectual flourishing, one toward intellectual life in general and another toward the appropriate role of women in it. With specialization, came an increasing belief in the separation of the "men's sphere" and "women's sphere." The industrial revolution and public transportation (stage coaches, trains, and later street cars) opened up careers outside the home, careers that were mostly men's. Men were supposed to participate in public life; women were supposed to remain in the home. Men and women were expected to have friends only within their own sex.

Some families believed, however, that education for women was appropriate to prepare them to be companions to men and to cultivate the next generation, so education for American women in the nineteenth century was more available than generally realized in the mid and late twentieth century. Girls' academies blossomed all over the North and Midwest, with a few in the South. Even in the 1820s "education that was as good or better than the run-of-the-mill men's colleges" was already available at the Troy Female Seminary led by Emma Willard in Troy, New York, at the Hartford Female Seminary led by Catharine Beecher in Hartford, Connecticut, and at the Ipswich Female Seminary led by Mary Lyon and Zilpah Grant in Mount

---

[4]Pnina G. Abir-Am and Dorinda Outram, *Uneasy Careers and Intimate Lives: Women in Science, 1789-1979*, Rutgers University Press, New Brunswick, 1989, pp. 2-3.

[5]ibid, p. 5.

[6]ibid, p. 5.

Holyoke, Massachusetts.[7] By 1839 Margaret Fuller could claim that women were taught more than men but had lacked men's career opportunities to use their education.[8]

Her lament was verified by Horace Mann in 1841, when he claimed that women teachers were paid less than women in factories and male teachers. Furthermore, teachers had the inconvenience of usually being "boarded around" in rural districts (living with various students' families, usually sharing their students' bedrooms). He reported that surveys indicated that the monthly income of male teachers in New York was $14.96 compared to $6.69 for females, in Pennsylvania $17.02 compared to $10.09, in Indiana $12 compared to $6, in Maine $15.40 compared to $4.80, and in Massachusetts $24.51 compared to $8.07.[9]

Catharine Beecher, Mary Lyon, and Emma Willard were dynamic leaders who wrote inspiring pieces for the public and thoughtful letters to each other. They sent their graduates to be teachers in faraway places, some of which did not have a literate inhabitant (in what is now the eastern United States). In her 1874 *Reminiscences* Catharine Beecher claimed that 13,500 students had been educated at Emma Willard's seminary, "a high proportion of whom had become influential teachers elsewhere."[10]

Many of these wrote back to their mentors about their lives as a single teacher alone in a frontier community where either nobody else, or almost nobody else, could read. Some of these letters provide fascinating reading in the twenty-first century. For example, one of Catharine Beecher's former students went to an Ohio town where in one room she taught 45 students, about half of each sex. Some walked three or four miles. "I board where there are eight children, and the parents, and only two rooms in the house. I must do as the family do about washing, as there is but one basin, and no place to go to wash but out the door. I have not enjoyed the luxury of either lamp or candle.... I occupy a room with three of the children and a niece who boards here. The other room serves as kitchen, parlor, and bedroom for the rest of the family.... The people here are very ignorant; very few of them can read or write, but they wish to have their children taught."[11] Universal literacy in our democracy came with considerable adventure to those providing it.

---

[7]Lori Kenschaft, personal email on 10/15/03; Barbara Miller Solomon, *In the Company of Educated Women*, Yale University Press, New Haven, CT, 1985, pp. 18-20; David Tyack and Elisabeth Hansot, *Learning Together: A History of Coeducation in American Public Schools*, Yale University Press, New Haven, CT, 1990, p. 43; Thomas Woody, *A History of Women's Education in the United States*, Volume 1, Science Press, 1929, reprinted by Octagon Books, Inc., New York, 1966, p. 352.

[8]Thomas Woody, *A History of Women's Education in the United States*, Volume 1, Science Press 1929, reprinted by Octagon Books, Inc., New York, 1966, p. 442.

[9]ibid, pp. 492-493.

[10]ibid, p. 313.

[11]ibid, pp. 485-487, quoting Beecher, *The True Remedy for the Wrongs of Women*, Boston: Phillips, Sampson and Company, Boston, 1851, pp. 163-167.

Mathematics played a crucial role in the women's academies of the early nineteenth century.[12] Emma Willard emphasized mathematics, and considered the introduction of higher mathematics to be "epoch-making" in the history of women's education. She taught herself increasingly difficult mathematical topics, then taught them to her students, and then handed their teaching to one of her students to free herself to study a still harder mathematical concept.[13] Catharine Beecher became known for her dynamic teaching of arithmetic, and wrote an arithmetic text, "which was published, and received favorable comment from Professor Olmstead of Yale."[14]

Both co-ed and women's colleges gradually provided access to higher education beginning in the 1840s. The new public secondary schools, sprouting vigorously in many American communities after the Civil War, were generally co-ed. By the last third of the century, there were a number of colleges open to women who had the time and money to pursue higher education. Furthermore, almost a third of the American women who earned college degrees between 1868 and 1898 went on to do graduate work, and many earned doctorates.[15]

However, the separation of men's and women's spheres meant that those women who were employed outside the home had special challenges. "In all professions, the work women did became 'women's work,' and the term always had negative overtones."[16] One way women could use mathematics was to apply it to "women's fields." Unlike the eighteenth century application of mathematics to the physical sciences (as in Franklin's and Banneker's almanacs), the new quantitative applications to the social sciences were largely pioneered by women.

Appropriate career opportunities, however, were not nearly as available for educated women as for their male peers. This did not preclude the possibility of research. Many late nineteenth and early twentieth century educated women devoted themselves to "social work" in an effort to use their economic and educational privileges. Social expectations that middle class men would support not only their wives, but also their unmarried daughters and sisters, freed a critical number of highly educated women not only to try to help those in need directly, but also to do the research prerequisite to eliminating the conditions that led to poverty and hopelessness.

The quantitative methods that were basic to this research were often eschewed by academic males. "[High-prestige male] sociologists considered quantitative work to be 'applied' and preferred to subcontract it, so

----

[12]ibid, p. 414.

[13]ibid, pp. 345-346.

[14]ibid, pp. 319-320.

[15]Linda Gordon, "Social Insurance and Public Assistance," *American Historical Review*, 97:1, February 1992, p. 36.

[16]Barbara Miller Solomon, *In the Company of Educated Women*, Yale University Press, 1985, p. 138.

to speak, to lower-status [female] workers," observed historian Linda Gordon. "Within the developing field of sociology, women's overrepresentation in this kind of research was such that quantitative studies were sex-typed as female. ... while male sociological scholarship remained more theoretical and qualitative." Gordon then adds, "Ironically, W. F. Ogburn, hired at the University of Chicago in 1927, is often credited with initiating quantitative sociology."[17]

After male sociologist Carroll Wright persuaded Congress to fund investigations into urban slum conditions in the 1890s, he then "subcontracted" the women of Hull House to conduct the Chicago survey. The results were so impressive that there are now *two* copies of the resulting report in the Montclair State University library more than a century later and a thousand miles away! Amid the touching and graphic accounts of the horrific living and working conditions near the University of Chicago in the 1890s, *Hull-House Maps and Papers* provide a detailed graph of the region with the nationalities of the inhabitants and another graph of their average wages. The original versions of the book showed the various nationalities and wage levels in different colors, but the MSU version is more prosaic.

The workers researching for *Hull-House Maps and Papers* went through the tenements, room by room, filling out a lengthy form about the inhabitants of each. Careful documentation of the computations is included. The math is not very sophisticated, but it is scrupulously explained. "In estimating the average weekly wage for the year, first the number of unemployed weeks in each individual case was subtracted from the number of weeks in the year, the difference multiplied by the weekly wage when employed, and the result divided by fifty-two; then the amounts received by the various members of each family, thus determined, were added together, giving average weekly income of the family throughout the year."[18] Such technical explanations are interwoven with social commentary. "The theory that 'every man supports his own family' is as idle in a district like this as the fiction that 'everyone can get work if he wants it'."[19]

Another report on servant women in 1892 addresses issues more directly relevant to women mathematicians. Lucy Maynard Salmon, a history professor at Vassar, carefully planned the questionnaire in consultation with Carroll Wright and another leading male sociologist. Five thousand packets of 5 to 25 forms were sent out to Vassar and University of Michigan alumnae, individuals who expressed interest in the work, and members of the American Statistical Association, the American Economic Association, and the Association of Collegiate Alumnae, which would later become the AAUW. Of these, 719 forms were returned directly from employees and 1025 from employers, which included reports on 2545 of their employees.

[17]Gordon, p. 40.

[18]*Hull-House Maps and Papers* by Residents of Hull-House, a Social Settlement, Thomas Y. Crowell & Co., Boston, 1895, reprint by Arno Press, 1970, pp. 7-8.

[19]ibid, p. 21.

A significant part of the report is devoted to discussing whether the responses are "representative" of the total population. Sampling theory was not yet developed, but Salmon was keenly aware of the issues involved. Her defense rests on matching comparable data with those collected in the 1880 census and asserting that since they are similar to those in the census, the new conclusions are plausible.

Lucy Maynard Solomon entertaining a group of students in her home, as was her custom. She is facing the camera at the far end of the table. Photo courtesy of Vassar College archives, Dean M. Rogers, archivist.

The major conclusion of this paper was the difference in what was needed to recruit more "good servants" as reported by employers and employees. The employers concentrated on their own interactions with the employees. However, when the employees were asked, "What reasons can you give why more women do not choose housework as a regular employment?," the three leading answers by a large margin were (1) Pride, social conditions and unwillingness to be called servants, (2) Confinement on evenings and Sundays, and (3) More independence in other occupations. Pay and "Lack of consideration by mistresses" placed only fifth and sixth on the list, each with about seven percent of the responses.[20]

Probably Salmon's most interesting discovery for modern readers is that the income available "for savings" of the domestic workers compared favorably with that of teachers. Most female household employees lived in the

---

[20]Lucy M. Salmon, "A Statistical Inquiry Concerning Domestic Service," *Publications of the American Statistical Association* (now the *Journal of the American Statistical Association*), 3:18/19, June-September 1892, pp. 89-118, p. 116.

homes of their employers and were provided food, room (a private room in 70 percent of the reported cases),[21] and "fuel and light." When the value of all this is added, and the cost of clothing and paying off the education that a teacher must have is subtracted from teachers' pay, the pay difference is negligible. Indeed six of the employee respondents were former teachers.[22] Salmon concluded, with convincing mathematical arguments, that the economic incentives for a nineteenth century woman to become a teacher were negligible or negative. Since teaching was the only employment routinely available to women with a high school or college education, financial incentives at that time to pursue higher education were minimal or nonexistent.

Yet many did, and the impulse to penetrate other professions, such as college teaching, was great. Even when they were successful, the financial rewards were not comparable with those of men, as the story of Maria Mitchell given below illustrates. Despite bleak employment prospects outside K-12 teaching, women pursued higher education in all fields, including mathematics. The charm of the subject, as every mathematician knows, exceeds the pecuniary rewards. Many nineteenth century women also knew they needed an income until they married, and teaching, even without economic incentives, seemed preferable to domestic or factory work.

It was common before the twentieth century for mathematics and astronomy to be linked. As in the social sciences, nineteenth century astronomy used women for the "mere" computational work. Of the 1205 Americans who Lankford and Slavings regarded as American "astronomers" before World War II (employment at an observatory, publication of research in astronomy, or recognition by other astronomers), 426 were women — more than a third. They were typically employed at "industrial" observatories. "Men observed at the telescope and carried out the final discussion of the data. Women measured spectrograms, computed start places or reduced photometric data."[23] In other words, women "did the math." However, half of these women had careers that lasted five years or less, and only twelve percent had careers longer than 25 years.[24]

Maria Mitchell (1818-1889) is the best known nineteenth century American woman astronomer. From her faculty position at Vassar College, from the time it opened in 1865 until her retirement in 1888, she was a role model and inspiration for young women, including Christine Ladd (discussed in Chapter 2). Mitchell strongly encouraged Ladd to pursue her interests in math and science.[25]

---

[21]ibid, p. 114.

[22]ibid, p. 103.

[23]John Lankford, and Rickey L. Slavings, "Gender and Science: Women in American Astronomy, 1859-1940," *Physics Today*, March 1990, pp. 58-65, p. 59.

[24]ibid, p. 63.

[25]Samantha Ragsdale, "Christine Ladd-Franklin," available at www.webster.edu/~woolflm/christineladd.html

Maria Mitchell with the first class of astronomy students at Vassar College in 1866. She is standing on the right with her hand on the shoulder of the student in the checked dress. Mitchell held overnight slumber parties for students called "Dome Parties" because they were under the observatory's dome. Photo and caption courtesy of Vassar College archives, Dean M. Rogers, archivist.

Mitchell grew up in Nantucket and was taught mostly by her father. In 1847 she became famous as the first person to sight a new comet, and two years later she became a "computer" with the newly established Nautical Almanac Office. When Matthew Vassar was founding the women's college that would bear his name, an emissary he sent to visit Miss Mitchell, returned with a glowing recommendation. She was hired, but her salary was only $800, compared to the men's salaries of $2500. She protested, along with the college physician, the other woman professional, but with no success. Mitchell wrote, "Devote myself more and more to my own department — try to be loyal to the stars but keep away from the administration as much as possible."[26]

Susan Cunningham (1842-1921), another of Mitchell's Vassar students, had a satisfying and prestigious career in mathematics and astronomy. On the basis of only one year of higher education, as a "special student" at Vassar College in 1866-1867, she joined the initial faculty of Swarthmore College at the age of twenty-seven when it opened in 1869. She began as an "instructor in mathematics," but became a full professor well before her retirement in 1906. "For most, and maybe all of her career, Cunningham

---

[26]Lankford and Slavings, p. 62.

Susan Cunningham, probably in the 1880s, was the mathematics department at Swarthmore College for years and also one of the founding members of the AMS. Photo courtesy of Friends Historical Library, Christopher Densmore, archivist.

was *the* Mathematics Department at Swarthmore."[27] In 1888 Swarthmore College awarded her an honorary degree of Doctor of Science (D.Sc.).

Swarthmore College was founded on a belief in the equality of the sexes, and Cunningham experienced more financial equity than Mitchell. "In 1870 there were three people with the title of 'Professor' and the one woman had the middle salary. Most of the faculty held the rank of teacher — eleven people, with salaries from $300 to $750. Only one (a male) was at $750. The next level was $600, including Cunningham. Several women had higher salaries than men."[28]

At her retirement, Swarthmore's President Joseph Swain said, "Susan J. Cunningham has the distinction of being the only one in the Faculty who has been connected with the College since its beginning in 1869. She is

---

[27]Christopher Densmore, Curator, Friends Historical Library, Swarthmore College, telephone conversation, December 1, 2003.

[28]Christopher Densmore, personal email, December 9, 2003.

energetic, forceful, and learned in her profession, and a thoro [sic] believer in the College.... She has, in season and out of season, been ready not only to serve the College, but to help individual students by giving to them her advice, her time, and in numerous cases her money."[29]

Her obituary reports that she "assisted in making the bed linen and in furnishing the rooms for the first students at Swarthmore." More dramatically, when the multipurpose building of the campus burned down in 1881, she "forgot herself and her belongings and thot [sic] only of aiding the students to get to safety. ...she lost her valuable library, the result of many years of collecting."[30]

The obituary reports that she was the "favorite professor" of the governor of Pennsylvania, a former governor of Delaware, "and many others." "Governor Sproul, at the dedication of the Sproul Observatory, declared that it was out of affection for his old teacher, Miss Susan J. Cunningham, that he came to present the Observatory to the College."[31] Sproul Observatory is still a major landmark of the College.

None of the ten American women who earned doctorates in mathematics in the nineteenth century obtained faculty appointments to universities granting doctorates. Before 1940, 239 American women earned doctorates in mathematics at three foreign and 34 different American universities. Most studied at strong institutions with fine advisors. However, during this time only 14 of these 34 American institutions hired and retained women mathematicians; of these 22 women, only five became full professors. Two of these five were at Bryn Mawr College, Charlotte Scott and Anna Pell Wheeler.[32] Thorough integration of women into the mathematical research community would not happen until the late twentieth century — although the numbers are still far from equal.[33]

Sofia Kovalevskaia and Christine Ladd-Franklin, the nineteenth century women mathematicians whose lives were outlined in the previous chapter, were innovators, but were not alone — although they surely must have felt alone at crucial times. However, they tried to find mathematical sisters. The cover of every Kovalevskaia Fund newsletter quotes Sofia Kovalevskaia: "... is it really possible not to stretch out one's hand, is it possible to refuse to help someone who is seeking knowledge and cannot help herself reach its source? After all, on woman's road, when a woman wants to take a path other than the well-trodden one leading to [traditional] marriage, so many

---

[29] "Dr. Susan J. Cunningham, Emeritus Professor of Mathematics Dies in her Swarthmore Home," *The Phoenix*, Swarthmore College, January 25, 1921.

[30] ibid.

[31] ibid, p. 4.

[32] Judy Green and Jeanne LaDuke, "Women in the American Mathematical Community: The Pre-1940 Ph.D's," *The Mathematical Intelligencer*, 9:1, 1987, pp. 11-23, p. 21.

[33] Allyn Jackson, "Has the Women-in-Mathematics Problem Been Solved?" *Notices of the AMS*, August, 2004, 51:7, pp. 776-783.

difficulties pile up. I myself encountered many of these. Therefore, I consider it my duty to destroy whatever obstacles I can in the paths of others."[34]

Ladd-Franklin clearly had similar sentiments. In 1893, she met a young woman, Mary Winston (1869-1959), at the International Congress of Mathematicians in Chicago. Felix Klein (1849-1925), the great German mathematician, had come to the Congress after consulting with German authorities and deciding that the great experiment of including women at the university should be done with foreign women and in mathematics, where, it was thought, "deception as to whether real understanding is present or not is least possible."[35] Winston seemed like a good candidate to Klein, but she lacked the money for travel abroad. Ladd-Franklin offered her a scholarship that enabled her to accept Klein's invitation.[36]

After she arrived, Winston wrote, "...everything is to be done very quietly. We are to go to Prof. Klein's private office before the regular time for changing classes so as not to meet the students in the halls and from there we are to go into the class." Two weeks later she wrote that she "received permission to study in the University of Göttingen."[37] Thus Mary Winston (later Newson), Grace Chisholm (later Young), a British woman who would become a mathematician, and Margaret Maltby, an American who aspired to study physics, became the first women to be admitted as regular attendees at lectures by the Prussian government. Winston completed her doctorate under Klein at Göttingen, and in 1897 became the ninth American woman to receive a doctorate in mathematics.

Mary Frances Winston Newson (1869-1959) then became head of the mathematics department at Kansas State Agricultural College until she married Henry Byron Newson in 1900. He was acting head of the mathematics department at the University of Kansas, and it was assumed that she would forsake employment for marriage. She did translate Hilbert's seminal 1900 Lecture at the 1900 International Congress of Mathematics for the *Bulletin of the American Mathematical Society* with his permission. She then gave birth to two daughters and a son. In 1910 her husband suddenly died of a heart attack, leaving her in serious need of an income.[38]

In 1913 she obtained a job at Washburn College in Topeka, Kansas, where she was one of two mathematicians. Her male colleague, without

---

[34]*Kovalevskaia Fund Newsletters*, available from Ann Hibner Koblitz, editor, Department of Women's Studies, Arizona State University, Tempe, AZ 85287.

[35]Judy Green and Jeanne LaDuke, "Women in the American Mathematical Community: The Pre-1940 Ph.D's," *The Mathematical Intelligencer*, 9:1, 1987, pp. 11-23, p. 15.

[36]Judy Green, "American Women in Mathematics — the First Ph.D.'s," *Newsletter of the Association for Women in Mathematics*," 8:1, April, 1978, pp. 13-15, p. 14.

[37]ibid.

[38]Betsey S. Whitman, "Women in the American Mathematical Society Before 1900: Part Three," *Newsletter of the Association for Women in Mathematics*, 13:6, November-December 1983, p. 10.

Mary Winston Newson with her daughters Caroline and Josephine at a family gathering in the summer of 1908 in West Virginia. This photo was taken 20 months before her husband died, and 18 months before the birth of her son. Photo courtesy of John Montgomery, grandson of Mary's younger sister Eugenia.

even a master's degree, was a professor, but she, with a doctorate earned under the great Felix Klein, was kept at the rank of assistant professor for eight years.[39] Finally, in 1921 she became head of the mathematics department at Eureka College in Illinois. In 1940 she was honored at the Women's Centennial Congress as one of 100 women who held positions not open to women a century earlier.[40] She retired in 1942, at which time the student newspaper observed that she was concluding 35 years of teaching college mathematics.

---

[39]Personal email from Betsey Whitman, August 2, 2004.
[40]Whitman, *AWM Newsletter*, 13:5, p. 10.

In the nineteenth century studying mathematics required determination and fortitude for most women. Mary Church Terrell (1863-1954), one of the first African American women to earn a bachelor's degree (from Oberlin in 1884), said in 1953, "It was held by most people that women were unfitted to do their work in the home if they studied Latin, Greek, and higher mathematics. Many of my friends tried to dissuade me from studying for an A.B. degree.... Further, I was ridiculed and told that no man would want to marry a woman who studied higher mathematics. I said I'd take a chance and run the risk."[41] She eventually did marry a magna cum laude graduate of Harvard University, Robert Heberton Terrell, a successful lawyer and later a judge. Her autobiography *A Colored Woman in a White World*[42] is fascinating.

Beyond marriage foreclosure, there was a genuine fear that studying, especially studying geometry, would affect a woman's basic health, as well as her reproductive abilities. When she received her doctorate in mathematics from Bryn Mawr in 1925, she heard an old woman's voice pipe up, "Well, it doesn't seem to have hurt her any!"[43] Marguerite Lehr emphasized to me this widespread nineteenth century belief.

However, there were less laudable motives for denying women access to mathematics. One example occurred when the United States government sent experts to "help" Native Americans educate their children. On their Oklahoma reservation the Cherokee tribe already had established schools that were advanced for the 1890s. The delegation from Washington arrived. "No wonder Cherokee homes are such a mess!," later generations remembered the agents as exclaiming. (One can wonder about how extensive was their home survey that led them to the conclusion that Cherokee homes were a mess.) "Their young women study Euclid!" The powerful Euro-Americans put a stop to that hazard for domestic cleanliness.[44]

Black women had little access to higher education in mathematics during the post Civil War period. Most schools and colleges focused on basic literacy and numeracy with the goal of preparing black men to be good citizens and black women to be good teachers and mothers. Almost all black colleges (antebellum and postbellum) opened as co-ed institutions, but undergraduate enrollment was small. In 1892 Fisk had 12 women in its entire liberal arts program. Howard had none, though it didn't exclude women by policy. Spelman College, opened in 1881 by two "Boston ladies," was the first institution to provide college level instruction specifically for African American women, but it put much more emphasis on career preparation,

---

[41]Jeanne L. Noble, *The Negro Woman's College Education*, Teachers College, Columbia University, New York, 1956, p. 23.

[42]Ramsdell Publishers, Washington, DC, 1940.

[43]P. C. Kenschaft, "An Interview with Marguerite Lehr," *Association for Women in Mathematics Newsletter*, 11:4, July-August, 1981, pp. 4-7.

[44]Robert Megginson, radio interview on Math Medley, September 12, 1998, "Native American Mathematics," available archived at www.webCT.com/Math.

especially teaching (the career available to professional women), than the colleges designed for white women.[45] This was at least partially because the black community needed teachers and black women needed to get out of field and domestic work. Until Bryn Mawr opened in 1885, none of the black or women's institutions offered doctorates.

Yale conferred degrees listed as Ph.D.'s in mathematics beginning in 1862, and Harvard began in 1873. Formal education for men had, obviously, a much longer tradition in Europe than in the United States; Oxford University dates back to the mid-twelfth century. Nevertheless (or therefore?), women found it more difficult to participate. A much-discussed article in the British *Fortnightly Review* of April 1874 by a Dr. Maudsley, "the well-known mental specialist," talked of the bad example of the "United States, where girls received the same mental education with boys, with the result that the American woman is physically unfit for her duties as a woman."[46] Nevertheless, the towering figure of early American women mathematicians, Charlotte Scott, was British. Before we turn to her, let us look briefly at three better known nineteenth century European women who were no doubt role models for her.

Caroline Hershel (Germany, then England, 1750-1848) had the good fortune to have a father who told her when she was young that she was too ugly to attract a husband, so she should prepare to support herself. She became a singer, an astronomer, and a mathematician, computing the locations of stars and nebulae. Her father and, especially, her older brother William were supportive of her career. On the other hand, **Sophie Germain** (France, 1776-1831) and **Mary Somerville** (Scotland 1780-1872) told later how their parents took away their books and candles so that they couldn't study at night. Germain's parents finally took away her clothing, so she studied math wrapped in blankets with smuggled candles and books. Somerville recounted that in her school days, "...I was enclosed in stiff stays, with a steel busk in front, while, above my frock, bands drew my shoulders back till the shoulderblades met. Then a steel rod, with a semi-circle which went under the chin, was clasped to the steel busk in my stays. In this constrained state I, and most younger girls, had to prepare our lessons."[47] Young women were to be decorations who attracted men. After they married, they were to devote their time to having and raising babies if they were wealthy, and also to cooking, cleaning, and raising food if they were among the vast majority. Women were assumed to have no time for studying or voting.

---

[45]Noble, p. 22.

[46]Barbara Stephens, *Emily Davies and Girton College*, Constable & Co., Ltd., London, 1927, p. 290.

[47]Mary Somerville quoted by Teri Perl, *Math Equals: Biographies of Women Mathematicians*, Dale Seymour Publications, 1978, p. 85.

Some men had loftier visions for women. Walter Scott (1779-1858) and his son Caleb Scott (1831-1919) were Congregational ministers who became presidents of two different colleges that trained such ministers. The Congregational Church was one of the "non-conformist" religions of Britain — not conforming to the Church of England. These men were non-conformists socially as well; they campaigned for freeing slaves and better treatment of the working classes and women.

Charlotte Angas Scott (1858-1932) had the good fortune to be the second child of Caleb, with a sister less than two years older. Shortly before Charlotte's seventh birthday, Caleb gave a talk to newly elected deacons, including some admonitions to their wives that indicate the kind of father he was trying to be. "God intended that childhood should have its dimpled cheek and its roguish eye and its merry laugh.... And when childhood is outgrown, let the innocent tastes and tendencies of youth not be all repressed and stifled in the iron mould of a conventionalism."[48]

The Lancashire College, of which Caleb was president, was widely known for its mathematics department, so Caleb was in a good position to hire fine tutors for his daughters. Alas, Charlotte's older sister died when she was barely nineteen and Charlotte was seventeen, leaving Charlotte to fulfill the dreams Caleb had for both.

And fulfill dreams she did! When she was eighteen she won a scholarship to Girton College near the Cambridge University campus. Girton College had been started by Emily Davies less than a decade earlier to provide England's young women their first opportunity for higher education. Cambridge University set (and still sets) final Tripos Examinations that students at all its colleges take after three years at the university. In 1872 three of the first Girton students obtained special permission, as the first women, to take the exams. They all passed, and thereby became "the Girton Pioneers." When Scott arrived with her ten classmates in 1876, it was customary to sing their praises on cold winter evenings:

> Whenever we go forward,
> A hard exam to try,
> Their memory goes before us
> To raise our courage high.
> They made old Cambridge wonder.
> Then let us give three cheers
> For Woodhead, Cook, and Lumsden -
> The Girton Pioneers!

Several stanzas continue in this vein, and then a final one that I found especially moving:

> And when the goal is won, girls
> And women get degrees,

---

[48] Caleb Scott, "An address to Newly Elected Deacons," delivered March 15, 1865, and now filed in the Lincoln Public Library of Lincoln, England.

We'll cry, "Long live the three girls
Who showed the way to these!
Who showed the way we follow,
Who knew no doubts and fears.
Our Woodhead, Cook and Lumsden -
The Girton Pioneers!"[49]

Lumsden's reminiscences, written in 1907[50], indicate they knew plenty of doubts and fears, but they continued anyway; they were truly courageous.

Cambridge did not grant degrees to women until 1948, but Charlotte Scott caused a great step forward in 1880. When she took her Tripos exams that year, women needed special permission to take them — which by 1880 had been occasionally and whimsically denied. Furthermore, they could not have their scores posted among the men's, a crucial matter when seeking jobs.

But Charlotte Scott, after eight nine-hour days of exams in the bitter cold (it was the cold she remembered decades afterward[51]), was in the eighth place in the entire university in *mathematics*. Newspapers throughout the country reported the amazing news. Three other Girton students also earned a "First" but because Scott's was in mathematics, hers received far more publicity than the others. Arthur Cayley, who would later supervise her graduate work, helped circulate a petition that women should have the rights to take examinations with men after a comparable time of study at Cambridge and to have their names posted among the men's in the order of excellence. Within a few months, over 8500 signatures had been obtained.[52] On February 24, 1881, the Cambridge Graces voted to grant women these two rights. A student at the newly-founded women's college at Oxford University celebrated the widespread impact of Cayley's and Scott's achievement when she broke into the dining room shouting, "We won! We won!"

Scott then became an instructor at Girton College, which meant that its students were no longer so dependent on the good will of men who might (or might not) agree to teach them mathematics. Previously some had agreed to come to Girton College, discreetly situated three miles from the main campus. A mathematics instructor had to be well motivated to take that hike! Some allowed the women to attend their lectures, but only if they would sit behind a screen so as not to distract the male students. Attending a mathematics class behind a screen obviously has serious disadvantages. The women would march behind the screen in a line, always attended by a chaperone. A later mistress of Girton College wrote to me, "Students had to pay extra to attend university lectures, and as the daughter of a

---

[49] E. E. Constance Jones, *Girton College*, Adam and Charles Block, London, 1913, pp. 28-29.

[50] *Girton Review*, 1907, p. 19.

[51] *Marguerite Lehr*, personal conversation, March 31, 1981.

[52] Jones, p. 31.

Congregational minister, she [Scott] was probably poor, but she could go as a chaperone to students without paying."[53]

There were non-academic problems with studying at Cambridge as well. That chaperone was not optional. Young women found on campus without a chaperone were summarily thrown into "The Spinning House" and charged with prostitution, their lives forever ruined. There had been a scandal shortly before Scott arrived at Girton because two Girton students presumably had been seen in a dogcart unchaperoned alone with a clergyman. It was eventually revealed that their companion had been a woman in mourning, and that was the reason for the all-black clothing.

After 1880 Charlotte Scott pursued her graduate studies with Arthur Cayley. "Professor Cayley gives her a high recommendation for her attainments and her capacity for original work," said the Bryn Mawr Executive Committee Report of July 7, 1884, as they considered her appointment to the founding faculty.[54] Since Cambridge would not grant degrees to women until 1948, Scott sat for a second set of exams and met a second set of standards for both her degrees. She was granted her B.Sc. in 1880 and her D.Sc. in 1885 from the University of London.

As the first native English-speaking woman to receive a doctorate in mathematics, what would she do now? Scott could have obtained a job in the secondary schools for girls that were popping up around England, but she was lucky and plucky. Martha Carey Thomas (1857-1935) had been a student in Baltimore when Christine Ladd-Franklin had finished her doctoral requirements at Hopkins and then had been refused the degree (see page 8). Thomas also had some inside information from her uncle, who was on the Hopkins board. She wrote at that time, "Her situation is the same as mine," and decided she would go to a more equitable institution. She received her Ph.D. summa cum laude from the University of Zurich in 1882 and visited each of the women's colleges at Cambridge University on her way home.[55] It seems likely that Thomas talked with Charlotte Scott at that time.

In 1885 Bryn Mawr College opened, complete with a graduate program, and Scott was offered the job as chair of its mathematics department. Actually, she was the only member of the mathematics department for a few years, but later she persuaded two other (male) mathematicians from Cambridge to join her.

How did a single woman from such protected circumstances dare to cross the ocean — a full week's trip, at least — to go to an unknown employer? Lack of alternatives was surely one reason. However, it seems likely that she talked about the United states with both Susan Cunningham (who spent

---

[53]Personal letter from Dame Mary Cartwright, March 18, 1981.

[54]Bryn Mawr archives.

[55]M. Carey Thomas, quoted in *The Making of a Feminist: Early Journals and Letters of M. Carey Thomas*, edited by Marjorie Housepian Dobkin, Kent State University Press, 1979, p. 278.

five summers at Cambridge while Scott was there)[56] and J. J. Sylvester (who was a close friend of Arthur Cayley), as well as Carey Thomas. Mail delivery was reliable in the late nineteenth century, and letter-writing was a more habitual means of communication than it was after telephones became common.

Nevertheless, there were surprises at her arrival. In a memorial article for Scott, her last student related that "...[she] arrived at Bryn Mawr late on a September evening in 1885. She rang the door-bell of Merion Hall, then the only Hall of Residence, and was amazed that the door was opened, apparently, by a white dress and apron, the dusky features of the wearer merging unseen into the darkness of the empty building in a manner very disconcerting to the unaccustomed English stranger."[57] During her first year at Bryn Mawr, there were only a few students, so the stakes were high for each. She had three advanced undergraduates and one graduate student, whose highest previous study had been differential equations.[58]

Scott attended the New York Mathematical Society meetings from their inception in 1888, joined as soon as membership was available to people outside New York in 1891, and she was on the original Council of the American Mathematical Society when it organized in 1894. She served another term on the Council from 1899 to 1901 and was the vice president of the AMS in 1905-1906 — the only woman to serve in that position until Mary Gray in 1976. Meanwhile, frustrated with the amount of time she was spending designing admissions examinations for so few students,[59] she helped organize the College Board and served as its first Chief Examiner in Mathematics, beginning in 1902.[60] She published research not only in the new American journals but in European journals as well.[61]

During the time of her influence, the American mathematics community didn't doubt that women could do mathematics. Indeed, the AMS held its spring 1922 meeting at Bryn Mawr to honor her. Two hundred people gathered to hear Alfred North Whitehead deliver the main address. Although he received invitations to speak at Columbia and Harvard and his trip across

---

[56]Susan P. Cobbs, "What's in a Name?" *Swarthmore Alumni Issue*, December, 1963, pp. 20-24, p. 21, quoting the Swarthmore College catalog of the late nineteenth century.

[57]Marguerite Lehr, "Charlotte Angas Scott: an Appreciation," *Bryn Mawr Alumni Bulletin*, volume 12, 1932, pp. 9-12, p. 9.

[58]P. C. Kenschaft, "Charlotte Angas Scott," *Women of Mathematics*, Greenwood Press, 1987, p. 196.

[59]Scott's letters in the Bryn Mawr College archives.

[60]College Entrance Examination Board Archives, New York, Document #8 1/10/1902, p. 43 and Document #12, 1/10/1903, p. 43.

[61]P. C. Kenschaft, "Charlotte Angas Scott," *Women of Mathematics*, Greenwood Press, 1987, reprinted in *A Century of Mathematics in America, Part III*, by the AMS, Providence, RI, pp. 241-252. A list of 27 of Scott's published works concludes this paper.

Charlotte Scott, (center front in white on a chair) first Chief Examiner of
Mathematics of the College Board in 1902 and the first mathematician
at Bryn Mawr College at its opening in 1885, with the first Bryn Mawr
class at a reunion. Courtesy of the Bryn Mawr Libraries, Gertrude Reed,
archivist.

the ocean took a week each way, he turned them down so as not to have
competing attractions in Scott's "neighborhood," as he phrased it.[62]

Throughout her career, Charlotte Scott worked hard to encourage women
in mathematics. When the American Mathematical Society (AMS) was organized in 1894, 12 of the founding 250 members, or under 5 percent, were
female. By 1907, the next time a complete list was published, 37 of the 548
members, or almost 7 percent were female, a significant increase in percentage and a tripling of the number. In April 1912, the *American Mathematical
Monthly*, then an independent journal, observed that although 50 of the 668
AMS members were women [7.5 percent], only five of the members of the
German Mathematical Society were women, and only one of these was a German woman. Emmy Noether's isolation in Germany was far more complete
than that of her American peers.[63]

---

[62]E. Putnam, "Celebration in Honor of Professor Scott," *Bryn Mawr Bulletin II*,
1922, pp. 12-14 and *Bulletin of the American Mathematical Society*, Notes 28, June 1922,
p. 274.

[63]Quoted by Frances Rosamond in "A Century of Women's Participation in the MAA
and Other Organizations," in *Winning Women into Mathematics*, MAA Committee on
Participation of Women, Washington, DC, 1991.

It is interesting, if somewhat depressing, to contemplate the influence of one person on the participation of women in mathematics. There was a higher percentage of identifiably women's names delivering papers before the AMS in 1905-1906 (5%) than in 1971 (3%).[64] Before 1928 over eight percent of the authors in the *American Journal of Mathematics* were identifiably female and 45 percent were identifiably male, so about 15 percent of the names identifiable by sex were female. A similar count for the 1970s revealed only 2.1 percent of the total were clearly female, but there were many whose gender I couldn't identify. If I restricted myself to those whose gender I knew, only four percent were women even though I could identify a higher proportion of women than men by their initials (due to my participation in the Association for Women in Mathematics by the time I did the count in the early 1980s). Women earned 14 percent of the doctorates in mathematics granted in this country before 1940, compared to only 5 percent of those awarded in the 1950s. But that is another story, in a time socially very different for both women and mathematicians.

Scott was the only woman on the first list of members of the New York Mathematics Society published in May 1891, but five more had been elected to membership before the end of that year. One was Susan Cunningham, and two others were primarily astronomers, **Mary Emma Byrd** (1849-1934) and Mary Watson Whitney. Both were strong-willed pioneers. Byrd resigned her position as director of the Smith College Observatory and Professor of Astronomy at Smith College in 1906 in protest of the college's accepting a $62,500 grant from Andrew Carnegie and John D. Rockefeller. She said the money was "tainted" because of the way the robber-baron benefactors had made their money. Afterward she taught for only one year, but then published articles, especially in *Popular Astronomy*, from her home in Kansas. She made an observatory station on her porch roof and sometimes used the astronomical instruments of the State University of Kansas.[65]

Mary Watson Whitney (1854-1938) attended Vassar College in its first year, 1865, and was also greatly influenced by Maria Mitchell. She then attended lectures of Benjamin Peirce at Harvard University, worked at the Dearborn Observatory in Chicago, and studied mathematics and celestial mechanics from 1873 to 1876 at the University of Zurich. The next five years "were perhaps the least satisfactory to her," according to a tribute after her death, because there was no position available where she could use her training and talents; she taught at Waltham High School in her hometown in Massachusetts. In 1881 Mitchell's health failed, and she invited Whitney to become her assistant at the Vassar College Observatory. When Mitchell

---

[64]P. C. Kenschaft, "Women in Mathematics Around 1900," *Signs*, 7:4, Summer, 1982, pp. 906-909, p. 906.

[65]Betsey S. Whitman, "Women in the American Mathematical Society Before 1900: Part One," *Association for Women in Mathematics Newsletter*, 13:4, July-August, 1983, pp. 10-14, p. 11.

retired, Whitney succeeded her as professor of astronomy and director of the observatory. It is reported that shortly before Whitney died, she said, "I hope when I get to heaven I shall not find the women playing second fiddle."[66]

Ellen Amanda Hayes (1851-1930) grew up in Granville Ohio, the granddaughter of original settlers there. She began teaching in a country school when she was sixteen and saved enough money to go to Oberlin College, from which she was graduated in 1878. She was principal of the women's department of Adrian College in Michigan for a year and then accepted a position as instructor of mathematics at Wellesley College, where she taught until she retired in 1916. A history of Wellesley College reports, "A dauntless radical in all her days, in the eighties she was wearing short skirts; in the nineties she was a staunch advocate of Woman's Suffrage; in the first two decades of the twentieth century, an ardent Socialist. After her retirement, and until her death in 1930, she was actively connected with an experiment in adult education for working girls. Fearless, devoted, intransigent, fanatical, if you like, and at times a thorn in the flesh of the trustees, who withheld the title of Emeritus on her retirement, she is remembered with enthusiasm and affection by many of her students."[67]

In 1912 Hayes was nominated for Secretary of State in Massachusetts on the Socialist ticket, the first woman to be a candidate for a state elective office in Massachusetts. Although women were not allowed to vote, she won more votes than any other Socialist candidate and 2,500 more than the nominee for Governor. That same year she addressed two thousand striking workers in the Colonial Theatre in Boston, urging them to continue their strike — no mean feat in those days preceding electronic amplification. In 1927 at the age of seventy-six, she was arrested for marching in protest of the execution of Nicola Sacco and Bartolomeo Vanzetti, thereby becoming a defendant in the American Civil Liberties Union's test case concerning the legality of the arrests. The case was won on appeal. Two years later she moved to teach at the Vineyard Shore School for women workers in industry.[68]

Little seems to be known about Amy Rayson, the other woman to join the New York Mathematical Society in its first year, except that she taught mathematics and physics at the Brearley School in New York from 1891 to 1898, and in 1899 became the joint principal of the School for Girls at 168 West 75th St. in New York City.[69]

---

[66]ibid, pp. 13-14.

[67]ibid, p. 12.

[68]Ann Moskol, "Ellen Amanda Hayes," in *Women of Mathematics: A Biobibliographic Sourcebook*, edited by Louise S. Grinstein and Paul J. Campbell, Greenwood Press, 1987, pp. 62-66.

[69]ibid, p. 12.

All six of these founding women (except perhaps Rayson) taught for a significant period of time at an institution of higher education serving women — all but Susan Cunningham at a woman's college. All apparently had a driving commitment to bettering the lot of women, although they expressed it in different ways.

Six more women were also founding members of the *American* Mathematical Society by 1894. **Ella Cornelia Williams** had been the first graduate student at Bryn Mawr when it opened in 1885. She taught mathematics at the Spence School in New York City, and was a regular attendee at the Society meetings from 1892 to 1903. **Ida Griffiths** was British but spent nine years from 1888 to 1897 teaching and studying in the United States. These two were the only women at the first summer colloquium of the AMS in 1896. (Scott always spent her summers in Europe.) Another British founding member of the American Mathematical Society was **Frances Hardcastle**, who came to the U.S. in 1892 to study at Bryn Mawr with Charlotte Scott. She was president of the Graduate Club at Bryn Mawr in 1895 and delegate to a conference of graduate students from twenty colleges and universities that year. However, she returned to Britain in 1901 without earning a degree at an American institution. **Fanny Rysam Hitchcock** earned a doctorate in chemistry in 1894 from the University of Pennsylvania, and was director of "the graduate department for women at the University of Pennsylvania" from 1897 to 1902, when she became director of Women's Studies. However, she retained her AMS membership until 1910.

Charlotte Cynthia Barnum (1860-1934) was the first woman to earn a Ph.D. in mathematics from Yale University, which she did in 1895. After teaching college mathematics for only one year, she held a succession of non-academic jobs, beginning with actuarial work. She then joined the Tidal Division of the U.S. Coast and Geodetic Survey until 1908. She helped with a biological survey for the U.S. Department of Agriculture from 1908 to 1916, after which she did various types of editorial work. She finally taught mathematics in a preparatory school from 1921 to 1923.[70]

Ruth Gentry (1862-1917) was one of Scott's first two doctoral graduates, receiving her Ph.D. in 1896. In 1891-1892, she studied at the University of Berlin; Scott tried hard to arrange for all her doctoral students to spend some time studying in Europe. Gentry wrote of her German experience, "I assume, on general principles, that there are students who look with disfavor upon anything pointing in the direction of co-education in Germany; what percent of the Berlin students belong to this class I have not the data for computing, but the number of those who have annoyed me I can reckon

---

[70]Betsey S. Whitman, "Women in the American Mathematical Society Before 1900: Part Three," *Association for Women in Mathematics Newsletter*, 13:6, November-December, 1983, pp. 9-12, p. 7.

to a nicety — the number is zero."[71] She taught at Vassar College from 1894 until 1902, when her health began to deteriorate. She then headed a mathematics department at a private school in Pittsburgh for three years, was a volunteer nurse, and traveled.

Betsey Whitman wrote in her 1983 report of women who joined the AMS before 1900, "All of the women in the study were remarkable. They pursued an education during a time when it was believed that women's brains were smaller than men's and that they were not suited for intellectual activity. [These women] helped to change the attitudes about the subordinate role of women that prevailed during the nineteenth century."[72]

Whitman did not mean to imply that all nineteenth century people believed that women were not suited for intellectual activity. Obviously, the twelve female founders of the AMS and the other women mentioned in this book not only believed that women could do challenging mathematics, but were determined to prove that fact. The personal sacrifices involved in such social proofs were considerable.

One striking characteristic of all twelve of the women who were on the original rolls of the American Mathematical Society was that (apparently) none married. All had crossed into the "men's sphere" by aspiring to learn mathematics at a high level and earn their own money; they knew that renouncing the joys of parenthood was part of the price. It seems likely that the twelve women among the founders of the American Mathematical Society in 1894 assumed that marriage was impossible for them. Indeed, from the 1870s through the 1920s between 40 and 60 percent of college graduates did not marry, at a time when only ten percent of all American women did not.[73] Most housekeeping activities required far more time than they would only a few decades later. Proving that women could hold their own intellectually with men, at a time when many doubted they could and every diaper had to be washed by hand and hung on the line, left little time for the traditional responsibilities of wives and mothers. However, the freedom to renounce marriage to pursue the life of the mind would become seriously challenged, as we shall see in the next chapter.

---

[71]ibid, p. 7.

[72]Betsey S. Whitman, "Women in the American Mathematical Society Before 1900: Part One," *Association for Women in Mathematics Newsletter*, 13:4, July-August, 1983, pp. 10-14, p. 10, and also "Women in the American Mathematical Society Before 1900: Part Three," *Association for Women in Mathematics Newsletter*, 13:6, November-December, 1983, pp. 9-12, p. 12.

[73]Carroll Smith-Rosenberg, *Disorderly Conduct: Visions of Gender in Victorian America*, Oxford University Press, 1985, p. 253.

CHAPTER 4

The Twentieth Century: Mathematics and Marriage

The "First Stage" of the feminist movement was in full swing by the early twentieth century and culminated with passage of the 19th Amendment to the United States constitution in 1920, which guaranteed access to the ballot box for women. There were still some inequalities, as the triumphant suffragettes soon discovered. "As one barrier falls, there is another," observed David Sadker recently.[1] The Equal Rights Amendment, immediately introduced in 1920, did not pass, and it failed again in the 1980s. As this is written, not only has the ERA not yet been passed, but the United States is one of the few countries of the 191 countries in the United Nations that has not yet ratified the Convention on the Discrimination Against Women.

My own impression is that the mathematical community has been more open to women than many, but our statistics show we still have a way to go.[2] The oldest institution of higher education in the country, Harvard University, still has not had a tenured woman on its regular mathematics faculty. (Deborah Hughes Hallett was a "Professor of the Practice," a position that was created for her, in which she specialized in undergraduate and remedial mathematics courses.[3] She is now a Professor of Mathematics at the University of Arizona.) In the 1920s one of Harvard's required courses for a doctorate in mathematics was taught by a man who refused to have women in his classroom. He allowed the door to be open, so women could sit outside, but they could not read the blackboard. That was well before the time of reproducible notes, so people who could not see the blackboard were at a great disadvantage. Nevertheless, some did earn doctorates in mathematics from Harvard during that time.[4]

With the vote came a softening of the separation of the sexes that had been so rigid in the late nineteenth century, and with this softening came the possibility that a woman did not have to choose between career and marriage. In 1932 Martha Carey Thomas (1857-1935), the second president of Bryn Mawr College, wrote a long and revealing letter to her beloved

---

[1]David Sadker on Math Medley, "Are Our Schools Failing Still?," June 19, 2004.

[2]Allyn Jackson, "Has the Women-in-Mathematics Problem Been Solved?," *Notices of the AMS*, August, 2004, 51:7, pp. 178-183.

[3]Deborah Hughes Hallett, personal emails in July, 2004.

[4]Alice Schafer, as told to her by a colleague at Wellesley College, recounted during Math Medley, December 1, 2001.

niece after the niece announced her engagement. "I have had several (eight, I think) in love with me and with one I was wildly in love, so wildly that I fled and never saw him for many years.... But my choice was made easy by the fact that in my generation marriage and an academic career was impossible. I knew myself well enough to realize that I could not give up my life's work..."[5]

The niece observes that her aunt had hoped she would follow in M. Carey Thomas' own footsteps, and had some reservation about marriage in general. However, the letter concedes, "On the pro side of the question we have the possibility that you and he will be able to make a 'genuine contribution' as the social workers say, to the all important burning question of whether a married woman can hold down a job as successfully as an unmarried woman. This must be proved over and over again before the woman question can get much further and I have set my heart on your making a success of it and so bringing great help to the '*Cause*'."[6]

This letter was written in 1932, when the possibility of combining marriage, motherhood, and career still needed to be proved "over and over again." We will see in Chapter 9 that the question of compatibility of career and motherhood may still be the burning issue of the early twenty-first century. In the mid-twentieth century, as I grew up in the two decades following Thomas' letter, I heard much discussion defending girls' education on the grounds that they might have to support themselves if their husband died. (The thought that I might not marry at all was unspeakable in the 1950s.) My mother's was the lone voice I personally can remember that suggested I might rightly aspire to "have it all" even if my husband did not succumb to an untimely death.

She didn't tell me about the other discussion raging in her youth. After women obtained the vote in the 1920s, men became worried that women were becoming too powerful politically, and sexologists linked their growing economic and political power with their "unnatural" personal relationships with each other. Unmarried women became suspect, politically and personally.[7] The flappers symbolized sexual liberation, not necessarily linked to political power, but sometimes. By the 1930s women students were expelled from college for staying out all night with a man — and for having too "intense" a relationship with another woman.[8] Some colleges explicitly prohibited women students from spending their nights in each others' rooms.[9]

---

[5] *The Making of a Feminist: Early Journals and Letters of M. Carey Thomas*, edited by Marjorie Houspian Dobkin, Kent State University Press, 1979, p. xv.

[6] ibid, p. xiv.

[7] Carroll Smith-Rosenberg, "The New Woman as Androgyne: Social Disorder and Gender Crisis, 1870-1936," *Disorderly Conduct: Visions of Gender in Victorian America*, Oxford University Press, 1985, pp. 243-349.

[8] Barbara Miller Solomon, *In the Company of Educated Women*, Yale University Press, New Haven, 1985, p. 162.

[9] Smith-Rosenberg, p. 281.

There was worried discussion about the effect of unmarried women faculty on women students, personally and politically.[10]

Also in the public sphere, many social pressures were thwarting the careers of intelligent women. In 1910 Ellen Amanda Hayes of the Wellesley mathematics department argued that two major reasons for the small number of women scientists included (1) social pressures that rewarded females for spending time on their appearance... and (2) the scarcity of good employment opportunities for females.[11] Employment opportunities have been a continuing problem, and I can remember as a teenager in the 1950s feeling resentful over how much time I felt "forced" to spend on appearance compared to the boys around me; it didn't seem fair. However, then (and now?) the apparent forced choice between mathematics and motherhood was worse.

A few women in mathematics before the mid-twentieth century did combine mathematical research and motherhood. Sofia Kovalevskaia and Christine Ladd-Franklin each had one daughter, but they were born after their mothers had earned doctorates and were nearing the end of their reproductive years. Marie Curie had two daughters, but both were born after she was well established professionally, and she had excellent support from both family and servants.[12] Her commitment to not wasting time in unproductive feminine activities was evident at her marriage ceremony, where she wore "no unusual dress," which was of "no matter to the groom who later amused himself at a banquet by calculating the number of scientific laboratories that could be financed through sale of the jewels adorning the female guests."[13]

Grace Chisholm Young (1868-1944), a British woman who spent most of her adult life in Switzerland, was the outstanding early exception to the "rule" of not combining mathematics and motherhood. However, she never earned money nor did she have her own paying job, and "in her letters she wrote that it wouldn't have been possible for her to do so."[14] Thus she was not literally entering the "men's sphere" and competing directly with men; her husband earned the family's income. Their arrangement was stated succinctly in a letter of William Henry Young to his wife. "The fact is that our papers ought to be published under our joint names, but if this were done, neither of us get the benefit of it. No. Mine the laurels

---

[10]ibid, p. 278.

[11]Ann Moskol in "Ellen Amanda Hayes," in *Women of Mathematics: A Biobibliographic Sourcebook*, edited by Louise S. Grinstein and Paul J. Campbell, Greenwood Press, 1987, p. 65, quoting Hayes in "Women and Scientific Research" in *Science* 32 (Dec. 16, 1910), pp. 864-866.

[12]Helena M. Pycior, "Marie Curie's 'Anti-Natural Path': Time Only for Science and Family," in *Uneasy Careers and Intimate Lives, Women in Science 1789-1979*, edited by Pnina G. Abir-Am and Dorinda Outram, Rutgers University Press, New Brunswick, 1989, p. 199.

[13]ibid, p. 198, quoting Eve Curie in *Marie Curie*, p. 207.

[14]Sylvia Young Wiegand, Will and Grace Young's granddaughter, in an email, July 12, 2004.

now and the knowledge. Yours the knowledge only. Everything under my
name now, and later when the loaves and fishes are no more procurable that
way, everything or much under your name." Will Young was president of
the London Mathematical Society from 1922 to 1924 and president of the
International Union of Mathematicians in 1929.

He kept his word, and in 1914 wrote in a footnote to one of his papers,
"Various circumstances have prevented me from composing the present paper myself. The substance of it only was given to my wife, who has kindly
put it into form. The elaboration of the argument is due to her."

Grace Chisholm Young in 1923. Courtesy of Sylvia Young Wiegand.

Together the Youngs produced over 200 research papers along with six
super-achieving children. "She completed all the requirements for a medical
degree except the internship.... She knew six languages and taught them to
the children, to whom she also communicated her love of music. Each child
played an instrument, and the family gave informal concerts together."[15]

[15]Sylvia Young Wiegand, "Grace Chisholm Young," *Women of Mathematics: A Bibliographic Sourcebook*, edited by Louise S. Grinstein and Paul J. Campbell, Greenwood
Press, 1987, pp. 247-254.

In the twentieth century, women mathematicians attained a series of "firsts." Some in the early part of the century also slipped in childless marriages.

Anna Johnson Pell Wheeler (1883-1966) was the first woman to give an invited address to the American Mathematical Society (in 1923) and also the first woman to give an AMS Colloquium lecture (in 1927). No other woman gave a Colloquium lecture until Julia Robinson in 1980.[16]

Before her birth, her parents and older siblings lived in a dugout hollowed from the side of a small hill, but she graduated from the University of South Dakota when she was only twenty years old. One of her mathematics professors there, Alexander Pell, recognized her ability and actively encouraged and helped her into a mathematical career. The year following her graduation she received a master's degree from the University of Iowa, and the next year a second master's degree from Radcliffe, the co-ordinate women's college of Harvard University. She studied at Radcliffe on scholarship for a second year, and then won the prestigious Alice Freeman Palmer fellowship with which she studied for a year at Göttingen University with Hilbert, Klein, Minkowski, and Herglotz.

That July (1907) she married Alexander Pell in Göttingen, despite her family's objections to her marrying a widower twenty-five years her senior. She taught two courses that fall at the University of South Dakota, but then returned to Göttingen without her husband to finish work on her doctorate. It seemed to be going well; the thesis was written and the defense was imminent. Then, apparently, there was a falling out with Hilbert, so she returned to the United States without a degree. Meanwhile, her husband had had a falling out with the administration of the University of South Dakota and landed a job at the Armour Institute of Technology in Chicago. She immediately enrolled at the University of Chicago and did a year's residency there studying with E. H. Moore and two astronomers. Her thesis written in Germany was accepted by Moore, and she was granted a Ph.D. in 1910.

She taught part-time at the University of Chicago that fall, but the following spring, her husband suffered a paralytic stroke. Until his death in 1920 she took care of him, supported them both, and continued her research. At first she substituted for him at the Armour Institute of Technology, but they refused to retain a woman on a full-time basis. For five difficult years she taught at Vassar College, but the teaching load was heavy. She was delighted to accept a position in 1918 at Bryn Mawr College, where time was provided for research. She succeeded Charlotte Scott as department chair in 1924. "There was a brief but happy second marriage [to Arthur Leslie Wheeler], followed by the death of her second husband in 1932."[17]

---

[16]Louise S. Grinstein and Paul J. Campbell, "Anna Johnson Pell Wheeler," in ibid, p. 244.

[17]ibid, p. 243.

Anna Johnson Pell Wheeler, c. 1904. Photo courtesy of Bryn
Mawr College Library, Barbara Grubb, archivist.

She was starred in *American Men of Science*, a great honor, and received two honorary doctorates. In 1940 she was selected by the Women's Centennial Congress as one of the one hundred American women to have succeeded in careers not open to women a century before.

Mina Rees (1902-1997) was the first woman to become president of the American Association for the Advancement of Science (in 1971) and also the first person to receive the Mathematical Association of American award for Distinguished Service to Mathematics (in 1961).[18] Indeed, she was the only woman to receive that award until 1991, when it was bestowed on Shirley Hill. (Since then, there have been several more women: Anneli Lax in 1995,

---

[18]Frances Rosamond, "A Century of Women's Participation in the MAA and Other Organizations," *Winning Women into Mathematics*, edited by Patricia Clark Kenschaft and Sandra Zarodny Keith, MAA, Washington, 1991, p. 34.

Alice T. Schafer in 1998, and T. Christine Stevens in 2004.)[19] In 1985 the City University of New York named its new graduate library after her.[20]

Rees' mother, Alice Stackhouse, had immigrated to the United States in 1882 from England after her father (Mina's grandfather) had become blacklisted because he was a union leader in the British coal mines.[21] Later that same year Alice Stackhouse married Moses Rees, an insurance salesman. Mina was the youngest of their five children, and when she was two years old, they moved to the Bronx in New York City.

"When I was in eighth grade in a public elementary school, I had marvelous teachers. One day one of my teachers, a man who was my current hero, said to me, 'Mina, you know, I think you ought to take the admission test for Hunter High School tomorrow morning.' I said, 'Hunter High School?' I had never heard of Hunter High School, but if he thought I should take the test, I would go down and take the test. I passed the test and was admitted. It was a superior school for gifted girls, and of course there was a mathematics department. And all of the girls studied mathematics."[22]

Rees then went to Hunter College, where she graduated summa cum laude in 1923. She was also president of her class and yearbook editor. The mathematics department asked her to stay and teach, but she felt she needed more education, so she took a job at Hunter High School and began graduate work at Columbia University.[23] Until then, she had felt no gender bias since she had been in a single-sex system.

"After I had my bachelor's degree, I studied at Columbia. When I had taken four of their six-credit courses in mathematics and was beginning to think about a thesis, the word was conveyed to me — no official ever told me this, but I learned — that the Columbia mathematics department was not interested in having women candidates for Ph.D.'s. This was a very unpleasant shock....

"I decided to switch to Teacher's College and take the remaining courses necessary for an M.A. there. A few years later, after I'd saved enough money, I went to Chicago. That was the only episode that raised the question about the appropriateness of mathematics as a field for women before I had my Ph.D. It was a really traumatic affair for me."[24]

After she had earned the master's degree at Columbia, she taught at Hunter College until 1943, except for her years at the University of Chicago,

---

[19]www.maa.org/Awards/gunghu.html

[20]Phyllis Fox, in "Mina Rees," *Women of Mathematics: A Biobibliographic Sourcebook*, edited by Louise S. Grinstein and Paul J. Campbell, Greenwood Press, 1987, p. 178.

[21]ibid., p. 175.

[22]Mina Rees, interview with Rosamond Dana and Peter J. Hilton in *Mathematical People*, edited by Donald J. Albers and Gerald L. Alexanderson, MAA, Washington, 1985, pp. 256-267, pp. 258-9.

[23]Phyllis Fox, p. 176.

[24]Rosamond Dana and Peter J. Hilton interview, p. 258.

Mina Rees receiving an honorary Doctor of Science from Wheaton College in 1964. Shown here with Richard P. Chapman (on the left), trustee and former chair of the board of trustees of Wheaton College and president of the New England Merchant's National Bank in Boston, and Dr. Nathan M. Pusey, president of Harvard University. Dr. Mina Rees was then dean of graduate studies at City University of New York. Photo courtesy of Graduate Center Archives, City University of New York, Julie Cunningham, Chief Librarian, John Rothman, archivist.

where she earned her Ph.D. in 1932.[25] "The decisive event in my life came in 1943, when I accepted a wartime job that introduced a whole new orientation into my career....

"Why do I call this change decisive? First, because it greatly broadened my awareness of unfamiliar fields of mathematics and my contacts with mathematicians; and, second, because it greatly increased my understanding of the character and activities of many of our educational institutions and of the structure and operations of the government, including the military establishment."[26] Why did she get this offer?

"It was not because I was an applied mathematician — my degree was in Abstract Algebra. It was not because I was a woman — there was no equal opportunity then. It was the good old buddy system. Let me explain.

---

[25] Phyllis Fox, p. 176.

[26] Mina Rees, "Women Mathematicians Before 1950," transcript of AWM panel in August 1978, organized, moderated, and edited by Pat Kenschaft, *AWM Newsletter*, July-August, 1979, 9:4, pp. 9-18, p. 15.

"I was at Chicago from 1929-1931. In the summer of 1930 I attended my first summer meeting of the mathematicians. . . . What I remember most clearly about that meeting was that I had breakfast with Marston Morse and G. D. Birkhoff. I found the experience overwhelming, and I was enchanted with mathematicians. . . . When I returned to New York, I continued my attendance at meetings, both winter and summer. And so it came about that, when Courant was a visiting lecturer of the Society, I met him at a meeting, and continued my acquaintance with him when he came to NYU. Though I was not a research mathematician, and though I soon learned that I couldn't understand much at the meetings, I did find them useful in giving me some idea of the directions that mathematical research was taking. I might add that I understand even less now."[27]

Rees' able service in the military during World War II led her to be invited after the war by the U.S. Navy to establish and lead the mathematical research program in the newly created Office of Naval Research (ONR). "When Rees went to Washington in 1946 to join the ONR, it was difficult to obtain housing. . . . She eventually located a hotel downtown that would rent her a room for two weeks at a time — all others would allow only a five day stay. Having to vacate her room regularly,. . . she used the occasion to travel to one or another of the nation's leading mathematics departments to consult with colleagues about research needs and opportunities."[28]

"My sex was only one of the problems that I had. I very much doubted that the mathematicians would want to receive support for their research from a military organization after the war was over. Initially, this judgement was right. But as time passed, mathematicians found the program a very desirable one."[29]

Rees was exceedingly successful in promoting mathematical research in the United States, and she received many honors as a result. In 1953 she returned to Hunter College as dean of the faculty. In 1961 she became dean of the graduate studies of the newly created City University of New York. She helped establish the Graduate Center of CUNY and became successively its dean, provost, and president (1969-1972). In 1970 she chaired the Council of Graduate Schools in the United States.[30]

In the 1978 panel, she said, "At our graduate school, women's admission to graduate study, access to fellowships, and acceptance on the faculty and in the administration seemed to be substantially without discrimination. On another front, I can report that, over the years, two other women have been appointed to head the Mathematics Branch of the Office of Naval Research

---

[27]ibid, p. 16.

[28]Homer Stavley, "Mina Spiegel Rees" in *Notable Women in Mathematics*, edited by Charlene Morrow and Teri Perl, Greenwood Press, Westport, CT, 1998, pp. 174-180, p. 177.

[29]Mina Rees in the AWM panel of 1978, p. 17.

[30]ibid, p. 18.

and that one of these was also made Director of the Mathematics Sciences Division."[31]

When asked in her eighties if she thought that there was a difference in the capacity of women and men to become mathematicians, Rees responded, "I don't believe that is true.... The eye on marriage is the background thing. In my family, that wasn't present. There was absolutely no parental pressure for me to marry. Each of us did what he or she pleased. That was not typical of American society, I think."[32]

"I don't care if there are a lot of women mathematicians, but if other girls have the same motivations I had — and I'm sure they do because there were so many of us at that time — I wish they wouldn't have irrelevant things interfering with their desires. It may well be that in our society a woman must sacrifice too much if she wants a career that offbeat. It didn't seem like a sacrifice to me because I had plenty of men friends, and I wasn't prepared to get married; that wasn't what I wanted to do."[33]

Nevertheless, Mina Rees did get married — at the age of 53. She met Leopold Brahdy, a physician, at a party in 1936. He said that he was going to Russia with a group to study life in that country and suggested she come along. She was planning to go to the Mathematical Congress in Oslo, so she added the trip to Russia to her plans.[34] They were married in 1955, and he died in 1977.[35]

Mina Rees' professional accomplishments and honors are amply documented elsewhere. Immediately after the election that would result in her becoming the first woman president of the American Association for the Advancement of Science in 1971, the *New York Times* published an article that included the sentence, "The modern breed of woman militants will no doubt take it for granted that male chauvinism was primarily responsible for denying members of their sex previous occupancy of the AAAS presidency."[36]

The trend of women Ph.D's in mathematics in the mid-twentieth century is a curious study in numbers. Between 1930 and 1934 there were 62 American women who earned a doctorate in mathematics; between 1955 and 1959, this number was 58. In the intervening five-year periods (between 1935 to 1954), there were 51, 43, 44, and 51 women recipients, respectively, less than ten per year on average.[37]

Although the numbers remained approximately steady, the percentage of American doctorates in mathematics that were awarded to women fell from

---

[31]ibid, p. 18.

[32]Mina Rees in the interview by Rosamond Dana and Peter J. Hilton, p. 259.

[33]ibid, p. 261.

[34]Phyllis Fox, p. 176.

[35]Introduction to Rosamond Dana and Peter J. Hilton interview, p. 257.

[36]December 31, 1969, quoted in Fox, p. 177.

[37]Margaret A. M. Murray, *Women Becoming Mathematicians, Creating a Professional Identity in Post-World War II America*, MIT Press, Cambridge, 2000, p. 5.

15.7 percent to 4.6 percent over this period. This is because the number of male recipients of doctorates in mathematics rose from 334 in 1930-1934 to 1,208 in 1955-1959, more than tripling.[38] Partially, this was the effect of "The Mathematician's War," as the chair of Bell Telephone Laboratories dubbed World War II.[39] For example German U-boats shot down about a thousand Allied ships early in the war with very little loss to themselves, but once radar and location analysis were developed, the U-boats themselves were essentially eliminated. The breaking of the secret code of the Germans by Allied mathematicians under the leadership of Alan Turing had drastic military consequences. I will always remember Isidor Rabi at the age of eighty-six saying, as he began a talk at Montclair State, "We did it because we were afraid Hitler would take over all of Europe. We were afraid he would take over England. That's why we did it! That's why we did it!" In his eighties he was apologizing emotionally to his audience for helping to initiate the atomic age. He then went on to say that at his first meeting with the military he thought to himself, "It's a good thing mathematicians and the military haven't talked before."

Of course, they had. Archimedes presumably sank invading ships with skillfully aimed catapults. However, the use of mathematics in World War II was vastly more effective — and horrifying — than anything that had preceded it. This would later cause concern among mathematicians such as Philip Davis, who wrote a chapter titled, "Beating Their Swords Into Fun and Games."[40] But in the 1940s the combination of patriotism and intellectual excitement was appealing to many mathematicians.

In World War II, women mathematicians played a significant role as men went abroad. Offices full of women served as "computers," and college women volunteered on weekends. Some did much more. **Grace Murray Hopper** (1906-1992) programmed the just-completed Mark I with Harold Aiken to make calculations that would help aim guns at their targets more precisely. After the war, she would envision and supervise the development of COBOL, the first high-level computer language, which is still in use. She also found a live bug that had disabled a walk-in computer (the early electronic computers made with vacuum tubes occupied at least one room), thereby giving rise to the computer expression "debugging." Divorced at the end of the war without children, she then devoted her life to the United States Navy, eventually rising to the rank of Commodore and becoming the oldest active officer in the Navy. She would close her public appearances with

---

[38]ibid, p. 5.

[39]ibid, p. 11, quoting Frank Jewett, in "The Mobilization of Science in National Defense," *Science*, 1942, 95, 225-241.

[40]Philip Davis, *The Education of a Mathematician*, A. K. Peters, Ltd., Wellesley, MA, 2000.

the statement that the highest privilege and honor of her life was serving in the United States Navy, and then would snap to a saluting position.[41]

Three somewhat younger women mathematicians who have received wide recognition for both their research and AMS leadership are Julia Robinson (1919-1985, see Chapter 2), Cathleen Morawetz, and Mary Ellen Rudin.

Cathleen Synge Morawetz (b. 1923) was the second woman president of the American Mathematical Society (1995-1997) and the first woman to become a director of a (private) mathematics institute, the Courant Institute (1984).

She grew up in Toronto, Canada, the daughter of Eleanor Mabel Allen Synge and noted mathematician John Synge and earned her undergraduate degree at the University of Toronto in 1945. Later that year she married Herbert Morawetz, a chemist she had met at the university, with whom she eventually had four children. Meanwhile, she had gone to Massachusetts, and in 1946 was granted a master's degree in electrical engineering from MIT. With the help of a family friend, her husband finally landed a job in New Jersey, after being told by many prospective employers, "We don't hire Jews."[42] At that time, it was taken for granted that she would move to join her husband.

When John Synge told his fellow-mathematician Richard Courant that his daughter had gotten married and had to relocate, Courant replied that his daughter too had just interrupted her career by getting married. "You can't help my daughter — she's in biology — but I can help yours."[43] Courant offered Cathleen Morawetz a job using her engineering background, but she soon started taking graduate mathematics courses. NYU, under the leadership of Courant, was far more encouraging to women than most institutions in mid-century. It was *the* leading producer of women Ph.D's. in mathematics during the 1950s.[44] Others included Betty Jane Gassner, Susan Hahn, Anneli Lax, Edith Luchins, Rebekka Struik, and Tilla Weinstein. "I didn't intend to go on in graduate school. . . but I got swept up by the — well, it was a very stimulating atmosphere that I had not experienced at either MIT or Toronto. And *that's* why I became interested in mathematics. . . . There weren't so many full-time graduate students; there were people like me, who were working on projects right within the group. And there was a

---

[41]Amy King with Tina Schalch, "Grace Brewster Murray Hopper," *Women in Mathematics: A Bibliographic Sourcebook*, edited by Louise Grinstein and Paul Campbell, Greenwood Press, Westport, CT, 1987, pp. 67-73, and personal recollections of Hopper's appearance at Montclair State in 1984.

[42]Teri Perl, "Cathleen Synge Morawetz," *Notable Women in Mathematics: A Biographical Dictionary*, edited by Charlene Morrow and Teri Perl, Greenwood Press, Westport, CT, 1998, p. 149.

[43]ibid.

[44]Margaret A. M. Murray, *Women Becoming Mathematicians: Creating a Professional Identity in Post-World War II America*, MIT Press, Cambridge, MA, 2000, p. 147.

Cathleen Morawetz and a grandson Eric Rubinstein motor their
sailboat through a lock in Muskoa, Ontario. Her two major non-
mathematical interests are her grandchildren and sailing. Photo
courtesy of Cathleen Morawetz.

really very wonderful, enthusiastic environment — a lot of mixing between
the faculty and the students. And so it was a great time."[45]

Both Cathleen and Herbert successfully pursued Ph.D.'s while producing
and caring for their first two children. The following year they went to
Cambridge for postdoctoral studies, he at Harvard Medical School and she
at MIT. Working with C. C. Lin built her self-confidence, and her first two
publications came out the year she spent at MIT. She and her husband
were then happy to get what turned out to be permanent jobs in New York
City, he on the chemistry faculty of Brooklyn Polytechnical Institute (now
Polytechnic University in Brooklyn) and she at New York University. Both
are now retired, she having risen through the ranks from department chair
to Director of the Institute.

In 1998 Cathleen Morawetz became the first woman mathematician to
be granted the National Medal of Science, also called the Presidential Medal
of Science, the highest honor our country awards to leaders in the behavioral,
biological, physical, and mathematical sciences. First granted in 1963, there
had been only 362 such awards up to and including the 1998 awardees.
In 2000 Karen Uhlenbeck became the second woman mathematician to be
thus honored. As of 2005, there have been only two women mathematicians

---

[45]ibid, pp. 147-148.

among the 417 awardees. Of these 417, 50 were mathematicians and 22 women; 13 of the 22 women are biologists.

Mary Ellen Estill Rudin (b. 1924) was the third woman vice president of the American Mathematical Society in 1980-1981.[46] She grew up in very rural Texas in a town that was accessible only via a 40-mile dirt road up a canyon. Only five students were in her high school graduating class. The scenery was magnificent, but play was mostly imaginary; children developed their imaginations in ways that would prove useful for a mathematician. Mary Ellen's only sibling was ten years younger, so she also learned to enjoy being alone.

Her father had fond memories of being a student at the University of Texas, so when she became the appropriate age, he drove her there himself. She had liked all her high school subjects and had no idea what her major would be. On the first day there she met R. L. Moore, who was doing registration for the mathematics department. He asked her a number of questions, discovered she used "if" and "or" correctly, and, as she now knows, decided to make her into a mathematician. He signed her up for the course she had already decided to take, and when she went to the first class, he was professor. It appears now that he rearranged his schedule to teach her a mathematics course every semester she was in college.

Moore's teaching method was to pose problems and have the students solve them. He would call on the less capable students first, and "let them fall on their faces. Then he would have me solve the problem for them. I was always the last person he would call on."[47] She went to the board and showed the class her solution. "It builds your ego to be able to do a problem when someone else can't, but it destroys that person's ego. I never liked that feature of Moore's classes. Yet I participated in it.... I was the killer. He used me that way, and I was conscious of being used that way."[48] "He built your confidence so you could do *anything*. No matter what mathematical problem you were faced with, you could do it. I have that total confidence to this day."[49]

She does not believe in the Moore method, even though it effectively builds confidence in the "killer" students. One disadvantage was that Moore's students learned only the mathematics revealed in the problems they themselves solved; she did not have a broad understanding of mathematics when she received a Ph.D. "I didn't even know what an analytic function was...."

---

[46]Rosemary McCroskey Karr, Jaleb Rezaie, and Joel E. Wilson, "Mary Ellen Rudin," *Women in Mathematics: A Bibliographic Sourcebook*, edited by Louise Grinstein and Paul Campbell, Greenwood Press, Westport, CT, 1987, pp. 190-192, p. 190.

[47]David J. Albers and Constance Reid, "An Interview With Mary Ellen Rudin," *College Mathematics Journal*, March, 1988, 19:2, pp. 115-137, p. 121.

[48]ibid, p. 123.

[49]Claudia Henrion, *Women in Mathematics: The Addition of Difference*, Indiana University Press, Indianapolis and Bloomington, 1977, pp. 84-94, p. 88, quoting Albers, Alexander, and Reid, *More Mathematical People*, Volume II, 1988, p. 288.

I never took an examination in mathematics in my life."[50] She had never read a mathematical research paper when she took her first faculty position. She makes sure her students know a great deal more mathematics by the time they leave her. "Of course, they're not always as confident as I was."[51]

Toward the end of her undergraduate years, she was still enjoying many fields, so she went to the vocational office for a battery of tests. They told her she was especially good at mathematics, and she responded that she didn't want to be a high school teacher. She didn't know anything else she could do with mathematics.

"They said, 'Just relax. They'll invite you to stay and go to graduate school.' And indeed within a week (I almost suspected that they had called the math department) I was offered an instructorship. So I stayed and went to graduate school. I am sure Moore would have caught me anyway. He knew exactly what he was going to do with me. He just hadn't told me yet."[52]

After she received her Ph.D. in 1949, Moore arranged for her to teach at Duke University, where she met Walter Rudin, another member of the Duke math faculty. They were married in 1953, and Rudin took a job at the University of Rochester. Wilder, an earlier Moore Ph.D., had arranged for her to have a grant to work with him at the University of Michigan, but when she wrote back that she was getting married and going to Rochester, he had the grant transferred to Rochester. "I always had this built-in family that took care of me.... It never occurred to me that it was slightly difficult to be a woman mathematician."[53] The University of Rochester hadn't known she was coming, but when she arrived, they gave her a calculus class to teach and a private office. "And that's the kind of job I have had all my life until 1971, when I became a full professor." She was allowed to teach the courses she wanted to teach, and not expected to do any committee or administrative work. "I often had grant money. It didn't make that much difference in my life though, since Walter always had a good job. But I was a mathematician, and I always thought of myself as a mathematician."[54]

In the first two years of their marriage, the Rudins had two daughters. Some years later they had two sons. At first they had friends helping with their two children. Before the birth of their third child, however, "I happened on an absolutely fantastic woman named Lila Hilgendorf. She had been the wife of a farmer and had had six children. She was wonderful with children.... One thing she did for me was absolutely fantastic. The first weekend after my retarded child was born, she said, 'Oh, I just have to have him for the weekend!' And he went to her house for the weekend for the rest of her life. Actually he lived at her house the last several years. So when

---

[50]ibid, pp. 125 and 126.

[51]ibid, p. 125.

[52]Albers and Reid, p. 121.

[53]ibid, p. 129.

[54]ibid, p. 130.

Mary Ellen Rudin teaching a class as a young instructor. Courtesy of the Mathematical Association of America, Donald Albers, and Mary Ellen Rudin.

people ask how it is, in my position, to have four children, I have to say that when you've got Lila, it's easy."[55]

In an interview more than a decade later, she reflected, "I think there are a fair number of women in my day who had the potential to become mathematicians, but who didn't become mathematicians because it didn't seem right to have someone help you with your children." Often it was the husband who was reluctant for his wife to get the needed help. Walter Rudin had grown up in Central Europe, where nannies were common. They realized that "the person who changes your diapers doesn't necessarily determine what you do in life." She also emphasized that the support she received from Walter's employers and from her Moore "family" were valuable, perhaps essential, for her research career. "The whole community support — family and other mathematicians' support — are needed in order to be a mathematician."[56]

Rudin's method of doing mathematics also contributed to her spectacular success in churning out new theorems and counterexamples. "I've never minded doing mathematics lying on the sofa in the middle of the living

---

[55]ibid, p. 130.
[56]Henrion, p. 91.

room with the children climbing all over me. I like to know, even when I'm working on mathematics, what is going on. I like to be in the center of things..."[57]

[When] the children were little, it was actually something very nice to do, to sit down with the little kids and let them do their thing while you sat and thought about mathematics in the same place. And you don't have to pay your entire attention to the child; the child goes about his business, just like you do... you think about it [a mathematics problem] for a few minutes, you go do something else, you come back. Actually, that's how one does mathematics a great deal of the time. It's not with continuous thought. You don't sit down and solve a problem in some finite number of hours without interruption. You work at it for a little while; you go away from it a little bit; you come back to it."[58]

She has produced over 90 research papers, a prodigious output for any mathematician's lifetime.[59] However, she refers to hers as the "housewife's generation."[60] She reveled in being a mother, and always took it for granted that she would follow her husband and enjoy the economic security that he provided. Her unusual happiness caused biographer Claudia Henrion to suggest that her model might be useful to both women and men. "Is it not possible for mathematicians to be part-time for certain segments of their career, and still be defined as professionals?.... Is it necessary to relegate family to a lesser priority in order to be defined as a real mathematician?"[61]

Other women were pursuing both careers and hobbies in mathematics beyond these comparatively famous women. The paucity of mathematical role models for girls and minorities reflects a lack of media attention to all mathematicians. Try asking your friendly person-on-the-street to name some mathematicians. When I ask my liberal arts college students to list as many mathematicians as they can — first individually, then in small groups, then as a class — they have never thought of more than ten in total, including Pythagoras, Newton, Einstein, the author of their text, and me. Recently, many never heard of Euclid. No wonder women and mathematicians are rarely noticed!

What was life like for less "famous" mid-twentieth century women mathematicians? Many were married, unlike their nineteenth century predecessors. Social possibilities had changed sufficiently so that a strong woman might have both a career and a marriage, although the options were less

---

[57]Albers and Reid, p. 133.

[58]Margaret A. M. Murray, *Women Becoming Mathematicians: Creating a Professional Identity in Post-World War II America*, MIT Press, Cambridge, MA, 2000, p. 180.

[59]Rosemary McCroskey Karr, Jaleb Rezaie, and Joel E. Wilson, "Mary Ellen Rudin," *Women in Mathematics: A Bibliographic Sourcebook*, edited by Louise Grinstein and Paul Campbell, Greenwood Press, Westport, CT, 1987, pp. 190-192, p. 190.

[60]Henrion, p. 85.

[61]ibid, p. 94.

than those of the twenty-first century, as these stories illustrate. Second class citizenship was not the same as total exclusion. Even if mothering and home-making were still their sole responsibilities (John Barrett's cooking reported below was a rare exception), innovations such as electric lights and irons, gas stoves, and vacuum cleaners helped middle class women combine domestic and career lives by the mid-twentieth century more easily than their grandmothers. Later, automatic clothes washers and dryers, dish washers, and frozen food would help even more.

The women who appear in this chapter, chosen mostly because of their organizational leadership, are atypical of mid-twentieth century women mathematicians in that none were divorced except Hopper. Margaret Murray's fascinating book *Women Becoming Mathematicians: Creating a Professional Identity in Post-World War II America*,[62] is based on interviews in the 1990s of 36 of the 200 American women who received a doctorate in mathematics between 1940 and 1959. In it, she suggests that the divorce rate of these women was comparable to the fifty percent divorce rate that was prevalent in the 1970s, around the time that most of the interviewed women were divorced. It may not be coincidental that the initial women who were elected to the top offices in the AMS and MAA had supportive husbands throughout their career, except for Dorothy Bernstein, who remained single.

The Mathematical Association of America, which focused on college mathematics teaching, provided a congenial professional organization for many women mathematicians. *The Monthly*, around which the MAA was formed, was founded in 1894 by Benjamin Finkel and his wife Hannah Cokeley Finkel. We know remarkably little about her, given that he once said she "helped in the proofreading of nearly every page."[63] When *The Monthly* fell onto hard times in 1914 and appealed to the AMS for sponsorship, it was refused.[64]

In 1915 ten women and 96 men met at Ohio State University and decided to form an organization serving college teachers of mathematics with *The Monthly* as its official journal. About twelve percent of the more than one thousand charter members were women. Two of these would eventually become vice president, Helen Abbott Merrill and Clara Eliza Smith; both were on the faculty of Wellesley College.[65] However, as with the AMS, the presidency was reserved for men until the late twentieth century.

Dorothy Bernstein (1914-1988) was the first woman president of the Mathematical Association of America in 1979-1980. She was the oldest of

---

[62]Margaret A. M. Murray, *Women Becoming Mathematicians: Creating a Professional Identity in Post-World War II America*, MIT Press, Cambridge, MA, 2000.

[63]Frances Novak Rosamond, "A Century of Women's Participation in the MAA and Other Organizations," in *Winning Women into Mathematics*, edited by Patricia Kenschaft and Sandra Keith, MAA, Washington, DC, 1991, pp. 31-53, p. 31.

[64]Murray, p. 7.

[65]Rosamond, p. 33.

five children, four daughters and one son, of Russian immigrants with no formal education. Four of them earned Ph.D.'s and the fifth an M.D.

Dorothy attended the public schools of Milwaukee, Wisconsin, and then her father mortgaged his home so she could attend the University of Wisconsin. At the age of twenty she received both her B.A. degree summa cum laude and an M.A. degree in mathematics, graduating first in a class of 2000.[66] The following year she did further graduate work at the same institution and taught undergraduates as a University Fellow. In 1935 she obtained a scholarship to Brown University.[67]

"So I came to Brown in 1935 and here became aware for the first time that some people made a distinction between men and women in mathematics. For example, I was assigned to teach a course in remedial algebra at Pembroke College, then a separate college for women at Brown, and Hugh Hamilton was assigned to teach the same course to Brown boys. When we discovered that I had three girls in my class and he had 45 boys, it seemed natural to both of us, he from California and I from Wisconsin, to make two classes of 24 students each. But the chairman, C. R. Adams, would not hear of the idea, saying that the Brown boys would not stand being taught by a woman instructor. I pointed out that I had taught boys in Madison the previous year, but nothing was done. We continued for a full semester — I with three girls and Hamilton with 45 boys." She then told of having an oral preliminary exam in two parts lasting eight hours by the entire Brown mathematics department, although some of her colleagues had only a two-hour exam and many only slightly more. A sympathetic faculty member told her that her exam was especially long for two reasons: she was a woman, and she had taken most of her courses at a Midwestern university.

Searching for her first job had its memorable aspects too. "...R.D.D. Richardson was Dean of the Brown Graduate School and also Secretary of the American Mathematical Society for many years. In his latter capacity, he was consulted by many people about hiring personnel — I have heard stories, perhaps exaggerated, that he was a one-man employment bureau for mathematicians throughout the country. I do know, however, that when I came to see him, as we all did, about a college teaching job, he took out a map of the United States, covered the region west of the Mississippi and said, 'You can't get a job there, because you are a woman.' Then he covered the part south of the Ohio River and said, 'And you can't get a job there, because you are Jewish.' So that left the Northeast quadrant. Well it happened that I heard of a job at Mt. Holyoke and after a visit to South Hadley, I got the position. When I told the Dean, he expostulated, 'But I had that job all reserved for Hamilton!' I was at Mt. Holyoke from 1937 to

---

[66] "Coon on Bernstein," Geraldine A. Coon, Professor of Mathematics, *Goucher Quarterly*, provided by archivist Sydney Roby.

[67] Ann Moskol, "Dorothy Bernstein," in *Women of Mathematics: A Biobibliographic Sourcebook*, edited by Louise S. Grinstein and Paul J. Campbell, Greenwood Press, Westport, CT, 1987, pp. 17-20, p. 17.

Dorothy Bernstein enjoying a difficult calculus problem with her students. Photo courtesy of Goucher College Archives, Julia Rogers Library, Sydney Roby, archivist.

1940, meanwhile receiving my Ph.D. from Brown in 1939. Then I returned to Wisconsin and was an instructor at the university."[68]

In 1942 she went to Berkeley in the war effort. "I remember Evelyn Fix and Elizabeth Scott working steadily to all hours of the night in order to compile long lists of figures which they would mail every morning to Washington." After eight months she left for the University of Rochester, where she stayed until 1959. She then went to Goucher College, from which she retired in 1982.

"I would like to speak briefly about the contrast between attitudes and opportunities for women with bachelor's degrees in mathematics in the late 1930s and... 1950," she said in her 1978 talk. "Before World War II the only opportunities open to them were high school teaching, a few civil service jobs doing mostly routine statistical calculations, a few low-level actuarial jobs, and graduate school with the remote possibility of a college teaching job at the end. This changed drastically after the war, for two reasons. During the war, women had taken jobs formerly held by men and had shown they could handle them, and also the computer explosion opened up many new areas to mathematics applications with many new jobs resulting from this.

---

[68]Dorothy Bernstein in, "Women Mathematicians Before 1950," panel organized, moderated, and edited by Pat Kenschaft, *AWM Newsletter*, July-August, 1979, 9:4, pp. 9-11, p. 10.

"On the other hand the attitude of women also changed. In 1950, most of the graduating mathematics majors, like most of their sisters, were interested only in getting married and raising a family. The numbers going to graduate school and entering professions decreased markedly. In contrast, before WW II, there was a slow but steady number of women going seriously into mathematics. For example, all six of the women who were graduate students at Brown when I was there continued in mathematics. Some married and some did not; but they are all, or were for many years, college teachers, industrial mathematicians, editors of mathematics journals, and so on.

"One final observation: There always has been a very nice, strong tradition of older women in mathematics helping younger ones as much as they could." She credited Julia Bower, Anna Pell Wheeler, Marie Weiss, and Marie Litzinger. "But then I can also say that, with a few glaring exceptions, the men I have known in mathematics have been equally kind and generous in their support."[69]

In 1962 Bernstein won a National Science Foundation grant to purchase the first computer at a women's college, which was installed at Goucher College. The following year she won an NSF grant for a Summer Institute on Computer-Based Mathematics for high school teachers. A representative of all but one of the public high schools in Baltimore County and four private schools attended a six-week course on campus during the summer of 1969. During the following decade she led an animated effort to introduce applied mathematics and computing into the mathematics curriculum. Throughout her career she was active in the local AAUP chapter and many campus committees, along with the regional and national activities that led up to her becoming the first woman president of the MAA. Her colleague wrote, "Whenever possible, she indulged in her favorite hobbies of gardening, canning and freezing."[70]

It is hard in the twenty-first century to understand the social pressures in the mid-twentieth century that caused women to marry despite the grim cultural punishments of marriage, motherhood, and even an engagement to be married. The disapproval and joking that was directed at "old maids" at that time was potent, but hard to record. It took fortitude to remain single as Dorothy Bernstein and most faculty in the women's colleges did. However, Lida K. Barrett, whose story follows, did marry, and experienced the typical treatment of professional women who chose motherhood over remaining single or marrying late in life.

Lida Kittrell Barrett (b. 1927) was the second woman to be president of the MAA. She grew up in Houston. Her father had lost a leg in a railway work-related accident when he was still a teenager. He was fitted with an artificial leg and much later was able to purchase the company that made his prosthesis. Barrett remembers him as someone who was "very good

---

[69]ibid, p. 11.
[70]Coon.

at numbers, really enjoyed numbers and games and things, and was very intelligent." Barrett's biographer Margaret Murray observes that in the first half of the twentieth century it was still possible for a man to have an excellent career without a formal education, but that was not true for women. Thus Barrett's mother campaigned for her two daughters to become highly educated.[71]

Both of her daughters went to Rice Institute (now Rice University) in Houston, where tuition was free in the 1940s. Lida graduated in 1946 at the age of eighteen. She worked for Schlumberger (an oilfield services provider) for a year, still living with her parents, and then accepted a position at Texas State College for Women (now Texas Women's University) in Denton. The department head there, Harlan Miller, had been the second woman to earn a doctorate under R. L. Moore, and she was eager for Barrett also to earn a doctorate. At the end of the 1947-48 academic year, Miller persuaded her to spend the summer in Austin studying at the University of Texas. When her protégé was offered a graduate assistantship for the 1948-1949 year, Miller said, "[There is] absolutely no point in your coming back here. You need to go to graduate school."

During her first year at Texas, she completed a master's thesis, decided to earn a Ph.D. with Moore, and met a fellow graduate student, John Barrett, her future husband. The following summer she again worked for Schlumberger, and the next academic year she declined the offer of an assistantship, choosing instead to work at the Defense Research Lab on campus. She was told in an interview to apply for a full fellowship, and she interpreted that to mean she would probably get one.

However, when she announced her engagement, she was moved down the priority list. "...because if I was getting married, they weren't going to waste a fellowship on me.... The two men who got [the fellowships] both got doctorates, but they got them after I got mine." She continued to enjoy the more remunerative job at the Defense Research Lab. However, when she actually married later that year, she was dismissed because of the anti-nepotism laws then in effect in Texas. "My husband was a full-time instructor." Her job was half time and "had nothing to do with the mathematics department.... The whole business of not getting the fellowship and getting booted out [of the lab] was just part of the culture of the time."[72]

They had married with the assumption that both would be earning money, so she picked up as much tutoring as she could find. The following fall John took a job at the University of Delaware. Although he had not defended her right to a fellowship, Moore highly recommended Lida to J. R. Kline at the University of Pennsylvania. At first she declined the assistantship he offered, took two courses, and tried to become pregnant. When this didn't work quickly, she accepted the assistantship in the fall of 1952.

[71]Margaret A. M. Murray, *Women Becoming Mathematicians: Creating a Professional Identity in Post-World War II America*, MIT Press, Cambridge, 2000, p. 51.
[72]ibid, pp. 138-140.

Lida Kittrell and her fiancé John Barrett listening to records, one of their favorite pastimes in those days. Photo courtesy of Lida Kittrell Barrett.

She was living in Newark, Delaware, and taking a train through Wilmington to Philadelphia daily. "... two stops to Wilmington, run down the stairs and up the other stairs, and twenty-two stops to Philadelphia and then take the trolley [to Penn].... I left home at 7:10 and got to campus at 8:30." Evening trips were a bit faster because there was a convenient express train from Philadelphia to Wilmington. Social life among the graduate students was limited because of her rigid schedule. John came up Wednesday afternoons for the seminar and the library, and they would go out to dinner with some of her fellow graduate students. She had excellent research skills that she had developed under Moore, and she had John for a back-up conversationalist at home.

She finished her doctorate in 1954. John Barrett deserves considerable credit for her doing so under such circumstances. "He kept house. He picked me up at the station every night and already had supper ready.... I don't know where I found such a liberated man in 1950!"[73]

Earlier she had turned down opportunities at Wellesley and Bryn Mawr to stay with her husband. She now continued efforts to start a family. Finally, they were successful in adopting three children between 1956 and 1961. However, John's kidneys were in trouble, and after a long-awaited transplant was rejected in 1968, he died in January, 1969. Throughout this time anti-nepotism rules prevented her from getting a secure tenure-track job, both when he was at the University of Utah and at the University of Tennessee. She was not allowed to hold any position in the math department

---

[73]ibid, pp. 140-141.

when he became department head so she started a successful consulting business, with Oak Ridge National Laboratory as one of her major clients.

John's death made Lida attractive to employers. She quickly joined the University of Tennessee full-time faculty, and the following year was made a full professor. "I was the third female full professor outside home ec, women's P.E., and nursing." In 1972 she was a natural choice to chair a special campus task force on women, which made recommendations about salary equity, child care, equal access to recreational facilities, and gender-inclusive language.

She then turned down an offer to become assistant dean, believing that her research, teaching, and consulting work were enough distractions from being the single mother of three children. However, in 1973, she did accept the position as head of the mathematics department, one of the first women in the country to hold such a post at a major university. "At first I didn't realize how much authority I really had. I'd always been the wife and the younger sister, and I had been impatient about all the things that needed to be done.[74] Now she could get things done, and Tennessee's national ranking improved substantially.

It effectively ended her research career, but there were satisfactions in being recognized as an excellent administrator. In 1979-1980 she took part in a program of the American Council of Education to identify senior academic women who might be interested in administration in higher education. In 1980, with all three of her children in college, she moved to Northern Illinois University to become an associate provost. The university had begun efforts to offer a degree in engineering, not just engineering technology; one of her duties was to assist in this effort. In 1987 she became dean of arts and sciences at Mississippi State University. From 1991 to 1995 she was a senior associate at the National Science Foundation.[75]

She then joined the West Point faculty. "It was great to end my career back in the classroom."[76] She now enjoys an animated retirement, more relaxing than working full-time, but still lively and engaged.

Lida Barrett observed that there were about twenty-five couples active in mathematics in the middle of the twentieth century, many of whom regularly came to national mathematics meetings. "... off the top of my head at the end of a long day," she could list fifteen of them in 2004: the Barretts (Lida Kittrell and John), the Haimos (Deborah Tepper and Franklin), the Rudins (Mary Ellen Estill and Walter), the Schafers (Alice Turner and Richard), the Neffs (Mary and John), the Jacobsons (Florence Dorfman and Nathan "she didn't have a doctorate but was very involved"), the Neumanns (Hannah and B. H.), the Robinsons (Julia Bowman and Raphael), the Todds (Olga Tausky and John), the Wyburns (Lucille S. and Gordon), the Struiks (Saly

---

[74]ibid, p. 220.
[75]ibid, p. 221.
[76]Lida Barrett, telephone interview, July 16, 2004.

R. and Dirk), and Josephine Mitchell and Lowell Schoenfeld. A bit later (early 1960s) they were joined by Judith and Paul Sally, Mary and Alfie Gray, and Louise Hay and Richard Larson.[77]

A glance through the 1956 Combined Membership List (of the AMS, MAA, and the Society for Industrial and Applied Mathematics) suggests Barrett's memory is correct. Each married woman is indicated with a "Mrs." followed by her husband's initials in parentheses behind their professional name, so it is easy to see which women were married and to whom, a consideration indicative of the importance of this information at that time. It is easy to identify many more women married to male mathematicians. I recognized the names of Natacha and Emil Artin, Ellen F. and R. C. Buck, Dorothy Maharam and A. H. Stone, and Rebekka Struick and Hans Freistadt.

In my early adulthood I remember being told that forty percent of married women mathematicians were married to male mathematicians. It was a matter of great interest to me, and I suspect that indeed someone told me that. I wondered how anyone would be able to compute such a statistic, but as I ponder this the 1956 CML with allegedly 12,969 names and addresses, it is clear that someone with sufficient motivation might actually determine whether this was true. It seems plausible from my perusal of the A's and B's.

When I asked Lida Barrett whether the couples socialized with other couples at math meetings, she said, "No, you ran around with your own specialty. I was with the topology group and John was with the analysis group."[78]

However, the Texas (UT Austin) Ph.D.'s did have their own beer party at the meetings and "provided a very good intellectual, as well as social, place for discourse. The Texas group looked out for each other." Remembering that her doctorate was from Penn, I asked if she were a member of the Texas group. "Yes, I was in that group. I can remember being in San Antonio when Wilder went out with the group. He wasn't president [of AMS] at that time, but at some other time. During a meeting at Columbia, G. T. Wyburn went out with us. He was currently president of the AMS and I was a new Ph.D. student. Lucille, his wife, had been a Moore student, but dropped out of the Ph.D. program when she married G. T. She had persuaded him to join a seminar of Moore's, and as a result he switched fields — I think from chemistry."[79]

In the 1950s the Joint Mathematics Meetings were between Christmas and New Year, and mathematicians typically stayed in dorms. During the Christmas meeting in Rochester the students left some calculus problems in Lida's dorm room to be solved. She also remembers that was the time that a beer party was announced, probably on the regular schedule. At

---

[77]Lida Barrett, personal email, April 26, 2004.
[78]Lida Barrett, telephone interview, July 16, 2004.
[79]ibid.

a formal meeting Saly Struik objected, because she didn't think women could go to beer parties. Lida said that she was going, and would drink beer. Afterward, she felt embarrassed to have responded that way in public. "That's the Texas in me."

For the 1953 summer meeting at Queens University in Kingston, Canada, Lida and John Barrett registered separately so they would show up as two registrants, and they were, therefore, given separate rooms. The rooms were side by side, so they rearranged the furniture. They had a sitting room and a bedroom, connected only by going into the public hall; the AMS did not object. At that meeting, newlyweds[80] Josephine Mitchell and Lowell Schoenfeld were denied a double room even though they were married. The AMS refused to allow them a double room because their last names were different. They and the Barretts had a hearty laugh over that together.[81]

Josephine Mitchell (1912-2000) and **Lowell Schoenfeld** (1920-2002) also faced discrimination that wasn't laughable. Born in Edmonton, Mitchell graduated from the University of Alberta in 1935, and earned her graduate degrees at Bryn Mawr. She then taught at several small colleges, but eventually in 1948 obtained a position at the University of Illinois. Schoenfeld spent his early years in New York City and graduated from City College in 1940. After earning his doctorate at the University of Pennsylvania, he taught at Temple and Harvard until he too joined the mathematics faculty of the University of Illinois. When they married in 1953, the university said her contract could not be renewed in 1954, although she had been there longer than he.[82]

Why? The reason given was the university's "anti-nepotism" rules. In 2005 Lee Lorch wrote, "Webster's New Collegiate Dictionary defines nepotism as, '... bestowal of patronage by reason of relationship rather than merit.' If Illinois had an anti-nepotism policy, rather than an anti-woman policy, it would clearly be inapplicable to Josephine and Lowell, since each had been appointed independently of one another, well prior to their marriage.... They would have had no reason to fear punishment for committing matrimony."[83] Lee urged me to obtain a copy of the university's rules in effect at that time. The following seems to be the relevant passage.

"As a general rule employment should not be given to more than one member of the same family, even though different departments are involved.... Departures from this policy have been authorized in emergency situations

---

[80]Lida Barrett, personal email, January 15, 2005.

[81]Lida Barrett, telephone interview, July 16, 2004.

[82]Some sources have indicated that she became tenured, but John Ewing referred me to Paul Bateman, who is retired from the mathematics department at the University of Illinois, having joined it in 1950. He attended the campus AAUP hearings about the Mitchell-Schoenfeld situation. In January, 2005, Bateman sent me a copy of a long letter he wrote about Mitchell in August, 2003. This letter provides convincing evidence that Mitchell had only renewals as an untenured Assistant Professor from 1948 to 1954.

[83]Personal email from Lee Lorch, January 16, 2005.

for exceptional reasons, but only for temporary periods. When a member of the staff marries another staff member..., the former is not asked to give up *his* position immediately, but is given reasonable time to make change."[84] (The italics are mine.) The university apparently felt magnanimous in giving Mitchell her final year. There was indeed a systemic policy against committing matrimony, independent of the qualifications of the offenders.

Josephine Mitchell as a new Master's Degree recipient at Bryn Mawr College, June, 1941. Photo courtesy of Alta Mitchell Bento, her sister.

During their final year at Illinois, Mitchell and her husband both protested. They appealed to the American Association of University Professors and the American Association of University Women. There was at least one AAUP hearing on campus. Their efforts were unsuccessful, and both resigned. For a while they wandered from one institution to another, but finally both

---

[84] "University of Illinois Business Policy and Procedure Manual," Urbana-Champaign, 12/1/52, provided by Debora Pfeiffer, Archival Reference Specialist, University of Illinois.

found positions at Penn State University, one of the few universities that would hire a couple.

In 1968 they moved to the State University of New York at Buffalo. They both had a avid interest in improving libraries and in the outdoors, especially hiking, canoeing, and studying wild flowers. At their deaths they left a "substantial bequest" to the AMS.[85] Also, the University of Alberta department of mathematical and statistical sciences received $1.6 million from Josephine Mitchell's estate.[86]

It wasn't until the 1980s that the Joint Mathematics Meetings would allow people to choose their own roommates without being monitored by the staff. Not being able to do so, young people argued, made it more difficult for people to attend meetings when they were poorest and needed the contacts of the meetings the most. I asked Lida Barrett in what ways women were treated differently at the meetings during her early years there. "I can't think of any. Women were on the program. I submitted papers for sessions and I never had any trouble with that." She adds that women were not invited speakers.

Lida Barrett is clearly much more bothered by the explicit racial discrimination of the mid-century. "The racial bias of the fifties affected everything." It wasn't until 1951 that blacks were allowed to attend the University of Texas — and that was the result of a court case. Let us turn to some stories of minority mathematicians.

---

[85] John Ewing, "Josephine M. Mitchell and Lowell I. Schoenfeld Gardens Dedication," www.ams.org/ams/garden-dedication5-03.html
[86] www.science.ualberta.ca/nav02.cfm/?nav02=16781&nav01=11471.

CHAPTER 5

African American Mathematicians from
the Eighteenth through the Twentieth Century

Even in the eighteenth century, when higher education was scanty in
the United States, some blacks were known for doing mathematics. The
earliest known African American mathematician is Thomas Fuller (1710-
1790). He was born in a part of Africa that was known for its inhabitants'
computational abilities. "...they easily reckon as exact, and as quick by
memory, as we can do with pen and ink..."[1] His obituary is worth quoting:

> Died: Negro Tom, the famous Africa Calculator, aged 80
> years. He was the property of Mrs. Elizabeth Cox of
> Alexandria. Tom was a very black man. He was brought
> to this country at the age of 14, and was sold as a slave....
> This man was a prodigy. Though he could never read or
> write, he had perfectly acquired the art of enumeration.
> He could multiply seven into itself, that product by seven,
> and the products, so produced by seven for seven times.
> He could give the number of months, days, weeks, hours,
> minutes and seconds in any period of time that any per-
> son chose to mention, allowing in his calculation for all
> leap years that happened in the time; he would give the
> number of poles, yards, feet, inches, and barley-corns in
> any distance, say the diameter of the earth's orbit; and
> in every calculation he would produce the true answer in
> less time than ninety-nine men out of a hundred would
> produce with their pens. And, what was, perhaps, more
> extraordinary, though interrupted in the progress of his
> calculation, and engaged in discourse necessary for him to
> begin again, but he would... cast up plots of land. He
> took great notice of the lines of land which he had seen
> surveyed. He drew just conclusions from facts; surpris-
> ingly so, for his opportunities. Had his opportunity been
> equal to those of thousands of his fellow-men... even a

---

[1]John Bardot's account, 1732, as quoted in http://www.math.buffalo.edu/mad/
special/fuller_thomas_1710-1790.html.

NEWTON himself, need [not] have [been] ashamed to acknowledge him a Brother in Science.[2]

Benjamin Banneker (1731-1806) is much better known, not the least
for the active current association that bears his name. Banneker's maternal
grandmother, Molly Welch, was an English milking maid who was accused
of stealing a pail of milk. She claimed that the cow kicked over the pail,
but she was transported across the ocean to Maryland where she was forced
to serve as an indentured servant for seven years. Unlike many of her less
fortunate contemporaries, she survived the seven years. (Indentured servants' masters had no incentive not to work their victims to death, unlike
slave-holders, who could hope for years, and perhaps generations, of labor if
they allowed their slaves the minimum needed to stay alive.[3]) Molly Welsh
managed then to purchase a small farm, and in 1692 she bought two slaves.
One of these, Banneker, had been a prince before his capture, and although
not as good a worker as the other, was "of bright intelligence, of very agree-
able presence, dignified manner, and contemplative habits."[4] Molly Welsh
eventually liberated both men and married Banneker, despite miscegenation
laws that said that white women who married "Negroes" could be punished
by becoming either a slave of his master or a servant to the nearby parish
minister.[5] Their daughter Mary married Robert, who had been captured in
Africa but whose master had freed him when he was baptized. When they
married, he opted to take his wife's surname. Benjamin was the oldest of
their four children and their only son.[6]

Molly Welsh taught her grandson to read and had a Bible shipped from
England so young Benjamin could read it to his grandmother. When Benjamin was six years old, Robert Banneker managed to purchase 120 acres
ten miles from Baltimore. Then he could send his son to a racially integrated
private school, where Benjamin received the fundamentals of an education.
Like many schools of its time, it was open only during the winter, and like

[2]"Thomas Fuller: A Precocious African," the *Columbian Centinial*, December 29,
1790, No. 707, p. 123. col. 32, Boston, Massachusetts, quoted in
www.math.buffalo.edu/mad/special/fuller_thomas_1720-1790.html.

[3]Lori Kenschaft, personal conversation, July 18. 2004. See also *American Colonies*
by Alan Taylor, New York, Penguin, 2001, pp. 142-44, or (for an extended discussion)
American Slavery, American Freedom: The Ordeal of Colonial Virginia by Edmund S.
Morgan, New York, Norton, 1975.

[4]Martha Ellicott Tyson (1795-1873), edited by her daughter Anne Tyson Kirk, *Banneker, the Afric-American Astronomer*, Friends' Book Association, Philadelphia, 1884, p.
10-11. Martha Tyson was the daughter of George Ellicott and says in an earlier piece
(written in 1836 and published in 1854) that she was in possession of "nearly every paper
left by Banneker."

[5]Silvio A. Bedini, *The Life of Benjamin Banneker*, Second Edition, 1999, Maryland
Historical Society, Baltimore, p. 17.

[6]Tyson, 1884, p. 11.

many boys of his time, Benjamin left school as soon as he was big enough to be a significant laborer on his father's farm.[7]

Despite becoming an able farmer in an isolated place, the young Banneker continued to read anything he could find and to learn from observation. In his early twenties, he took apart a watch and apparently with only that knowledge built a clock that chimed the hours until his death.[8] It was of great interest to the neighbors and others.

When Banneker was 27, his father died and it became his turn to run the family farm. He was an "industrious and thriving farmer" with horses, cows, and many hives of bees. His ample orchard was known for miles around. He and his mother lived comfortably in the cabin built by his father.[9] During winters and other free time he studied mathematics and read as many books as he could borrow.

In 1772 his life changed when the Ellicott family moved in nearby and began building a flour mill. The Banneker farm was a major source of food for the workers. Banneker watched the mill's construction with the keen interest common among his neighbors, but with more understanding. His clock was already famous, and a natural friendship grew between the Ellicotts and Banneker.[10] George Ellicott saw Banneker's interest in mathematics and lent him three books, two of which consisted of tables. Without instruction, Banneker mastered the books so well that he found errors in them.[11] Ellicott urged him to begin the calculations needed to write his own almanac.[12]

In 1791 George's cousin Andrew Ellicott was invited to lead the group that would survey the "Federal City," later to be called the District of Columbia. He may have been the best surveyor in the country, but he needed an assistant. He asked George Ellicott to join him. George declined, but suggested that he ask Banneker. Andrew did so because of Banneker's knowledge of "practical astronomy," his experience in calculating day-to-day positions and motions of heavenly bodies, and the lack of a better candidate, even though Banneker had to be taught surveying. Banneker was excited by the offer, so shortly after dawn on February 7, 1791, he and Andrew Ellicott set off by horseback for the longest trip that Banneker would ever take. That evening they arrived in Alexandria, Virginia, which was then one of the three busiest seaports in the county.[13]

---

[7]ibid, pp. 13-14.

[8]ibid, p. 22.

[9]Martha Tyson, "Sketch of the Life of Benjamin Banneker," Maryland Historical Society, 1836, p. 5.

[10]Tyson, 1884, pp. 23-25.

[11]Brawley Benjamin, *Early Negro American Writers*, originally published by the University of North Carolina Press, 1935, republished by Books of Libraries Press, Freeport, NY, p. 76.

[12]Tyson, 1884, p. 28.

[13]Silvio A. Bedini, *The Life of Benjamin Banneker*, Second Edition, 1999, Maryland Historical Society, Baltimore, pp. 109 and 113-115.

After a few days of sightseeing in this amazing city, during which time
Ellicott hired laborers and purchased horses, they set up a surveyors' camp
within the limits of the prospective Federal City. There for two months
Banneker slept in the observatory tent with the finest telescopes and measuring instruments of the time. One of his duties was caring for a precise
timepiece on a carefully leveled stump of a tree that had been cut down
for this purpose. He spent his nights making astronomical observations and
doing calculations, which were checked each morning shortly after dawn by
Ellicott, who then supervised his laborers for the rest of the day seven days
a week. Meanwhile, Banneker could nap between making observations of
the sun to establish the correct time for the regulator clock. Finally in
late afternoon he could usually get some uninterrupted sleep. This arduous
schedule for a sixty-year-old in the District of Columbia winter "aggravated
Banneker's aches and pains, often causing him considerable distress."[14]

However, the work was exciting, and he stayed with it until late April.
There are few surviving records of his activities there. Martha Tyson (1795-
1873), daughter of George Ellicott, wrote in the mid-nineteenth century that
he was well received by the others and invited to sit at the table with them,
but he declined, and another table was set for him in the same room so that
his meals could be served at the same time as theirs.[15]

One oft-repeated twentieth century story not mentioned in any nineteenth century references claimed that Banneker and Ellicott were assistants
of L'Enfant, the lead designer of the city, and when L'Enfant left in a pique,
Banneker's notes provided enough detail so that he could reproduce them
in their entirety.[16] However, Silvio Bedini, a highly respected twentieth
century scholar, denies this story, first by noting that L'Enfant was hired
well after Ellicott was launched into surveying the District, so they worked
independently,[17] and secondly by the fact that Banneker left the scene in
April 1971, ten months before L'Enfant departed.[18] The scarcity of surviving records makes the latter argument inconclusive. It is possible that
Banneker returned the following winter to help, even though no records of
that visit survive. It is clear that some of Banneker's contemporaries wanted
to erase his memory (a fire two days after his death would destroy many of
his personal records) and Bedini reports threats during his lifetime.

It seems likely that L'Enfant, while making the plans for the capital
city, would have had to collaborate with Banneker, who was making the
basic measurements of the land. This could have happened easily during
Banneker's first winter in the Federal City and possibly also in early 1792,

---

[14]ibid, pp. 116-125.

[15]Tyson, 1884, p. 37.

[16]Will W. Allen, *Banneker, the Afro-American Astronomer*, Books for Libraries Press,
Freeport, New York, first published in 1921, reprinted in 1971, p. 14, for example.

[17]Bedini, p. 126.

[18]ibid, p. 136.

shortly before L'Enfant left. It does appear that L'Enfant took his preliminary plans back with him to France, so someone else wrote the final layouts.
Decades later Martha Tyson wrote that Andrew Ellicott, "...under the orders of General Washington, then President of the United States, located the
sites of the capitol, the president's house, treasury, and other public buildings. In this, also, Banneker was his assistant."[19] Since Banneker's home
was near the route taken by Andrew Ellicott as he traveled from Washington to his home in Philadelphia, it is possible that he stopped in to consult
with Banneker without paying for these consultations; this would explain
the lack of surviving records. As mentioned above, it is also possible that
records were destroyed.

In April 1791 Banneker was understandably concerned about his health,
so when one of Ellicott's younger brothers arrived to join the team, he felt he
should return to the comforts of his home. He waited until Andrew Ellicott
took a trip to his family in Philadelphia, and rode with him as far as George
Ellicott's. When they arrived, Banneker was clearly "reanimated by the
kindness of the distinguished men with whom he had mingled."[20]

He dived into his intellectual work with renewed energy, and late in 1791
he completed the computations for an almanac that predicted astronomical
events for 1792. He sent a handwritten draft of the first edition to Thomas
Jefferson with a long, articulate, passionate letter dated August 17, 1791,
pleading for compassion toward "my brethren" and recognition of the equal
abilities and value under God of those of African descent.[21] Jefferson responded, "Nobody wishes more than I do to see such proofs as you exhibit
that nature has given to our black brethren talents equal to the other colors
of men... nobody wishes more ardently to see a good system commenced
for raising the condition, both of their body and mind, to what it ought
to be...". He then reports that he has taken the liberty of sending the almanac to Monsieur de Condorcet, Secretary of the Academy of Sciences at
Paris... "because I consider it as a document to which your whole color had
a right for their justification against the doubts which have been entertained
of them."[22] Unfortunately, Condorcet felt it necessary to go into hiding at
about the time Jefferson's package should have reached him. When he tried
to escape, he was captured by the revolutionaries and the following day
was found dead, so Banneker's work was never presented to the Academy.[23]
However, both Banneker's letter and Jefferson's reply were later published
in a widely distributed pamphlet.[24]

---

[19]Tyson, 1884, p. 37.

[20]ibid.

[21]Allen, pp. 21-27, Bedini, pp. 158-164, Brawley, pp. 79-83; Tyson, 1884, pp. 39-45.

[22]ibid.

[23]Bedini, pp. 167-169.

[24]Bedini, p. 164.

Although several efforts to get his almanac published in 1790 had been fruitless,[25] in 1791 Banneker's reputation soared and he obtained a prestigious publisher for his almanac, the firm of William Goddard and James Angell in Baltimore. They arranged for other outlets in Philadelphia and Alexandria. (It may have helped that Benjamin Franklin died in 1790, removing serious competition for reliable almanacs.) Their introduction says it contains "the Motions of the Sun and Moon, the true places and aspects of the Planets, the Rising and Setting of the Sun, and the Rising Setting and South Place and Age of the Moon.... Days for holding the Supreme and Circuit courts of the United States, as also the usual courts in Pennsylvania, Delaware, Maryland, and Virginia; also several useful Tables and valuable Recipes... with interesting and entertaining Essays in Prose and Verse, the whole comprising a greater, more pleasing and useful variety than any work of this kind and price in North America." They asserted it "must be considered an extraordinary effort of genius — a complete and accurate Ephemeris for the year 1792, calculated by a sable descendant of Africa who, by this specimen of ingenuity evinces to demonstration that mental powers and endowments are not the exclusive excellence of white people..."[26]

The editors included an introduction by James McHenry, a physician who had been a member of the Continental Congress, General Washington's private secretary for two years, and a writer of the U.S. Constitution. At the time, McHenry was a Senator from Maryland to the U.S. Congress.[27] His introduction is our only surviving contemporary account of Banneker's life.[28] "His father and mother were enabled to send him to an obscure school, where he learned, when a boy, reading, writing, and arithmetic as far as double fractions, and to leave him at their deaths a few acres of land, upon which he has supported himself ever since by means of economy and constant labor, and preserved a fair reputation.... Mental exercise formed his chief amusement, and soon gave him a facility in calculation that was often serviceable to his neighbors...". McHenry added that three years previously George Ellicott had lent him a book on astronomy, two books of tables, and some astronomical instruments, "and from thenceforward he employed his leisure in astronomical researches."

McHenry then challenged the prevailing wisdom of his (and our?) day. "In every civilized country, we shall find thousands of whites liberally educated and who have enjoyed greater opportunities for instruction than this negro [who are] his inferiors in those intellectual acquirements and capacities that from the most characteristic features in the human race. But the system that would assign to those degraded blacks an origin different from

---

[25]Bedini, p. 172.
[26]Tyson, 1884, pp. 46-48.
[27]Bedini, p. 169.
[28]Bedini, p. xiv.

the whites... must be relinquished as similar instances multiply."[29] With such an introduction from a luminary and the help of various anti-slavery societies, the almanac sold widely, and Banneker rapidly became famous.[30]

The second year's almanac did not include McHenry's introduction, but did include the letters to and from Thomas Jefferson. It also included a proposal for a Department of Peace that has been attributed to Banneker,[31] but Bedini reports that Dr. Benjamin Rush republished it later as his own writing.[32] Almanacs with Banneker's astronomical computations were published for six consecutive years, through 1796 with predictions for 1797. During those six years, there were at least 28 editions of which examples still survive.[33] Then publication apparently stopped, although Banneker continued to do complete computations until 1802, and fragmentary computations until his death. Bedini questions why such a popular almanac was discontinued, noticing that the competition became livelier and wondering if Banneker met deadlines less predictably as his health deteriorated. However, then Bedini writes, "The reign of Banneker's almanacs perfectly coincided with the origin and demise of the Maryland Society for the Abolition of Slavery." The Society was not directly involved with the almanacs, but as the anti-slavery movement faded, it may have been harder for a black man to obtain a publisher, perhaps because it became more risky for the publishers. Bedini reports that Banneker himself faced violence and threats after 1797.[34]

Banneker's nights beginning in 1790 were occupied with observing the heavens, and since he had never married, there was little point in working so hard on the farm by day. He used actuarial computations to decide that he had a fifteen year life expectancy. Estimating the cost of the farm at 180 pounds, he offered the farm to George Ellicott for a lifetime annual pension of twelve pounds, keeping only his small house, garden, and orchard for himself (to go to Ellicott at his death).

The nights of the 1790s he spent "wrapped in his cloak and lying on the ground in contemplation of the heavenly bodies." At dawn he would sleep, "but he does not seem to have required as much sleep as ordinary mortals. Still cultivating sufficient ground to give him needful exercise, he might often be seen hoeing his corn, cultivating his garden, or trimming his fruit trees. Sometimes he would be found watching the habits of his bees." Other times he sat under his chestnut tree and played the flute or violin; he "had some skill in using either of these instruments."[35]

---

[29]Tyson, 1884, pp. 48-51. A surprisingly different version appears in Bedini, pp. 182-184.

[30]Bedini, pp. 184-5.

[31]Brawley, pp. 83-86.

[32]Bedini, p. 190.

[33]Bedini, p. 206.

[34]Bedini, 239-240.

[35]Tyson, 1884, pp. 34-35.

Benjamin Banneker
Courtesy of Photographs and Prints Division, Schomburg Center for Research in Black Culture, The New York Public Library, Astor, Lenox and Tilden Foundations

Banneker was described as "of black complexion, soft and gentle manners, though manly, and with uncommonly pleasing colloquial powers." His appearance gave no trace of his mixed blood.[36] Martha Tyson, daughter of George Ellicott, marveled in 1836 that none of Banneker's contemporaries had written his biography. "He appears to have been the pioneer in the movement in this part of the world toward the improvement of his race; at a period of our history when the negro occupied the lowest possible grade in the scale of human beings, Banneker had struck out for himself a course, hitherto untravelled by men of his class, and had already earned a respectable position amongst men of science. But from those who

---

[36]Tyson, 1884, p. 30, The quote is from a letter from her uncle, Thomas Ellicott.

were the witness of his success, we cannot now ask information concerning him."[37] Martha Tyson's daughter wrote in 1884 that George Ellicott was "the warmest friend of this extraordinary man," and that her mother had done much research about Banneker and talked with "all such aged peoples had known Banneker." Alas, Martha Tyson, like her father, did not live to have her memoirs of Benjamin Banneker published, but her daughter completed the work that her mother and grandfather would have wanted.[38]

"His life was one of constant worship in the great temples of nature and science," wrote Martha Tyson, who worshipped in the same Friends' Meeting room with the aged Banneker during her first eleven years. "In his early days, places of worship were rare. As they increased in number during his later years, he would occasionally visit those of various denominations. He finally gave a decided preference for the doctrines and form of worship of the Society of Friends, whose meeting-house at Ellicott's Mills he frequently attended."[39] His father had been baptized into the Church of England, but Friends (Quakers) had provided both his elementary education and the books that were the seed of his mature flowering.

After 1802 his health declined, and during one serious illness, he specified that as soon as he died, the gifts of George Ellicott should be returned to him along with a number of Banneker's own writings and other possessions. On October 9, 1806, "he strolled forth, as was his custom, to enjoy the air and the sunshine and the view... He met an acquaintance, with whom he conversed pleasantly for awhile, when, suddenly complaining of feeling sick, they immediately turned to his cottage. He laid himself upon his couch and never spoke again. In a little while his mortal frame lay dead."[40]

On the same day, a nephew carried out Banneker's instructions. "Being himself the messenger who conveyed to Ellicott's Mills the tidings of his uncle's death, he arrived at the house of George Ellicott driving a cart, in which was the oval table on which all Banneker's calculations were made, a large number of scientific instruments, and many books on varied topics." He also delivered a volume that contained Banneker's own writings. His sisters also took his Bible. Their promptness turned out to be fortuitous because while the gravesite rites were being performed two days later, Banneker's house took fire and quickly burned to the ground. "His clock and all other evidences of his ingenuity and scholarship were consumed in the flames."[41]

Fortunately, many people had visited his home and clock, especially during the decade when he was producing his almanac. Some left records that indicate his gracious, simple lifestyle. "We found the venerable star-gazer under a wide-spreading pear-tree laden with delicious fruit. He came

[37]Tyson, 1836, p. 7.

[38]Tyson, 1884, pp. v-vi. (Martha Tyson died in 1873 and this book was edited by Anne Tyson Kirk, her daughter.)

[39]Tyson, 1884, p. 67.

[40]ibid, pp. 68-69.

[41]ibid, pp. 70-72.

forward to meet us, and bade us welcome to this lowly dwelling. It was built of logs one story in height, and was surrounded by an orchard. In one corner of the room was a clock of his own construction, a true herald of departing hours."[42] Benjamin Banneker was a not only a scientist of amazing achievements, but also a remarkable human being.

As Banneker was well aware, most of his race was enslaved, but there were some other lucky ones who pursued education vigorously.

Patrick Francis Healy (1834-1910), born a century after Banneker, apparently was the first African American to earn a doctorate. He was the son of an Irish immigrant owner and one of his female slaves, but Healy's father freed all their nine children when he died. Patrick was able to leave Georgia and travel to Holy Cross College in Massachusetts. When he graduated in 1850, he joined the Jesuits. He was sent to Europe where he received his doctorate from Louvaine University in Belgium. In 1866 he returned to teach philosophy at Georgetown, which was then both a preparatory school and a college. Healy worked hard to prepare Georgetown to become a university, including placing new emphasis on science. In 1874 he became president of Georgetown University, the first African American to be president of a predominantly white university.[43]

A generation younger than Healy, Edward Bouchet received the first doctorate granted to a black within this country in 1876. It was in physics, not math, but he did teach math.

Edward Alexander Bouchet (1852-1918) became the first black to receive a doctorate from an American university in any field in 1876; it was from Yale. He was the sixth American of any race to earn a Ph.D. in physics.[44]

Bouchet grew up in New Haven, Connecticut, the only son and youngest of four children of a recently freed slave. He attended one of the three schools open to black children, an ungraded school with never more than 30 students, and received most of his elementary education from Sarah Wilson. After two years in New Haven High School and two years at a school that prepared young men for Yale College (from which he graduated first in his class), he entered Yale, and was graduated Phi Beta Kappa in 1874. He was the sixth in his class of 124 students, and its only black, the first black to be graduated from Yale.[45] A Philadelphia philanthropist, Alfred Cope, then paid for him to continue at Yale toward a doctorate, which he was awarded two years later.

---

[42]Memoir of Susan Mason by the Daughter, R. Mason, long out of print but quoted in Tyson, 1884, pp. 56-57.

[43]http://memory.loc.gov/ammem/today/jul31.html from The Library of Congress.

[44]www.math.buffalo.edu/mad/physics/bouchet_edward_alexander.html.

[45]ibid.

Bouchet taught physics and chemistry at the Institute for Colored Youth in Philadelphia from 1876 to 1902. The ICY had been founded by the Society of Friends because African Americans were not admitted to any of the city's other high schools. Alfred Cope served on the board and was determined to provide a fine science program at ICY; his support of Bouchet's doctoral study was indicative of that determination. Most people who taught physics at that time also taught mathematics, so Bouchet probably did too.

He was fired when the Institute discontinued its college preparatory program and the all-white board replaced all the Institute's teachers with instructors committed to industrial education. It was "at the height of the DuBois-Washington controversy of industrial vs. collegiate education."[46] His application to join the faculty of Hampton Institute was not successful,[47] so the following year Bouchet taught "physics and mathematics" in St. Louis at the first high school for blacks west of the Mississippi. After that he had a series of jobs, including that of a customs inspector, manager of a hospital, and administrator in educational institutions. At the age of 64 he became principal of the Lincoln High School in Gallipolis, Ohio. Ill health forced him to retire five years later, although some reports indicate he then spent some time teaching at Bishop College in Marshall, Texas.[48] Finally, he returned to New Haven, where he died in his childhood home. He never married or had children.[49]

"My favorite recreations are walking and rowing," he wrote as an old man.[50]

Kelly Miller (1863-1939) was apparently the first African American to pursue doctoral studies in mathematics. He was the son of a slave woman only one generation removed from Africa and a free black man in South Carolina. At the time of his birth in July 1863, his father was serving in the Confederate Army as a conscript, the South's way of "disposing of free Negroes to keep them from stirring up mischief during the war," as his son later observed. When the reluctant soldier returned, he, as a tenant farmer, was able to send his children to school. Kelly Miller later referred to himself as one of the "first fruits of the civil war;" he was one of the first blacks to learn reading, writing, and arithmetic in the public schools. Later he praised the Northern teachers who came South to teach in these schools as "a band of heroes... who sowed the seed of intelligence in the soil of ignorance and planted the rose of virtue in the garden of dishonor and shame..."[51]

In 1878 a minister helped the young man to be admitted to Fairfield Institute, a secondary school founded by the Northern Presbyterian Church.

---

[46]ibid.

[47]Ronald Mickens, personal email, January 29, 2005.

[48]http://www.princeton.edu/~mcbrown/display/bouchet.html.

[49]www. math.buffalo.edu/mad/physics/bouchet_edward_alexander.html.

[50]Negro History Bulletin, 31:8, December 1968.

[51]Julia Boublitz Morgan, "Son of a Slave," *Johns Hopkins Magazine*, June 1981, pp. 20-26, pp. 20-21.

Two years later Kelly Miller competed for and won a scholarship to Howard University, which was then 13 years old. The New England Missionary Society provided the scholarship, a train ticket, and ten dollars. Two years later he entered the "collegiate department," also at Howard. While working in the U.S. Pension Office to support himself, he achieved an outstanding academic record. He also saved enough to buy a farm, which he gave to his parents when he graduated in 1886.

He then took the civil service exam and went off to New England to wait tables for the summer. Legend has it that when he received the telegram offering him a full-time job in the Pension Office, he dropped his tray of dishes and took the next train back to Washington. In his government position, he met Simon Newcomb, who was the Naval Observatory astronomer in charge of the Nautical Almanac and also a professor in the Johns Hopkins mathematics department. Newcomb helped Miller obtain tutoring in mathematics, French, and German since Hopkins required fluency in both languages for admission to the doctoral program. A year later Newcomb helped Miller to be admitted to the Hopkins doctoral program in mathematics.[52]

Miller described his introduction to Hopkins. "Upon enrollment I was ushered into the room of President Daniel C. Gilman, a dignified courteous gentlemen, who received me graciously. He stated that I was the only colored student that the University had ever admitted, and being one among many I would naturally be the subject of observation. He stated that all the opportunities and facilities of the University would be open to me, and all the rest depended upon myself."[53]

"Cool, calculated civility," were the words Miller used to describe how he was treated on campus. He "met with no classroom embarrassment on the part of either students or professors." On the other hand, no students invited him to study with them except once. Miller persisted for two years in this chilly climate, studying analytic geometry, differential equations, quaternions, spherical and practical astronomy, and celestial mechanics, among other topics. It was neither lack of ability nor emotional factors that caused him to abandon his doctoral studies after two years. The B&O Railroad stocks that were the financial bedrock of the university foundered in 1887, and in 1888, the tuition was raised from $100 to $125. Miller hung on for one more year, but could not find the funds to remain further.[54] Our country's first doctorate in mathematics for an African American was apparently delayed for over 25 years for the lack of $25. If one had been granted before the suffocating effect of the Jim Crow laws descended, would others have soon followed? Kelly Miller was definitely the kind of human being that would have reached out to pull others through.

He immediately had a teaching position in a Washington, D.C. high school. Soon thereafter he joined the faculty of Howard University, where

---

[52]ibid, p. 22.
[53]ibid, p. 22.
[54]ibid, p. 22.

Kelly Miller. Photo courtesy of Moorland-Spingarn Research Center at Howard University archives, James Stimpert, archivist.

he stayed for the rest of his career. From that vantage point, he campaigned ardently for education for all African Americans. He contributed articles to *The Atlantic Monthly, Popular Science Monthly, Educational Review, Crisis*, and the *Journal of Negro Education*. He helped edit the latter two. For many years he wrote a weekly letter to the editor that appeared in more than 100 newspapers, including the *New York Times*, the *Washington Post*, and the *Baltimore Sun*. Several of his letters were read into the Congressional Record.

In 1908 he wrote, "When a child learns the multiplication table, he gets a clear notion of intellectual dignity. Here he gains an acquisition which is his permanent, personal possession, and which can never be taken from him."[55] In 1900 the U.S. Commissioner of Education asked Miller to contribute a chapter on "The Education of the Negro" to his annual report. Miller was a friend of both W.E.B. DuBois and Booker T. Washington, and supported both intellectual and vocational education. He said education

---

[55]ibid, p. 22.

had two aims, "to develop the faculties and powers of the mind [and] to prepare the individual for the work he has to perform." His 128-page report included an analysis of current textbooks. "Whatever is creditable to the negro is merged in the credit of the general population, while the odious and repugnant stand out in bold relief. Some special corrective influence is necessary in order that the negro may not despise himself, for no class of people who despise themselves can hope to gain the respect of the rest of mankind."[56]

He married Annie May Butler, a teacher in the Baltimore Normal School. She left her profession when she married, but became known for her hand-painting of fine china. They had three sons and two daughters. All five earned their bachelor degrees at Howard and had professional careers. One of their daughters taught mathematics at Miner Teachers' College in Washington. The eldest son earned a master's degree in physics at Clark University, but his race prevented him from obtaining a position for which he was well qualified. He became a doctor and was founding editor of the *Howard Medical News*. He regretted this decision because he preferred mathematics and physics to medicine. Another early African American mathematician was lost due to racial discrimination.[57]

When the United States entered World War I, Kelly Miller wrote an open letter to President Wilson decrying the decision to send troops abroad while refusing to get involved with the race riots in Memphis and East St. Louis. His letter sold 250,000 copies, but the government branded it "demoralizing." President Wilson did not respond to it and refused to see a black delegation that came to the White House to discuss its issues.[58]

When he was 75, he established the Moorland-Spingarn Research Center at Howard University as a center for historical materials on African Americans. He once boasted he was the best gardener in the District of Columbia. When asked what he felt to be his most important achievement, he replied that he had planted a seed that developed into a full-grown tree.

Susie Johnson McAfee (1889-1974) is another nineteenth century African American who might have earned a doctorate in mathematics if she had not encountered blatant racism. She was the sixth of the eleven children of two former slaves, Robert Johnson and Rachel Lucas Johnson. Robert Johnson had been about twelve years old at the time of Emancipation, and told his grandchildren vivid stories about the horrors of slavery. While Susie was growing up, he owned a 100-acre farm in Texas, which he had bought for $1.50 an acre with the aid of a mortgage. He raised all the family's food, "with cattle for both milk and beef," and enough cash cotton

---

[56]ibid, p. 24.
[57]ibid, p. 25.
[58]ibid, p. 26.

to pay for his children's college education. He had a pasture area for the cattle and a wooded area to provide fuel for cooking and winter warmth.[59]

Robert's oldest child was Walter Samuel Johnson, who became a physician in Chicago. The next three, two sons and a daughter, all lived long enough to go to college, but each came home from college sick and died. The youngest five were daughters who lived long lives. All went to college, but none had a professional career.

In 1912 Susie Johnson graduated from the normal school at Wiley College in Marshall, Texas, and took the Texas teachers' examination. "She wanted more than anything to be teacher," said her son Walter.[60] She did extremely well in all parts of the exam, except on her spelling paper, which was lost. Her father was told that for fifty dollars, it could be found. "My grandfather looked them straight in the eye and said, 'I paid to educate her, and I'll be damned if I'll pay to get her a job.'"[61] Remembering the atrocities of slavery, he was not willing to collaborate with this form of subjugation. His daughter's career was ended before it began. (The family and I had always considered this story an example of racism, but an historian of the nineteenth century, Lori Kenschaft, informs me that such corruption was very common at the end of the nineteenth century and early in the twentieth, regardless of race.[62])

Susie Johnson married Luther Ford McAfee, who had graduated from Texas College in Tyler, Texas, where he had studied Greek, Latin, and carpentry. He too loved math and helped his children both with their Latin translations and their high school math. He was a farmer, businessman, and carpenter. When Susie was pregnant with their third son, Cecil, she convinced Luther to trade farms with one in Marshall, Texas, near her alma mater, so that their children could conveniently go to college. Marshall had two black colleges, Bishop College (now closed) sponsored by the Baptist church and Wiley College sponsored by the Methodist church.

"She taught *us!*" exclaimed her son Walter.[63] All nine of her children (six sons and three daughters) who survived infancy went to Wiley College. The majority — five — graduated as math majors. Two were chemistry majors, one son and one daughter. Another son was three years into the successful completion of a mathematics major on the GI bill after serving abroad during World War II, when his wife left him. He became extremely depressed and couldn't finish college. He did marry a second time and

---

[59]Cecil McAfee, Susie's third son, telephone interview on November 4, 2003.

[60]Wiley, Ed, "Mathematicians' Success Underscores the Value of Parental Participation," *Black Issues in Higher Education*, January 19, 1989, p. 14.

[61]ibid.

[62]For further information, she recommends *Religion, Race, and Reconstruction: the Public School in the Politics of the 1870s*, Ward M. McAfee, Albany, State University of New York Press, 1998. There was some reform movement in the early twentieth century, but 1912 was not far enough into these reforms "to make me think the pattern had become exceptional."

[63]Walter McAfee, Susie Johnson McAfee's second son, telephone interview in 1987.

Susan Johnson McAfee. Photo courtesy of Cecil McAfee.

became a successful electrician, working with HUD urban renewal in Detroit. The ninth child, a son, rebelled from the family tradition and majored in physical education in college. However, in middle age he returned to school to study mathematics and became a middle school mathematics teacher. Susie Johnson McAfee had one hundred percent success in interesting her *nine* children in mathematics!

The story does not stop there. Her third son Cecil (1916-), who was a principal for 37 years after being a high school mathematics teacher, had two sons and five daughters. All five daughters completed math majors. The oldest four are mathematics teachers, but "the baby" (aged 51) is a computer analyst with a government munitions plant in Alabama.[64] One can wonder what would have happened if Susie Johnson McAfee had been allowed to take the path of Marjorie Lee Browne (1914-1979), who became a teacher after college, gradually earning a doctorate in mathematics (from the University of Michigan in 1949), and serving as the mentor of many more African American mathematics professionals. Denied her rightful career, Susie Johnson McAfee became, as far as I know, the outstanding mathematical parent.

---

[64]Cecil McAfee, telephone interview on November 4, 2003.

Euphemia Lofton Haynes (1890-1980) was the first black woman to earn a doctorate in mathematics. She was born within a year of Susie Johnson McAfee, but was a fourth generation Washingtonian and the daughter of a prominent dentist and financier of black businesses, so she was "unhampered by financial constraints."[65] In 1909 she graduated from Miner Normal School with distinction, and in 1914 from Smith College with a major in mathematics and a minor in psychology. In 1917 she married Harold Appo Haynes, who became a principal and then deputy superintendent in charge of "colored schools" in Washington, D.C. The couple had no children.[66] In 1943, at the age of 53, she received a doctorate in mathematics from Catholic University of America under Aubrey Landrey, 22 years after the degree was first granted in any field to African American women.[67]

She taught in the public schools of Washington D.C. for 47 years and part-time at Howard University. During those 47 years, she taught first grade, high school mathematics at Armstrong High School and English at Miner Teachers' College, served as mathematics department chair at Dunbar High School, became a Professor of Mathematics at Miner Teachers College, where she established the mathematics department, and then at the (renamed) District of Columbia Teachers College, where she served as chair of the Division of Mathematics and Business Education. After retiring in 1959, she joined the Washington, D.C. Board of Education, serving as its president from July 1966 to July 1967, the first black woman to hold this position. During her time on the school board she was an outspoken critic of the D.C. system's segregation and "track system," which placed students in either academic or vocational programs, presumably depending on ability. Both were abolished by Judge Skelly Wright in June 1967 while Haynes was board president. Also while she was president, the machinery was set up for collective bargaining rights for Washington, D.C. teachers.[68]

At a presentation during her 55th Smith College reunion in 1969 she wrote about her philosophy of supporting students in their own search for a role in the world.

> "...the large number of drop-outs, the general unrest in the schools, the inability to secure and hold competent teachers, indicate the need for a re-examination of public education.... We admit there is a need for change. The question is what form it must take.
>
> "...Both the parent and the teachers must become the companion to the youth in his search for an understanding

---

[65] Johnny Houston, "Spotlight on a Mathematician: Euphemia Lofton Haynes (1890-1980)," *Newsletter of the National Association of Mathematicians*, 32:4, Winter, 2001, p. 2.

[66] ibid.

[67] Barbara Solomon, *In the Company of Educated Women: A History of Women and Higher Education in America*, Yale University Press, New Haven, 1986, p. 137.

[68] Scott Williams, www.math.buffalo.edu/mad/PEEPS/haynes.euphemia.lofton.html

of his world and of his place in it — indeed an understanding of self. . . it is our responsibility to provide for him the
opportunity to express his thinking, to act with freedom
and to face danger. Only in this way can he establish for
himself a self image which commands not only his respect
but the respect of his peers. He and his parent. . . and his
teacher must become companions in learning. . . "[69]

Euphemia Lofton Haynes, c. 1960, the first black woman to
get a doctorate in mathematics (in 1943). Photo courtesy of
The American Catholic History Research Center and University Archives at the Catholic University of America, Washington, D.C., The Haynes-Lofton Family Papers, Patrick Cullom,
archivist.

This 1969 presentation anticipates some of the educational thinking of
the subsequent 35 years. Her exploration was the starting point for an interview three years later with Mary Jo Deering of Smith College. In that 1972
interview she told an interesting story reminiscent of more recent NCTM

[69]Euphemia Lofton Haynes, "The Identity Crisis," presented at the 1914 class reunion
at Smith College, May 30, 1969. Provided (with the above interview) by Heather Morgan,
from the American Catholic University Research Center and University Archives.

writings, which for several reasons seems worthy of a significant direct quote here.

> My brother died in 1958.... He was dying in Chicago, and I was head of the math department in Teachers College. I had, of course, the top students and I had a very good class of young men and I did this: I said, "I'm going to be away over every weekend as long as there's a breath in my brother's body. Maybe I'll go on Thursday and be back on Monday or maybe I'll go on Friday and come back Wednesday, but I'm going to be gone. I don't want any class president. I want you to work together. We'll take one day and determine what are the problems involved in this particular question in mathematics that we are considering here and now. And then you'll go to work on that as a class. I don't want any 'A' student; I don't want any 'F' student. I'm not interested.... I want everybody free to express himself, to do any kind of work that will contribute to the solution of the problem....
>
> ...they met at their regular class hour and they did this type of work. ...after a bit the president [of the college] came to me and he said, "What does this mean? They tell me you miss classes two or three days a week."
>
> ...I said, "I do go over the weekend. I'll either take the last two or the first two days,... but part time I'm away."
>
> He said, "You can't do that. You just can't do that."
>
> I said, "Okay, go right ahead. Do anything you're ready to do. Dismiss me, discharge me, anything you're ready to do... because this is what I'm going to do as long as there's a breath in my brother's body. It started because I wanted to be there. But right now, I see what these boys are getting, and I hope he lives a long time because they're getting a lot more than they are when I'm here."
>
> "You just can't do it."
>
> "Well, you know your job. You do what you have to do..."
>
> So what he did was visit the class.... He didn't say anything to me for quite some time... the class understood what he was trying to do. And they worked accordingly. From things they said, I don't think they made him too comfortable at all... they weren't interested in whether he knew or not what they were doing, but they did their work. Then he took one of the teachers in with

him to visit, and he said he'd never seen any better work anywhere in his life than these young people and what they were doing.... Everybody was interested in the problem and they didn't care whether you knew more about it than I did or not, and so it was a very good experience.... He came back and complimented me on it.[70]

In that 1972 interview Haynes also said, "My mother was so successful as a mother because she believed in me." In answer to a question if there was discrimination at Smith when she was there, she said, "I don't think so... we were not conscious of it, if so." She observes that there were very few "brown-skinned girls" there; a reader might conclude the discrimination was in the admission process. Later she commented, "I have been a mathematics scholar all my life, through high school, through college, and then to get my doctor's degree in mathematics. ...I didn't expect to get my doctor's degree, never, in mathematics, but I wasn't surprised in other areas because I enjoyed it so much."[71]

Around 1980 I tried to interview all African American women who had earned a doctorate in mathematics; I knew a few at the beginning and located others by asking each subject for new names. Haynes was still alive while I began this process, but none of the twenty-one I located before the publication of my first article knew her, so she was omitted.[72] I omitted three others because they did not know the networked twenty-one, but they or a friend did read the October 1981 *Monthly* in which my article was published, so I promptly learned of my oversight. When the article was republished in the April 1982 *Journal of African Civilization*,[73] they were included. But Haynes had a stroke and then died shortly before the publication of my *Monthly* article and apparently none of her friends read it, so it was not until 2001, twenty years later, that the first black woman to earn a doctorate in mathematics became recognized by the mathematical community.

Why?

It was certainly not that Dr. Haynes was a hermit. She received the Papal medal "Pro Ecclesia and Pontifex" for her service to the church and her community in 1959 and was president of the Washington Archdiocesan Council of Catholic Women from 1964 to 1966. She was elected a Fellow of the American Association for the Advancement of Science in 1962. At her death, which followed her husband's by two years, she left $700,000 to Catholic University. In her name there is a professorial chair in the

---

[70]Euphemia Lofton Haynes, interview with May Jo Deering, October 26, 1976, in the home of Haynes in Washington, D.C., provided by Heather Morgan.

[71]ibid.

[72]Patricia C. Kenschaft, "Black Women in Mathematics in the United States," *American Mathematical Monthly*, 88:8, October, 1981, pp. 592-604.

[73]Patricia C. Kenschaft, "Black Women in Mathematics in the United States," *Journal of African Civilizations*, 4:1, April, 1992, 63-83.

Department of Education, an annual colloquium, and a perpetual student loan fund.

Her neglect can be partially explained by the racial segregation of educational institutions, the financial starvation of the black system, and the fact that Haynes worked entirely in the black system. The expense of transportation and telephones in the early and mid twentieth century, along with overwork (also due to lack of resources), kept the black mathematical community fragmented. When Wade Ellis, Sr., joined the Oberlin faculty in 1949, he apparently became only the second African American mathematician to teach at a predominantly white institution. The first was a century (!) earlier, when Charles Reason spent a year on the mathematics faculty of Central College in Cortland County, NY.[74]

Haynes' lack of recognition by the mathematical communities, however, is also due to the systemic exclusion of African Americans, especially in the South, from meetings of the mathematical societies during her career. Meetings were held in institutions (hotels, colleges, and universities) that would not provide food or lodging to blacks, or even allow them to attend lectures. Haynes was already long retired by the time of the first meeting of the National Association of Mathematicians in 1969 that caused the subsequent networking among blacks.

There were attempts to integrate these meetings during her lifetime. The first recorded such attempt was during the MAA meeting in Nashville in 1951 in connection with the official banquet lecture by president Saunders MacLane titled, "What Makes Students Think?" Lee Lorch was then department chair at Fisk University in that city. He and three African American colleagues, Evelyn Boyd (later Granville), Walter Brown, and H. M. Holloway, came to the meeting and were able to attend some of the scientific sessions. Employees of a publicly financed institution would have risked being fired by such audacity, but Fisk was private, so their risk was not so great. However, the day before the banquet, the chair of the arrangements committee cancelled their banquet reservations.[75]

Professors Lorch and Boyd requested that President MacLane withdraw from the banquet or state his objections to discrimination publicly. He declined on the basis that such action would be discourteous to the hosts. The Fisk faculty then wrote to the MAA board of Governors requesting that the organization change its by-laws to provide "explicit and effective protection of the rights of all members to participate fully, freely, and equally in the affairs of the organizations without regard to race, creed or color."[76] Instead,

---

[74]James A. Donaldson, "Black Americans in Mathematics," *A Century of Mathematics in America, Part III*, American Mathematical Society, Providence, RI, 1988, p. 451.

[75]Sylvia T. Bozeman, Etta Z. Falconer, Abdulalim A. Shabazz, Harriet J. Walton, and J. Ernest Wilkins, Jr., "A History of Minority Participation in the Southeast Section," April 1995, available at the headquarters of the Mathematical Association of America, p. 7.

[76]ibid, p. 11.

the board passed a *resolution* affirming its intention to ban discrimination[77] and requesting the President to consult with Section officers "to determine the best means for avoiding discrimination."[78]

President MacLane sent letters to "54 people, including the sectional officers and governors from the regions most directly affected and a number of other members of the Association chosen to represent differing opinions on this topic." Three months later he had 32 replies. He reported that, "About 20 replies said in essence, 'I heartily approve the resolution passed by the Board of Governors at its September meeting.'" Some pointed out that other organizations have opened to "negroes" and several attended. Another told about an interracial professional meeting in an office conference room with lunches sent in.

Others were not so encouraging. "When a section meets at an institution, the section is not the host, but is a guest. A guest is obligated to work for the welfare of the host as long as he is a guest." Slightly more helpful was another Southerner who wrote, ". . . we might consider the matter of discontinuing the social functions and holding only meetings to which anyone could be admitted. Several others suggested canceling the banquet, but one called this idea "a retreat," writing, "I. . . have lived here all my past life, and all my teaching has been in this state. I am eager that we go forward." President MacLane concluded his report with a quote of a "distinguished Southern mathematician," who said, "I feel that such discrimination should end, and that the way to stop it is just to stop."[79]

Later that winter President MacLane sent a letter to the section officers saying that he had determined it was possible "to conduct the scientific, business, and social affairs of the Association without discrimination as to race, creed, or color" but that this would require "careful planning in advance and consultation with the host institution in question." MAA Secretary-Treasurer Harry Gehman sent a copy of this report to all predominantly "Negro" colleges. In another December 1951 letter Lorch suggested interracial planning. The result of all this activity is that apparently no African Americans attended any Southeast Section meetings in the remainder of the 1950s.

The next known attempt was in April 1960 by Lonnie Cross (now Abdulalim Shabazz), who was then chair of the mathematics department at Atlanta University. He was scheduled to present a paper at 3:24 P.M. Earlier that afternoon he arrived at the Section meeting at the University of South Carolina in Columbia with a colleague from New Delhi, India, and two graduate students, one of whom was "so-called white." When the group presented confirmed reservations at the Wade Hampton Hotel, they were told to "wait a minute" while their rooms were made ready. About a half

---

[77]Published in the *American Mathematical Monthly*, November, 1951, p. 661.

[78]Bozeman, Falconer, Shabazz, Walton and Wilkins, p. 7.

[79]ibid, 14-16, reprinting the report of President Saunders MacLane to the Board of Governors of December 28, 1951.

hour later an assistant manager told them that the Wade Hampton would honor only the reservation of the "white" man, but would help the others get reservations in the Nylon Hotel (a colored hotel) some distance away.

"Such arrangements are unsatisfactory to us," responded Cross, and sought out the local MAA officers. They corroborated the manager's statement that they could attend the sessions of the meeting, but not any social event. C. L. Seebeck, Secretary-Treasurer of the Southeast Section added, "We regret that South Carolina's law prevents your full participation in our meeting. We want you to attend and participate to the extent you can. About 90% of the membership feels as you do and is with you, but times are such that they cannot openly say so."

The group from Atlanta University left. As they did so, Cross abandoned his plans to present a paper and stated, "In view of the fact that the Southeast Section of the Association is operating contrary to the enunciated national policy..., we cannot remain at this meeting. We would be less than human beings to do so... we ask you, Professor Seebeck... to explain to those at this meeting our reasons for leaving.... As a member of the Association, I shall continue to do all I can to make the policy of the national body a reality in the Southeast Section."[80]

He then wrote a press release that was highly quoted in the national African American press. Forty-four years later he observed, "We didn't want that kind of attention, We just went to give a paper and have a good weekend." He said he hadn't a clue about what would happen until he arrived. "Of course, I knew that the United States was a white supremacist country, but I had no idea this kind of activity was going on in the MAA and AMS." That concluded his attempt to participate for decades. "Our appetites for the Southeast Section was destroyed when we had to walk out of the meeting."[81]

Abdulalim A. Shabazz (b. 1927) was born Lonnie Cross in Bessemer, Alabama. He grew up in Alabama, but when he was fourteen, he went to Washington, D.C., in search of a better education. For a while he lived with his grandmother, both of them in one room in a rooming house, sharing a bathroom and kitchen with others. When he turned sixteen, he obtained working papers and an evening job as a clerk at the United States Department of War. Now able to support himself, he began living alone "with the help of God." Another clerk asked him to meet her husband. After he did, they invited him to live with them as an older brother to their two sons and a daughter. He paid a small rent, but it was a much more satisfactory arrangement than living alone.[82]

---

[80] "Atlanta University Professors and a Graduate Student Leave South Carolina Mathematics Meeting in Protest of Discrimination," press release issued by the Department of Mathematics, Atlanta University, Georgia, April 4, 1960, provided by Abdulalim Shabazz on 10/27/04.

[81] Abdulalim Shabazz, telephone conversation, 10/27/04.

[82] ibid.

After graduating with honors from the fabled public Paul Lawrence Dunbar High School, he won a scholarship to Lincoln University in Pennsylvania, where he earned an A.B. in mathematics and chemistry in 1949 in spite of the fact that he was drafted into and served honorably in the United States Army Airforce for one year. Two years later he received an M.S. in mathematics from M.I.T. After working a year and a half as an assistant mathematician in the Cornell Aeronautical laboratory in Buffalo, New York, in 1953 he began working toward a doctorate at Cornell. In the summer of 1954 he saw an ad for which he was eminently qualified, but when he arrived, they took one look at him and told him the job was taken. "That convinced me I had to get that piece of paper called a Ph.D."[83] He worked hard the next year, and in 1955 was awarded a Ph.D. in mathematics from Cornell University.

After graduation, he felt called to social change, and took a job in a rug cleaning business. However, his body was so injured after the very first day that he decided to go back to mathematics. He saw an advertisement for a Research Mathematician and phoned the given number. "Come on down," was the response. They were clearly shocked to see him, but they liked his credentials, so they offered him the advertised job with the Metals Research Laboratory of the Electro Metallurgical Company in Niagara Falls. While he was there, he didn't realize they were doing nuclear research and engaged in making nuclear weapons; the scientists would pose problems and he would set them up in the form of mathematical equations.[84] In the fall of 1956 he left to join the faculty at Tuskegee Institute.

In 1957 he became chair of the mathematics department at Atlanta University. It was only a graduate school at that time, and there were only two students in mathematics. "During the six-year period 1957-63, when I was chairman of the department, 109 students graduated with master's degrees in mathematics," Shabazz later wrote. "More than a third of them went on to earn Ph.D. degrees in mathematics or mathematics education. Many of them went on to produce students who earned Ph.D's in mathematics. Now it is estimated that nearly 50 percent of the roughly 200 African American mathematicians in the United States resulted either directly or indirectly from Atlanta University's 109 master's degree recipients between 1957 and 1963."[85]

In 1961 Shabazz became a Muslim, changed his name, and became politically active. He was accused by the Atlanta University president of being a communist, and in 1963 he left the university.[86] He spent twelve years in Washington, D.C., as the Director of Education of the University of Islam #4, and then taught in Chicago, Detroit, and Mecca, Saudi Arabia.

---

[83]ibid.

[84]ibid.

[85]Paul Cody, "Affecting Eternity: Abdulalim Abullah Shabazz, Ph.D. '55," *Cornell Magazine*, April 1994, p. 62.

[86]ibid.

Meanwhile, he married, had two sons and a daughter, raised them with his wife, and divorced. He then adopted two Ethiopian boys whom he raised alone. Both are now mathematicians.

In 1986 he returned to what would soon become Clark Atlanta University, following a merger of Atlanta University and Clark College. The math department was in terrible shape; many students were considered incapable of doing even basic mathematics. He insisted that the undergraduate department offer higher level mathematics courses. When his colleagues said they weren't ready, Shabazz responded, "Give me the very worst ones you have, and I'll show you that they can be taught." He again served as Chair from 1990 to 1995. In 1990 only 35 undergraduates were majoring in math, but by 1992, there were 155 undergraduate mathematics majors.[87] No mathematics B.A./B.S. degrees were granted in 1990 and only one M.S. degree, but in 1995 there were 23 B.A./B.S. degrees and 23 M.S. degrees granted in mathematics.

Abdulalim A. Shabazz (right) at a 1999 conference of the African-African American Summit in Accra, Ghana, with fellow-delegate James Donaldson, who was then interim president of Lincoln University and is now Dean of the College of Arts and Sciences at Howard University. Photo courtesy of Abdulalim A. Shabazz.

---

[87]ibid.

From 1997 to 2000 he was chair of the Mathematics and Computer Science Department at Lincoln University, his alma mater. During his first year as chair, he led a complete revision of the mathematics curriculum and established a 4-year B.S./M.S. degrees program in mathematics. That was the first time in the 144-year history of the university that a higher degree in any science had been offered. Suddenly, he was dismissed from his position as department chair, ironically while he was in Washington accepting the National Mentor Award from President Clinton.[88] On the web one can read an interview that he gave shortly afterward. He indicates he was dismissed because he maintained high standards and strongly advocated hiring more blacks, although other reasons were alleged.

Shabazz has received several other outstanding honors from a variety of sources, including the "Mentor Award" of 1992 from the American Association for the Advancement of Science, the Lifetime Achievement Award of the African American Educators of California, and NAM's Distinguished Service Award in 1994. (NAM, the National Association of Mathematicians, supports African American mathematicians and aspiring mathematicians, especially at the collegiate level.) He continues as Professor of Mathematics at Lincoln University at the age of 77.

In 2004 he remembered with regret the 1954 Supreme Court decision requiring racially integrated schools, a regret he felt even then. "The majority population got the entire control of our education. Rather than equalize the support, they got rid of our teachers and educational administrators. Before 1954 all the teachers and administrators in our Southern schools were colored — and usually as well an assistant superintendent who supervised our schools. Now only six percent of the teachers nationwide are African American and 85 percent are European American. Our children are at the mercy of teachers who don't understand them and aren't inclined to teach all of them properly. Especially our young men are affected; black boys are feared by their non-black teachers."[89]

Individual black mathematicians who tried to leap the color bar typically had a very different experience from Gloria Hewitt's as reported in Chapter 2. Many reported an isolation similar to that of Kelly Miller's in the nineteenth century at Hopkins. Dr. Vivienne Malone Mayes, who, like Hewitt, studied under Lee Lorch and was inspired by him to pursue a doctorate in mathematics, wrote a moving account of her experience at the University of Texas, reminiscent of that of Kelly Miller's eighty years earlier at Hopkins. "My mathematical isolation was complete."[90]

Yet there were signs of progress, especially for black women. In 1920, when American women were first able to vote, only about twenty percent

---

[88] www.math.buffalo.edu/mad/PEEPS/Shabazz_abdulalima.html

[89] Abdulalim Shabazz, telephone conversation, October 27, 2004.

[90] Vivienne Malone Mayes, "Black and female," *Newsletter of the Association for Women in Mathematics*, 5:6, 1975, pp. 4-6.

of the graduates of predominantly black colleges were women. By 1940, a majority were women.[91] This was at a time of increasing college attendance for black males too, and the Supreme Court decision of 1954 mandating total integration of all K-12 public schools brought hope that a new day was dawning. Indeed, the introduction of the 1955 book *The Negro in Science* included the sentence, "Whether or not this monograph should have been written at such times as these when the trend is so pronouncedly away from racial delineation is a moot question."[92]

Lack of resources continued, and continues, to be an omnipresent problem for African Americans with legitimate American aspirations. The inadequate funding of the segregated black schools in which most were educated before and after 1954 took a terrible toll. The lack of compliance with the 1954 Supreme Court decision meant that many youngsters were confined to inadequately supported segregated schools long after they had ceased to be legal.

Furthermore, the shock of first experiencing integrated education in college or graduate school could only be withstood by people with tremendous ability and stamina. That so few African Americans earned doctorates in mathematics compared to their proportion in the American population reflects the double onslaught of the inequitable resources and the emotional impact of segregation. Nevertheless, twenty-four of the first twenty-five African American women who earned doctorates in mathematics were educated in segregated K-12 schools — even though Corlis Powell Johnson began school three years *after* the 1954 Supreme Court decision.

Elayne Arrington (b. 1940) was the sole exception, and she went to otherwise all white schools. Arrington's story reveals why the inadequately funded segregated school produced more black female mathematicians in the years following the Supreme Court decision than integrated schools with many more resources. The year that she was valedictorian of her Pennsylvania high school was the only year that the class president, instead of the valedictorian, gave the graduation speech. She was not allowed to be a cheerleader or drum majorette with her high school band — and certainly not an angel in the Christmas play! She adds with relish that both her daughters won national contests in baton twirling.

The isolation did not end when she was an engineering student at the University of Pittsburgh. "They were not friendly and I didn't ask them any questions, lest they think that I was not capable of doing my own work. In effect, I was isolated, and it was me against all of them... the worst effect of my undergraduate experiences was the lack of intellectual exchange with my peer group." When she graduated from the University of Pittsburgh,

---

[91] Jeanne L. Noble, *The Negro Woman's College Education*, Teachers College, Columbia University, New York, 1956, p. 28.

[92] The Calloway Hall Editorial Committee, Morgan State College, *The Negro in Science*, 1955, p. 173.

her class standing was not listed because women were not included — reminiscent of Charlotte Scott's treatment by Cambridge University eighty years earlier. She had to compare her average with the men on the list to discover where she stood.[93]

In 1974 she joined the Department of Mathematics and Statistics at the University of Pittsburgh as an assistant professor. Since 1993 she has been a Senior Lecturer in that department.

The first gathering of black mathematicians in the South took place in 1969, supported by a grant from the National Science Foundation obtained with the help of Southern white male mathematicians. Thus the National Association of Mathematicians was born, dedicated to helping and supporting minority mathematicians. Gradually NAM became more visible at national conferences, and its newsletter connected mathematicians and aspiring mathematicians inexpensively.

Not all successful mathematicians earn doctorates. Many pursue satisfying and respected careers with only a bachelor's degree in mathematics. However, mathematicians — female and male, black and white, doctoral or not — receive little attention in the American media. This leaves young people without role models and a general ignorance of mathematical careers. (One can cogently argue that there is widespread ignorance about mathematics itself, despite its alleged inclusion in all elementary school curricula.) As Delores Spikes, later Chancellor of the Southern University system in Louisiana, said in the 1978 AWM panel of black women mathematicians that sparked my interest in the subject, "I would suggest that the mathematical community initiate a massive public media campaign. I think we ought to help the public understand what our problems are and what the possible solutions are."

In an effort to learn more about both black mathematicians and how mathematics is used in our economy, I obtained one class of released time in 1985 and 1986 to survey black mathematicians of New Jersey. I located the subjects by networking, starting with the few black mathematicians that I already knew, mostly former students, and asking each subject for the names of more. Since New Jersey is a relatively representative state with both rural and urban areas, and a swing state in national elections, the findings here may be somewhat indicative of larger trends. I located about 150 black people with at least one degree in mathematics, and received 75 responses, 26 written mail-backs and 49 telephone interviews with people who did not mail back the questionnaire.

What did I find? Most spectacular, perhaps, was the discovery that all but one were happy with themselves and their careers. Again and again I heard people say that they were glad they had majored in mathematics.

---

[93]Patricia C. Kenschaft, "Black Women in Mathematics in the United States," *American Mathematical Monthly*, 88: 8, October, 1981, pp. 63-83, p. 76.

(This finding was corroborated a decade later when I sent out question-naires to all graduates of my department at Montclair State and received 455 responses; over 90 percent were working in mathematics and enjoying their careers very much or enormously. Only three percent were seriously unhappy with their careers, or lack thereof.[94]). The one exception was a black woman making more than $60,000 annually in the mid-1980s. (This is equivalent to over $100,000 in the early twenty-first century.) Her complaint was the sense of alienation that she felt as a black person in an all-white business context. I suspected that if she were truly discontent, she could have moved, but perhaps she thought that anywhere there was satisfying work, her isolation would have been similar.

Another startling discovery was the surprisingly large number of black mathematicians contrasted with the few that any one of them knew. When I told subjects that I had located as many as thirty black mathematicians in New Jersey, most were amazed. Yet I located about 150 African American residents of New Jersey with at least one degree in mathematics. At the rate I was going, I estimated that if I had been able to continue, that num-ber might have doubled. However, except for those employed in essentially African American school districts (of which there are quite a few in New Jersey), none knew more than five other African Americans interested in mathematics, and most knew only one or two. The contrast between their sense of isolation with the reality of their significant population in our small state was moving. It is uncomfortable to feel alone, and when it is needless, it is sad as well.

A crucial finding was the accessibility of mathematical careers to first generation college students. Mathematics provides a good career path for people without an academic family background. Almost a quarter had no parent who started high school, and a majority had at least one parent who had not graduated from high school. However, most talked with appreciation about their parents' love of learning. (It seemed to me that an unusual number of the parents were still married, but, unfortunately, I did not have that as a formal question on the schedule.) Only four of the 75 had two parents who had graduated from college. Of these, two had two parents with master's degrees, and a third had two parents with doctorates. Two had ten siblings each and two parents who had never attended college, although one of these also had one sister who was a teacher.

What about money? Twenty-eight each of the teacher and non-teacher respondents answered my questions about their income and birth year. The median age of the teachers was 41 and their median annual income was $32,000 (equivalent to $54,000 in 2001). The median age of the non-teachers was only 34 and their median salary was over $40,000 (i.e., $70,000 in 2005).

---

[94]Patricia C. Kenschaft, "What are They Doing Now?," *The College Mathematics Journal*, May, 2000, 31:3, 193-199.

Four reported incomes above $60,000 ($100,000 in 2001) and ten more in the fifties.

How representative are these data? Most who seemed to be evasive were cooperative and friendly when tracked down, and apologetic for being so busy and elusive. Only one seemed to resent my intrusion into his life. He was retired, and said that because he had been born in Africa, he was not part of the problem, and since he was retired, he was not part of the solution. He was clearly exasperated with aspects of American culture, especially a tendency not to work hard.

The other three retirees grew up in the American South and were devoting their retirement to solving "the problem," using their mathematical knowledge to inspire and teach young people. Mae Tate, the only retired woman, described her early career as "a computer." As a teenager, she wanted to prepare to share her life with Harold Tate, who, by the mid-1980s, was a retired engineer with whom she organized tutorial and speaking programs for black youngsters. However, in her youth the only professions available to women were nursing and teaching. Teaching mathematics was closest to Harold's dream of becoming an engineer, so that was Mae's aim. By the time she was in college, World War II was raging and there was a great need for the mathematical computations that many believe enabled the Allies to win the war. She never taught, but became a Mathematician and Computer Specialist, spending the last thirty-two years of her career at Fort Monmouth. Dr. Walter McAfee, son of Susie Johnson McAfee, had also been at Fort Monmouth, concluding his career as Chief Scientific Advisor to the Electronic R&D Command. Dr. Edward Carroll had been director of two Ph.D. programs at New York University, one for mathematics supervisors in the public schools and the other for mathematics educators in colleges.

Three open-ended questions had much more complex answers than those about job satisfaction, parental education, and income: "What was the effect of racism on your career?" "Why did you become interested in mathematics?" and "What can be done to bring more blacks into mathematics?" The career paths were so varied, and perhaps so far from the theme of this book, that they have been relegated to an appendix (see page 211).

Many commented that the effect of racism on their careers cannot be separated from its effect on their educations and lives. Their substantive answers varied enormously. Several said that the impact had been both positive and negative, and it was hard to weigh the balance. Seven of the younger respondents suspect that their race has been an asset because of special scholarships, quotas, and affirmative action. On the other hand, the older ones had many stories of jobs evaporating as soon as they appeared for interviews, only to be filled by white candidates the following day.

"The most insidious racism is when it affects your thinking about yourself," said Dr. Eldon McIntyre sharply. Many of both sexes talked about the emotional strain of being the only black among dozens of whites, no matter how understanding the surrounding professionals try to be. Without my prodding, several women volunteered that racism was the primary problem when they were students, but after college graduation they were more affected by sexism than racism. The only respondents who claimed that race was not a factor in their careers were those who worked in all-black school systems.

A disturbing trend was the consistency of the complaints about racism in graduate school, both from current graduate students and from those who had been to graduate school previously. Several said that graduate education was the most racist environment that they had experienced.

"Why did you become interested in mathematics?" also had many answers. About a third remembered enjoying it from a very young age, some adding that their family or an elementary school teacher had generated the interest. More than a quarter named a specific teacher or subject in secondary school, and almost as many said it was because math was their easiest subject. Two studied mathematics because they like to obtain a definite answer, another for "the challenge," and one because it conferred the most status in his native country in Africa. One was drawn in by "the NASA Space Club of the 60s and Star Trek," and another by playing arcade games in high school. One ended up in the field because he worked so hard to overcome his fear of mathematics.

Several said that they pursued mathematics because it was the best way to help others. One high school teacher said she was determined to help "my people" and that determination enabled her to struggle through a math major although it was very difficult for her. She became a highly respected teacher in a challenging urban high school — making less than her husband does collecting tolls at the Lincoln Tunnel.

Only seven made the choice for mathematics at college or later. One reported she had signed up for nursing but the quota was full for her first semester; she took a math course while waiting for the nursing program to open, and "I never got around to returning." Another actually earned a degree in nursing, but discovered she didn't like that career, so she returned to study math. One of the men had been pre-med, but didn't have the financial resources to go to medical school. Two had been studying engineering and one was pursuing philosophy before they switched to math in college.

One of my former students had never expected to go to college until he was surprised to receive an Equal Opportunity Fund federal scholarship. Until then he had never thought seriously about his future. While he was taking remedial algebra at Montclair State, he suddenly decided "to make something of myself." I remember him as an incredibly hardworking Calculus 2 student. By then he had convinced himself that only consistent hard work was needed for him to have a successful career in mathematics. At the time of the survey, he was well launched in a remunerative industrial career.

The leading answer (by almost *half*) to "What can be done to bring more blacks into mathematics?" was to improve the elementary school mathematics education of all American children. If American children continue to be taught by unprepared non-specialists, those growing up in homes where mathematics is taught daily will have a tremendous advantage by the time they reach teachers prepared in mathematics. Thus any ethnic group that is underrepresented in mathematics is doomed to remain so until we change our approach to elementary education. This overwhelming response had a dramatic impact on my own career, since it came as a complete surprise, made sense, and, when I became involved, seemed clearly true.

What is needed? Two wanted to change the elementary mathematics curriculum, but most were more concerned with approach than with content. One asserted that "mathematics is a natural interest" squelched by an unfriendly environment and emphasized, "[We need] more certified, enthusiastic teachers." Several advocated math specialists no later than fourth grade. One middle school teacher told of his frustration at having to teach other subjects too, when the need for good middle school mathematics teaching is great and he feels a compelling desire to do it full time. The middle school teachers were full of ideas for making math exciting. The theme of making math fun was recurring. "Forget the dolls, the soldiers,... and the toy guns. Buy them games that make thinking *fun*."

The far-trailing second answer, from 14 respondents, to the question of how to bring more blacks into mathematics was "Provide role models." One, a non-teaching role model, keeps a file box of teachers' names and addresses on his desk and frequently sends them ideas or flyers that he thinks might help their students. I might have planted the concern for role models simply by doing my survey, but the fact that each of my subjects knew so few of the others emphasized how unavailable role models are.

A number of respondents commented that many people outside mathematics can't understand why they work so intensely for such long hours. How do we teach people not to give up? A math-based career necessarily involves a struggle. One said that he often prays with college and graduate students that they will have the strength not to give up, and in his experience such prayers have always had the desired result. A sterner approach was taken by one who told about climbing trees as a child in the South to watch KKK demonstrations, and was now one of the highest paid in the group. He said of today's young people, "They have a golden opportunity, but they aren't willing to pay their dues." Several decried "the distractions" of high school. One bemoaned, "The peer pressure in high school is unreal," and another, "By the time they're in high school, they're involved with sports — or drugs." Another observed with irony, "Basketball was not a game developed in Africa." He also reflected that men who enjoy mathematics are suspected of being "sissy" and women of being "mannish," a no-win situation for everyone.

Five said that family influence, especially in the pre-school years, is crucial. Parents should help their children learn to associate math with fun before they enter the classroom. Another five focused on the high school years, one wishing that counselors would advise students to study mathematics as often as cosmetology. Five others said that the influence of mathematics teachers is most important. (When I interviewed 21 of the first 25 black women to receive doctorates in mathematics, *every one* said that they had had some secondary school teacher who told them they were gifted in math and it would be worth their struggle to pursue a career in it.) Two suggested special summer and weekend programs and two others pleaded for more scholarships and other financial support.

Thus there were seven major conclusions from this study, now almost twenty years old. (1) Mathematics graduates have satisfying careers, feel good about themselves, and are glad they pursued mathematics. (2) There were at least 150 black people in New Jersey with degrees in mathematics in the mid-1980s, despite the widespread belief, even among them, that there were far fewer. (3) Mathematical careers are accessible to first generation college students; only a minority of the respondents had a parent who had graduated from high school and almost a quarter had no parent who had *started* high school. (4) Salaries of mathematics graduates are consistently middle class. (5) Discrimination against blacks is still serious, and blacks are brainwashed at all ages to believe they cannot achieve. The most racist environment in New Jersey is graduate education. (6) However, an individual with stamina and family support who overcomes this brainwashing can achieve. The choice for mathematics can and does occur at all ages up through college. (7) Mathematics teaching in elementary schools is woefully inadequate, and is seen by this group as the primary reason for minority underrepresentation in mathematics.

How many of these are still valid? I personally am acutely aware of how appallingly poor most elementary math education is in northern New Jersey, despite efforts in the past two decades. It is much more apparent to me than it was twenty years ago that children in families that teach mathematics to preschoolers are at an enormous advantage compared to children of parents who don't have the time, interest, or knowledge, and that this advantage compounds as the youngsters grow. It does not require a high school education to provide adequate preschool mathematical nurturing, but it does require considerable interest, knowledge, and joy in mathematics. Teachers favor students who are eager to learn; I can't plead innocent of this tendency.

Many black people I respect still observe much too much discrimination. The perception that the worst racial discrimination was in our graduate programs is truly unsettling. I am not aware of any similar study of black mathematicians in one geographic area. It seems past time for another.

Meanwhile, the good news of conclusions (1) through (4) and (6) are worth shouting far and wide. Mathematics is a way! All the respondents, whether they were middle school teachers, research mathematicians, or highly paid industrial mathematicians, felt good about themselves and what they were accomplishing. It seems appropriate to urge every middle school and high school in the country (perhaps elementary schools too) to display the attractive poster of African American mathematicians that is free for anyone who promises to post it.[95]

Perhaps it is worth repeating what Delores Spikes said in 1978, "I would suggest that the mathematical community initiate a massive public media campaign. I think we ought to help the public understand what our problems are and what the possible solutions are." Both society and many individuals would benefit from such a campaign.

---

[95]Contact William Hawkins, bhawkins@MAA.org, SUMMA (Strengthening Underrepresented Minority Mathematics Achievement), MAA, 1527 Eighteenth St., Washington, D.C. 20036, 800-741-9415.

CHAPTER 6

Latino Mathematicians

In 1992 Luis Ortiz-Franco, a professor of mathematics at Chapman University in California, decided it was time to provide role models in mathematics for young Latinos. With that as a goal, he laboriously went through the entire Combined Membership List of the American Mathematical Society, the Mathematical Association of America (MAA), and some smaller mathematical organizations. How many Latinos, he wondered, were among them? If he wanted to contact them, would he have an overwhelming job to get responses from all of them? There were about 30,000 members of the MAA alone at that time, and thousands from other organizations who were not MAA members. He counted sixty-five identifiably Latino last names — less than 0.2 percent of the total.[1] At that time more than 10 percent of the United States population was Latino. By 2003 this had jumped to 15 percent, making Latinos the largest "minority" population in the United States.

Why are there so few Latino mathematicians? A report released in late 2001[2] concluded that about 91.8 percent of "white non-Hispanic" Americans graduated from high school in 2000. High school graduation rates that year were 94.6 percent for Asian/Pacific Islanders, and 83.7 percent for African Americans, but only 64.1 percent for Latinos. The differences start long before graduate school.

Ortiz-Franco points out that Latinos are often educated in the United States' poorest districts with inadequate resources, but this tends to be true also of African Americans. They often have teachers with appallingly poor education in mathematics, but this is true of many American children. However, it affects those already disadvantaged more than those whose parents teach them math at home. Latinos have the added disadvantages of cultural and language gaps, and the lack of role models. Ortiz-Franco has been working to remedy the latter, and his book of biographies of Latino mathematicians will be published by the MAA.

There are other, perhaps more easily remedied, obstacles for Latinos. One is high school advising against mathematics. When Ortiz-Franco first came to the United States at the age of sixteen, he told his high school counselor in Los Angeles that he wanted to take algebra. "You can't," was the reply. Without telling her, he made some investigations, found an

---

[1] Luis Ortiz-Franco on Math Medley, May 21, 2004, "Latinos in Mathematics."

[2] *New York Times*, Friday, November 16, 2001, from the Associated Press.

algebra class that was available when he had time in his schedule, went to it, and sat down. The teacher helped him enroll. By the time of mid-term grade, he had an A average. His counselor then discovered that he was surreptitiously taking algebra, and had the grace to congratulate him on his A.

He has now heard of several similar stories of Latinos who eventually became mathematicians.[3] One can only wince at the number who accepted their counselor's statement that they "couldn't" take algebra, or some higher level of mathematics.

William Vélez, now Distinguished Professor of Mathematics at the University of Arizona, did a simpler survey in 1978. How many Latino research mathematicians were there in the Southwest, the area with the greatest concentration of Latinos is in the United States? Getting in touch with all of the Ph.D.-granting departments was not an overwhelming job, and he discovered there were seven Latino research mathematicians in total — no two at the same institution. They were Efraim Armendariz, who is still at the University of Texas at Austin; Joaquin Bustoz, Jr., at Arizona State University, now deceased; Richard Greigo at the University of New Mexico, now retired; David Sanchez at UCLA, now retired; Richard Tapia, who is still at Rice University in Texas; William Torres at New Mexico State University, who left after a few years to install irrigation systems near his home community; and himself.[4] Vélez missed Francisco J. Samaniego, a statistician at the University of California at Davis. Samaniego earned a Ph.D. in mathematics in 1971 from UCLA and taught in the Davis mathematics department until 1979, when the department split and he joined the new statistics department.[5] (Nobody pointed him out to Vélez, a hazard facing all surveys such as his in 1978 and mine this year.) Each of these men has worked hard to bring more minorities into mathematics, but each is working alone. At the remaining universities, there are far fewer Latino students.

As I contemplated repeating Vélez's survey in 2004, the question of "defining the problem" arose. What was the "Southwest?" That was easy. Vélez defined it as the states of California, Arizona, New Mexico, and Texas; therefore, so would I. Should immigrants from Spain and Argentina be included? If so, why not immigrants from Italy and Nigeria? This was harder. Richard Tapia's response to my question was articulate and enlightening:

> In education, when we use "Latino" in the sense of under-
> representation, we usually mean someone who is a product
> of this country: if not born in the USA, at least raised and
> educated in the United States. Foreign born and raised
> Latinos do not count. If they did count, then we would

---

[3]Luis Ortiz-Franco on Math Medley, May 21, 2004, "Latinos in Mathematics."

[4]Celestino Fernandez and W. Y. Vélez, "Underrepresentation in the Sciences: Chicanos and Native Americans," *Proceedings of the Conference on the Status and Issues of Chicano Native American Participation in the Sciences*, Boulder, CO, 1978.

[5]Francisco J. Samaniego, personal email on January 13, 2005.

just be talking about foreign immigrants like those from any other foreign country. The distinction is critical because foreign Latinos do not have the same life experiences that we domestic Latinos have had. They did not experience or have to deal with what I call "U.S. raised extra baggage": being told I am different, and that our kind can't do this or do that, or that I won't make it.

Then we do not see role models, so after moments of failure, we have to question why we fail and at least confront the issue, "Maybe they are right." Having confidence, feeling that you belong, and seeing others like you are very powerful and probably necessary. Mainland Puerto Ricans (so-called New Yorkicans — my wife is one) have the same problems. However, those from the Islands are completely different. I had one of my Island Puerto Rican students tell me that she did not see herself as a minority because she never saw herself as different from anyone else growing up in Puerto Rico. The extra baggage life experience can not be minimized.

Those domestic Latinos whose ancestors came to this country for economic reasons (e.g., Mexicans and Puerto Ricans) have similar extra baggage experience. However, by and large the life experiences of the Latinos whose ancestors came here for political reasons (e.g., Cubans and Salvadoreans) are different and this difference allows them to be much better represented. Indeed many of their parents were successful professionals in their home country.

I often ask a Latino to watch the movie, "Stand and Deliver" and then tell me what it is about. If they can't explain the movie, then I see they can't help me in my outreach activities. However, if they really understand, then they can be, and often are, a great help. Recently, one of my Colombian students told me that he thought that it was a senseless story and did not understand why so many people thought that the movie was great. It is clear that he can not help me in my outreach.

While Chicanos or Mexican Americans are the bulk of the Latino population, I do not have trouble including other Latinos if they are indeed products of this country.[6]

Vélez corroborated that this was the philosophy of his 1978 survey, and Ortiz-Franco used the same in his 1992 survey, so these were the definitions I used in 2004. Alas, the number of Latinos, thus defined, has hardly increased in the doctoral-granting mathematics departments of the Southwest,

---

[6]Richard Tapia, email on June 4, 2004.

although the nationwide percentage of Latinos in the U.S. population has grown from five percent to fifteen percent, and they tend to be concentrated in the Southwest. Perhaps I should add that now Francisco J. Samaniego is one of three who reported to me in doctoral-granting statistics departments in the Southwest. I also kept a record of the number of "Latinos" as defined by the administration of my own university — which includes immigrants from Spain who had their entire education outside the United States. They do, perhaps, help provide role models, if not personal understanding of American problems. Alas, even this broader definition yields only about 26 more. More details of my survey will be included in Chapter 10, "Minorities in Mathematics Now (2004)."

Meanwhile, it should be emphasized that mathematicians pursue satisfying careers outside doctoral-granting departments — in industry, government, and the more than 2000 non-doctoral-granting institutions of higher education such as the one in which I teach. Many Latino mathematicians are included among these. The lack of role models visible to young Latinos is not just because they are underrepresented, but also because most mathematicians are not visible to the public. In particular, Latino mathematicians in every region of this country are hidden from public view, busily pursuing their active careers without appropriate notice. It would be healthier if all young people (not just Latinos) could see mathematicians at work.

William Vélez believes the established mathematics community is not acting responsibly toward Latinos. He tells a symbolic story with passion. He had an excellent Latino student, a mathematics major at the University of Arizona, who wanted to pursue graduate study in mathematics. The student was turned down for *admission* by the University of California at San Diego, the University of California at Santa Barbara, and UCLA.

"What happened to him?" I asked.

"Amazingly, he went to UC Berkeley on a fellowship," Vélez responded.

"I have to tell you, I'm still steaming about this incident. How can these universities that sit in *huge* populations of Mexican Americans turn down a well-qualified student from that population? I find this to be amazing and unconscionable. We could go on for hours, talking about incidents like this of the inattention of the mathematics community to the members of our population."[7]

The discrimination that Vélez himself faced when he was young was more than "inattention." He applied to work for the National Security Agency, since his mathematical specialty was cryptography. "At the exit interview, they told me that if I worked for them I couldn't have contact with foreign nationals. I told them, 'I live on the border. You can't be serious about this.'

"'No,' they said. 'Here's the rule. Are you willing to comply?'

---

[7]William Vélez, Math Medley interview, December 8, 2001, "Every College Student Should Be a Mathematics Major."

"In the end I said that I couldn't." His parents had emigrated from
Mexico, and he regularly visited aunts, uncles, and cousins a short distance
across the border from Tucson where he lived. He was shocked at the policy,
but refused to give up his family life for a job. "I had satisfied the minimum
requirements. I had security clearance already and my mother was a citizen.
But they would not hire me. The effect of this is that they were excluding the
Chicano population from being employed at the National Security Agency.
Now this particularly annoyed me, because I was fine to be sent to Vietnam.
But now that I was educated and could address the technological problems
that confront us, I was not allowed to participate in this enterprise. I should
point out that the National Security Agency no longer feels this way, but
this is an example of rules they once had that kept us out of employment."[8]

Despite the obstacles facing every wave of immigrants and a few special
to the late twentieth century, Chicanos (from Mexico) and other recently
arrived Latinos have participated at all levels of mathematical activity, including the highest levels of research. Innumerable Latinos are in K-12
education; among those who have amazed me with their ability to teach
and inspire pre-high school youngsters mathematically are Olga Torres in
Tucson, Arizona; Hector Garcia in Hayward, California; and Milo Novelo in
Harlem, New York City. Grace Davilla Coates spent her childhood following her Mexican parents around the United States. They worked as migrant
workers and could not provide stable schooling for their children. She taught
for a while, and is now director of the International Family Math Program.

Luis Ortiz-Franco (b. 1947), as mentioned above, arrived in the
United States from Mexico when he was sixteen. His father and older sister
were already here, and a married older sister remained behind in Mexico. His
father packed paper for a waste company at minimum wage. Four younger
siblings came with Luis and his mother, who promptly got a job in a shoe
factory.

After fighting for his right to take college preparatory mathematics, he
spent two and a half years in high school, doing well enough to be accepted
by UCLA. He quickly realized he had received a below average education at
Lincoln High School in Los Angeles, and that this had happened to most
Latinos. Knowing he couldn't make change alone, he decided to start the
first Latino student organization on campus. Some school records were accessible to the public, so he painstakingly sorted through twenty-eight thousand cards, one for each student. Among these he found sixty-five Latinos,
who joined with him in a new student organization, the United Mexican
American Students (UMAS), which later evolved into what today is known
as MECHA. Also while in college, he became active in the United Farm
Workers, led by Cesar Chavez. He participated in picket lines protesting
unfair employer practices.

---

[8]ibid.

After graduation in 1969, Luis Ortiz-Franco went to Reed College in Portland, Oregon, for a year and earned a master's of arts in the teaching of mathematics. That was the year of the Kent State tragedy. He joined the protest demonstrations on the Reed College campus in May of 1970.

In June he returned to his family in Los Angeles, getting ready to become an instructor in a special program for minorities at UCLA in mid-September. The program served four minority groups, selecting high-potential students who did not meet UCLA's academic requirements and providing remedial help. For two years he taught mathematics in the Latino component of the program.

Meanwhile, on August 28 he joined a Chicano Moratorium, a demonstration against the war in Vietnam. He reports that a *quarter* of the casualties in Vietnam were Latino people, although in those days only five percent of the United States population was Latino. He points out that a similar pattern happened in Iraq. The first casualties were Latino non-citizens, whom our government "generously made citizens posthumously."[9]

The demonstrations on August 28, 1970, were broken up by the police and culminated in riots. Luis Ortiz-Franco woke up on the sidewalk during the evening of August 30 with no memories of the previous two days. He was missing his driver's license. He had double or triple vision in one of his eyes. His family had been searching for him in vain. His health wasn't good for the next couple of years, but eventually improved.

After his instructorship at UCLA, he directed a program at San Diego State serving migrant farm workers' children. He recruited them and helped locate financial and academic support services. He then realized that if he were going to continue to work in academia, he should get a doctorate. In 1977 he was awarded a doctorate in mathematics education by Stanford University. He then spent one year at the University of New Mexico initiating a program and writing a grant proposal for a grant that was awarded after he left. The next year was spent at the Southwest Regional Educational Laboratory in Los Alamitos, California.

In 1979 the National Science Foundation (NSF) flew him to Washington for a job interview. While in Washington, he visited a friend who set up an interview for him at the National Institute of Education (NIE), part of the Department of Education. Both the NSF and the NIE made offers, and he chose the one from the NIE. He enjoyed the opportunity to live in Washington, D.C., but as his three year appointment drew to an end, he wanted something more exciting.

He returned to California in February 1983 to become a full-time volunteer for the United Farm Workers, collaborating directly with Cesar Chavez. Full-time volunteers, including Chavez himself, were provided (with their families) room and board and $15 a week for incidentals. He found that

---

[9]Luis Ortiz-Franco, Math Medley, May 22, 2004, "Latinos in Mathematics."

"full-time" meant he did not have any time for professional conferences, although occasionally he found time in the evenings to referee articles for the *Journal of Research in Mathematics Education* and other NCTM journals.

Cesar Chavez handled the political discussions, and Dr. Luis Ortiz-Franco did the mathematical follow-up in the negotiations with growers, nit-picking about salaries and benefits. That August he met another UFW volunteer, lawyer Judy Weissberg. In November they were married, and they now have a daughter and a son.

Late in 1983, they left the UFW to be with his family as his father's health declined; he died on January 4, 1984. Luis was quickly able to pick up a job as research co-ordinator for the Chicano Research Center at UCLA, but he kept his eye out for something more permanent. In 1986 he joined the mathematics faculty of nearby Chapman College, now Chapman University, where he has become a professor of mathematics.

Luis Ortiz-Franco, on his 1991 holiday card, with his daughter Rebeca Xochitl, his son David Tizoc, and his wife Judy Weissberg Ortiz on the Chapman University campus in Orange, CA. Photo courtesy of Luis Ortiz-Franco.

He has since been involved in research and writing about Latinos in Mathematics. He is co-editor of the book, *Changing the Faces of Mathematics: Perspectives on Latinos*, published in 1999 by the National Council of Teachers of Mathematics. It is the first book focusing on Latinos in mathematics published by a professional society. It includes contributions from over a dozen Latinos. Ortiz-Franco's own chapter details how Latino mathematics achievement as measured by the National Assessment of Educational

Progress test came closer to the United States average between 1972 and 1992. Since during this time Latinos' median family income fell even farther below the U.S. average, his analysis raised questions as to the connection between income and educational achievement. The Mathematical Association of America will publish his volume of biographical sketches of Latino mathematicians based on surveys following his 1992 search of the Combined Membership List.

Most Latino leaders in mathematics are not first generation immigrants. It takes a while for most families to gain enough economic stability for a member to pursue higher education. Graduate work in mathematics is, obviously, yet another step.

William Vélez (b. 1947) was born in Tucson, Arizona, but both of his parents were born in the state of Sonora in Mexico, just across the border from Arizona. His father, a mechanic, died when Bill was only nine, so the mathematician-to-be grew up in poverty. His mother worked three jobs to support her four children.

The "good news," according to her son, is that in 2004 Julia Vélez was still working four days a week at the age of ninety-four. She sometimes complained about her failing mental abilities because she could no longer compute the seven percent sales tax in her head and had been reduced to using paper. She has lived a good life.

However, when her son became of age, the Vietnam War was raging, and he was called to go. He vividly remembers March 25, 1968, when he said good-by to her and his fiancée Bernice as they stood side by side. He had been scheduled to be graduated from the University of Arizona and married that June, but the Navy activated him in mid-semester. He was in the Gulf of Tonkin aboard the U.S.S. Yorktown by April. The ship was leaving Hong Kong to return to Vietnam, and suddenly an announcement came that instead they were returning home. He managed to talk to Bernice on a ham radio. He told her he was coming home in a month and asked if she could reschedule the wedding. In one month she organized a wedding for over three hundred people. On July 20, 1968, they were married, but before long he was again sailing the Pacific. Fortunately, the University of Arizona gave him half credits for the semester he had half completed, and that was enough to allow him to graduate in absentia before his wedding.

Four years earlier he had entered the University of Arizona in September 1964. Three weeks into this semester he dropped calculus and enrolled in five units of easier math: college algebra and trigonometry. His semester grade was D in both math and chemistry. "I was mortified. I thought I was going to be a failure.... I was angry at myself for having dropped calculus. It hurt my pride. So, I took calculus the second semester. That semester I also spoke with a Navy recruiter and he told me that if I could survive two years of college I could become a pilot in the Navy. I thought that was better than returning to pump gas at my cousin's gasoline station. So I signed up."[10]

"After that first semester I changed my ways.... Though I was never a good student, I earned a C in calculus the second semester. In my third semester I took second semester calculus. Two great things happened that semester. I earned an A in calculus, and I met Bernice. I instantly fell in love with her. The feeling was not mutual. A common friend, Linda Valenzuela, had to convince Bernice to accept a date with me." It was during his second year of college that he decided to get a doctorate in either mathematics or physics. "I chose math because after looking at the physics schedule, it appeared that I would have to take a year of senior lab. Since no experiment of mine had ever worked in any lab course, I thought that was a recipe for disaster."[11] Later that year he told Bernice he was going to be a mathematician, that it was a long and arduous journey, and she might want to look around for an easier match. She didn't.

"She was madly in love with me," he observed in 2001. She stayed with him through his devotion to mathematics. He describes Bernice as someone who improves the quality of life for her family and other people. "We live a wonderful life."[12] They have a grown daughter and son and two grandchildren.

He threw himself into his study, and not only earned a doctorate in mathematics, but pursued a successful career in research and teaching, and eventually became a distinguished full professor of mathematics at the University of Arizona — the same institution where he had dropped Calculus 1! The University of Arizona designates two distinguished professors each year in recognition of their work with undergraduates. These professors are honored, a short videotape is made of their lives, and their salary is increased by five thousand dollars a year.

Vélez's department provides him with funds to hire a student assistant to arrange for every minority student who attempts calculus to have a twenty-minute appointment with him. He first praises the student for what they have already accomplished to be accepted at a university. Then he asks what they expect to be their major. If the student gives a prompt answer, he discusses ideas for doing well in that major, including a pep talk about the value of continuing to take mathematics to prepare for a career using that major. If the student is undecided, he says, "Then I'll put you down for a math major."

"What! But I just failed Calculus 1!"

"So did I. But the second time, I got a C, and then I did even better, and now I'm a distinguished full professor. Why not you? Besides, if I put you down for a math major, then you have to come see me every semester.

---

[10]William Yslas Vélez, personal email, May 23, 2004.

[11]ibid.

[12]William Vélez in a personal interview with the author, December 3, 2001.

I'll be your advisor if you remain a math major, or until you choose one that
you want more."

He believes he has been successful when students choose another major
because it has been a conscious choice, made after knowing that mathematics
was available. However, he is also pleased by the number of math majors
he recruits this way. Math is a good major for anyone, and bcause their
numbers are so low, each minority math major adds significantly to the
pool of African American or Latino mathematicians.

William Vélez giving the keynote address in October 2003 in
Albuquerque, New Mexico at the thirtieth anniversary celebra-
tion of the Society for the Advancement of Chicanos and Native
Americans in Science. Photo courtesy of Abid Kureshi.

William Vélez has worked at the national level too. He has been the Governor representing minorities on the Board of Governors of the Mathematical
Association of America and president of the Society for the Advancement
of Chicanos and Native Americans in Science. SACNAS for several decades
"has provided a strong national leadership in improving and expanding opportunities for minorities in the scientific workforce and academia, mentoring college students within science, mathematics, and engineering, as well
as supporting quality pre-college education."[13]

When I asked him how much discrimination he had faced after he became
an established mathematician, he said, "None. Once I was a professional
mathematician, there was no discrimination." However, the path toward a

---

[13]SACNAS website, www.SACNAS.org

tenured job in mathematics provides plenty of obstacles, and there are few hands reaching out to help young Latinos along the way.

"One thing I found extremely motivating was reading biographies of mathematicians and physicists. I did a great deal of reading when I was an undergraduate.... I was just enamored of the whole idea of being lost in thought, of being given this opportunity by society to be able to *create* new things. So this is the enterprise I belong to. I'm just absolutely *thrilled* that this country was able to support me so that I could have a position like the one I have now."[14]

"Mathematics is equitable. It is interesting and it is difficult for everyone, but the profession is not as equitable.... I'm teaching the honors course in calculus this semester. There are twenty-six students and twelve are female, and extremely bright.... We are, I think, doing a better job of opening up opportunities to the female population in the profession, but we are not doing as good a job for the minority population. We have a long way to go before there is any kind of equity in the profession for the minority population."[15]

Not all Latino Americans are immigrants or children of immigrants. Some have been here longer than most of us. For example, the ancestors of Cleopatria Martinez have lived in what is now New Mexico for thousands of years. When the Spanish explorers first came to the Southwest, they intermarried with the local population and imposed some aspects of their culture, including their language. At the end of the Mexican War in 1848, Mexico ceded most of Arizona, New Mexico, Utah, Nevada, and California to the United States for a payment of fifteen million dollars. The daily life of the residents did not change much.

Cleopatria Martinez's (b. 1948) parents spoke Spanish and thought of themselves as being "Mexican," although they and their ancestors lived in northern New Mexico, hundreds of miles within the United States. However, she grew up in Denver, Colorado, because her mother, Mary Jean Martinez, decided after her divorce to raise her family in a different location and moved there with her children. With only a third grade education, she had to live in the projects. "She worked very hard," remembered her daughter. "She is a wonderful person." She would even walk five miles to her job to save the carfare for her three children.

She was determined that her children would have an easier life, and told them that education was the way out of poverty. When she began school, little Cleopatria did not know English, but she learned it quickly. Soon she found herself being called to the principal's office as a translator when a student or parent did not know English. She enjoyed this, but wondered why she was entrusted with so much responsibility.

---

[14]William Vélez, Math Medley radio show, December 8, 2001.
[15]ibid.

Cleopatria Martinez and her mother, Mary Jean Martinez.
Photo courtesy of Cleopatria Martinez.

As a child, she studied very hard to get good grades. She succeeded most of the time, but remembers acutely one exception. An English teacher assigned the class to write about "something interesting." This was novel; she had always been told to write about something specific before. She thought about this quite a while, and wrote the most interesting paper that she had ever written about the most interesting topic she could think of.

When the grade was a D, friends urged her to ask the teacher why it was so low so she could do better next time. Cleopatria did so, and the teacher said the paper was not "interesting." The student concluded that "interesting" was completely subjective, and she wasn't going to excel in language courses. Furthermore, history was solely about events and dates, with no attention to people of any kind. Nor did it ever mention even dates and events that affected "my people." On the other hand, all teachers graded mathematics uniformly; if an answer was right, all teachers graded it right. "Mathematics is not fickle. It's not like a fickle lover."[16]

---

[16]Cleopatria Martinez, Math Medley radio interview, April 14, 2004, "Reflections of a Latina Mathematician."

High school students from the projects did not consider going away to college; it was remarkable enough if someone went to college at all. Cleopatria Martinez went to the University of Denver, and graduated with a major in mathematics. Then she became a high school mathematics teacher in the Denver public schools. While teaching, she began graduate work at the University of Colorado in Boulder, and before long she had earned a master's degree in mathematics education.

She enjoyed the beauty of mathematics enormously. "I can get lost in another world — the world of a math problem — for two hours and not remember this world," she comments. On the other hand, she remembers another incident that confirmed her opinion of non-mathematical education. One of her education professors assigned a book to read and asked the class to write a paper about "innovative ideas" based on the book. Remembering her earlier experience, Martinez wrote three papers as soon as she had finished reading the book. She handed in the most innovative very early and asked for the professor's evaluation. He said it wasn't innovative at all. She wondered if he had read the book. She then handed in the in-between paper, and he said it was better. On the due date, she handed in the routine paper where she had just spouted party lines, and got an excellent grade. She decided to stay with mathematics.

After receiving her master's degree, she got a job at a nearby community college, married, and had three daughters. At the same time, she pursued her doctorate at the University of Colorado in Boulder, saying to herself, "Let's do it all." In 1980 she was granted a Ph.D. in bilingual mathematics education.

Years later, when she was on the faculty of Phoenix College in Phoenix, Arizona she decided she wanted to become the evening coordinator. She talked with several of the eighteen full-time faculty in the mathematics department, and they encouraged her to apply. She made an appointment with the department chair, and told him of her aspiration. He looked her directly in the eye and said, "I don't think it's a good idea."

"Why not?"

"Evening director is a direct step to becoming the department chair, and I don't think you are good enough for that." She could hardly believe what she was hearing. This was not behind her back, but directly to her face. Not good enough! She had felt a lot of discrimination because her skin was dark and her first language Spanish, but this level of open hostility was new. She bided her time through another department chair, and then when the job was open again, put her name in as a nominee for chair. Her former adversary responded by nominating himself, but when it became obvious to him that she was going to win an election between them by a considerable margin, he withdrew his name. She was unanimously elected chair, a position she retains as this is written.

When asked how she feels about her career, she responds that she regrets the lack of Latino role models. When she was young, she wanted to help save lives by becoming either a brain surgeon or a heart surgeon — but she had never heard of a Latino who was a surgeon. She did know that her father, whom she had never met, was a teacher, so Latinos could be teachers. Alas, she never had a Latino teacher in her entire education. Nor does she have a colleague at Phoenix College "like me." She likes her colleagues. "They are wonderful people and teachers. But it would feed my soul to be working with a Latino."

One of the outstanding Latino leaders in mathematics repeatedly expresses similar sentiments. He has traveled in many national circles, which he enjoys, but misses having the companionship of people "like me."

Richard Tapia (b. 1939) is the first native-born Latino to be inducted into the National Academy of Engineering (1992). His parents were born in Mexico and came to the United States as teenagers in search of educational opportunities for themselves and their future five children. Dr. Tapia went through the Los Angeles public schools and attended a community college in Los Angeles, the first of his family to attend college. He received B.A., M.A., and Ph.D. degrees from the University of California at Los Angeles. Thus his entire education was in the public institutions of Los Angeles. He believes he had a fine education, and worries that today's youngsters growing up in cities are not being provided the quality of education that was available at public expense when he was young.

Richard Tapia with his '57 Chevy Bel Air in his garage at his Houston, Texas, home. This picture appeared with the article about him in the *Chronicle of Higher Education*, March 28, 2003, which observes that now that he no longer drag races, he collects and preserves cars. Photo courtesy of Greg Smith. The article is available at http://chronicle.com/free/v49/i29/29a01201.htm.

His research field has been optimization in its many forms. He has been a central figure in helping our complex economy produce safer, more environmentally sound products at minimum cost. He is now professor of computational and applied mathematics at Rice University. His career has paralleled the development of sophisticated computers. He observes, "We could do more with yesterday's computers and today's mathematics than we could with today's computers and yesterday's mathematics."[17] He is very concerned that the public, politicians, and educational leaders do not seem to understand adequately that the newly developed mathematics is essential for using modern computers (or even old computers) efficiently; he believes that financing hardware (particularly new computers for schools) at the expense of helping teachers learn mathematics does not make sense.

Richard Tapia's commitment to family is legendary. In June 2000 he was the keynote speaker at a SIAM (Society of Industrial and Applied Mathematics) annual conference at the University of Puerto Rico. He took with him not only his sixteen-year-old daughter and a significantly older son, but also his wife who is in a wheelchair and his aged mother. Another mathematician at the end of the conference told him that his conversation with Tapia's mother at a celebrity dinner "was the best conversation that I have had for weeks."[18] Although she never completed high school herself, 85-year-old Magda Tapia had wide-ranging interests and seized every opportunity for informal education, including traveling whenever possible with her famous son. He wonders how much of his success is really his parents' and his Mexican American background. He speaks of social events throughout his life as always including people of all ages. "To me, inclusion is just a part of life."

He laments the lack of tolerance of boredom and failure by today's young people. "Adversity and failure to me are the part of life that allow you to appreciate, enjoy, and go onto the successes you also have.... I have a keen feeling for what is important and what is not important in my life because of the adversity I have experienced." He talks about adversity (including failure) as providing perspective on what is important in life.

Personal tragedy has also played a significant role in Richard Tapia's perspective. The first of his three children died in an automobile accident at the age of twenty-one. At the time she was a very good student at Rice University and a professional dancer in New York City. "In her eulogy at her funeral, I said, 'Yes, it was a short life, but she did so much in her short life... perhaps in equilibrium she did as much.... Her short life was a life of contribution.'"[19] Her life and death are a major part of who he is and his conviction that one must live life despite adversity.

---

[17]Richard Tapia, Math Medley interview, July 22, 2000, "Underrepresentation: K-12 Education and the Cities."

[18]ibid.

[19]ibid.

Four years earlier, his wife had contracted multiple sclerosis. "She is in a wheelchair now, and she says, 'I would take this ten times over if I could have Cercé back'.... Being confined to a wheelchair is not even *close* to the pain she has experienced at the loss of a daughter.... Yet I look forward. I'm happy to talk about it. I'm happy to use the name Cercé. I am proud and I take pleasure from thinking of the moments I spent with her and her successes. It's a part of me."

His wife's coping with multiple sclerosis has provided Richard Tapia with many entrees into medical research. The couple's determination to keep her as lively as possible has brought both of them opportunities for innovation. His research in related fields has resulted in his becoming an adjunct faculty member at Baylor College of Medicine.

"If there is one thing I want to say, it is that not enough people — especially professors and teachers — tell students they *can*! I will say to a student, 'You're good. Are you going to graduate school?' They will say, 'Nobody ever told me I am good before. Besides, I get B's and sometimes C's.' So? I got B's too. But I'm creative and that's what matters. I'm creative in many ways. When we were in high school, my twin brother and I did drag racing. We had to use physics to figure out what would happen. It was very creative."

As part of the admission process at Rice University, he has insisted that the difference between a 1200 and 1600 on the SATs has no predictive value. Everyone with an SAT score above 1000 is in the same pool; other criteria are more important. One of their best students got only a 980 on the SATs. He looks for creativity and determination. They interview students to find "that spark," and he puts applicants in a room and watches them solve math problems together.

Under Tapia's leadership through his Center for Excellence and Equity in Education, Rice University has become a leader in providing higher education for Latinos and African Americans. Through his efforts, there are minority students in all thirteen of the science, engineering, mathematics, and technology departments on campus. Rice has an outstanding percentage of minority Ph.D. graduates in the mathematical sciences — thirty percent — compared to about five percent nationwide.[20] This increase is most startling when compared to the fact that between 1992 and 1995 no minority students were granted a Ph.D. from Rice University. Today there are fifty-seven minority students in Rice Ph.D. programs.

Richard Tapia has served on many national committees and panels, including the National Science Board, the governing body of the National Science Foundation (1996-2002) and the National Research Council's Board

---

[20]In 2004, 12 African Americans and 13 Latinos (about 5.7 percent together) were among the 441 U.S. citizens who received doctorates from U.S. institutions, according to the "2004 Annual Survey of the Mathematical Sciences" in the February 2005 *Notices of the AMS*, 52:2, p. 243. Data for the previous two years are given near the beginning of Chapter 10.

of Higher Education and Workforce (1992-). He regrets how few "people like me" he meets in such circumstances.[21] He has authored or co-authored two books and more than eighty papers. The varied honors bestowed on him include the Presidential Award for Science, Mathematics, and Engineering Mentoring from Bill Clinton (1996), a Peace Award for Education from the Spiritual Assembly of the Bahai's of Houston (2000), Professor of the Year from the Association of Hispanic School Administrators, Houston Independent School District (1994), Distinguished Scientist of the Year Award from the Society for the Advancement of Chicanos and Native Americans in Science (2000), and the 2004 Distinguished Public Service Award of the American Mathematical Society.[22]

"I'm a product of an inner city. I have been fortunate to end up with some influence at the national level. What haunts me is that there are so very few people with my background in positions of leadership. I'm not trying to blame the system, or the people, or anybody. I'm just saying the fact is that as I get to the national level, there are no people who understand my situation, my plight, my public education, my inner-city East Los Angeles upbringing... which I think is a critical issue. We have to understand what's happening in the cities. If you look at the underrepresented groups, they live in the cities.... And what's happening in the cities is something we have to understand if we are going to change this problem.... I don't want to get into the situation where we have a permanent underclass. And I think the divide — the digital divide if you like — is getting wider between those who have and those who have not. It's not so much an issue of fairness as of the health of an economy. If you have a permanent underclass, you are going to have troubles with the economy, so it's everyone's problem."[23]

All of the Latino mathematicians studied by Luis Ortiz-Franco, William Veléz, and me have made a significant contribution to recruiting and mentoring younger Latino mathematicians. However, Manuel Berriozábal, professor of mathematics at the University of Texas in San Antonio, has started an enormous and growing program.

Manuel Berriozábal (b. 1931) was born in San Antonio, Texas. His father was Mexican and his mother was of German descent. His father worked in optical houses, starting as a lens grinder and working up to become an inspector. He then became a licensed optometrist in the late 1940s; at that time a college education was not required in Missouri to become an optometrist.

---

[21]Richard Tapia, Math Medley interview, July 22, 2000, "Underrepresentation: K-12 Education and the Cities."

[22]"A Brief Biography for Richard A. Tapia," http://www.caam.rice.edu/~rat/biography.html

[23]Richard Tapia, Math Medley interview, July 22, 2000, "Underrepresentation: K-12 Education and the Cities."

When Manny was an infant, the family moved to Independence, Missouri, where he grew up. After earning a B.S. from Rockhurst College and a Ph.D. from UCLA in 1961, he joined the faculty of Tulane University, where he was the dissertation advisor of four Ph.D. students. In 1966 he moved to the University of New Orleans, and in 1976 he became a professor at the University of Texas at San Antonio, the city where he had been born, his wife had grown up, and where he still had many relatives.

In 1979 Manuel Berriozábal started the Texas Prefreshman Engineering Program ("TexPREP") with fifty students, whom he personally taught. As more students were accepted into the program, he gradually relinquished daily personal contact with the students. As director of TexPREP, his time was increasingly taken with outreach so that by 1986 he had to leave the teaching to carefully selected mathematicians and scientists. By 2002, Tex-PREP had served 10,000 students in San Antonio alone for at least one summer, another 10,000 in the rest of Texas, and 6,000 others in Latino-rich communities on twelve campuses in eight states.[24]

Almost 80 percent of the students served by TexPREP are minority, and a slight majority are female. It offers an eight-week, all-day summer program that largely occupies the students' entire summer. Nevertheless, it has had an 85 percent retention rate. Students start typically after sixth grade, when they take a rigorous course in logic. In succeeding summers they study intensely computer science, problem solving, and writing. Students are selected among those with A and B averages in school for their eagerness to learn and to "make something of themselves."

Manny Berriozábal visits every TexPREP site every year, and tries to meet with each class for an hour, his favorite activity. He tells the students about unsolved problems, typically the Goldbach Conjecture and twin primes, and offers a $10,000 reward if one of them solves one of these problems. He tells them if they do, they will become famous immediately, they will probably be given a doctorate immediately, they will make him famous, and they will make TexPREP famous.

TexPREP costs a lot of money, and the policy has been to keep the program free to the students so that economics are not a deterrent. Indeed, there are some stipends available to compensate families for summer income that their daughter or son is not earning. Raising money takes a great deal of the director's time. There are public and private benefactors, monetary donors and in-kind supporters (especially of classrooms by educational institutions), and small and large benefactors. The state of Texas is a major benefactor. In San Antonio alone there are 70 benefactors, and 150 throughout the state of Texas.[25] All of this takes not only recruitment, but also extensive reporting.

---

[24]prep-usa.org/portal/main/

[25]Manuel Berriozábal, Math Medley, October 26, 2002, "Best Practices in Mathematics Education."

Manuel Berriozábal and his wife Marie Antonietta Berriozábal with a poster of an outstanding American. Photo by Roberto von Ellerreider, courtesy of Marie Antonietta Berriozábal.

The annual survey of present and past participants in TexPREP shows that about 90 percent take Algebra 2, 60 percent take pre-calculus, and 30 percent take calculus in high school. By 2002 there were about 11,000 former students of college age or older. Of these, 5,380 responded to the 2002 annual survey. Of the respondents, 99.9 percent were high school graduates, and the senior college graduation rate was 90 percent, 51 percent with science, mathematics, or engineering majors. Among the college graduates, 76 percent were members of underrepresented groups, and 71 percent of the science, mathematics, and engineering graduates were members of underrepresented groups.[26]

Each year TexPREP sends not only a general report of the annual statistics, but also disks of its students to appropriate prospective employers — those who might want to provide summer employment for high school or college students, and those who are glad to find a promising pool of new college graduates.

Manuel Berriozábal was the first Governor for Minorities on the MAA Board of Governors, and has served on Congressional and other national advisory panels. In the late 1990s he served on an expert panel sponsored by the United States Department of Education to evaluate mathematics programs. He was the only mathematician on that panel and did not support any of the panel's assertions that a mathematics program was "exemplary"

---

[26]Manuel Berriozábal, personal email, May 26, 2004.

— because there had been no survey to confirm the alleged later academic achievement of their graduates.

He is concerned with the country's overemphasis on computers and calculators — which TexPREP does sometimes use. "They are not nearly as important as intellectual activity.... We must stop giving our children fuzzy math programs that emphasize process over content. Furthermore, we need to support programs that stress the acquisition of self-esteem through hard work, commitment and achievement and oppose those that stress the acquisition of self-esteem as an end of itself."[27]

Manuel Berriozábal's wife Maria Antonietta Berriozábal has served repeatedly on the San Antonio city council. In 1991 she ran for mayor, being defeated only in a run-off. In 1998 she ran for Congress in the Democratic primary, but lost to the current incumbent.[28]

Manny tells a wonderful story that makes a fine conclusion for this chapter "I was walking from my parking area at the university to my office and as I was going there, I felt a tightening of my chest which spread over my right arm. When I got to my office, I called my doctor. He immediately advised me to go to the downtown Baptist hospital in San Antonio, and at the emergency room they would be expecting me because he would call me in. So I got down there and I still had the tightness in my chest and arm. They took an electrocardiogram. There was no apparent damage, but they did put me in bed. A few minutes later a young staff cardiologist comes up to my bed and says, 'I'm Judas Penosa. You may not remember me, but I was in the 1981 Prep program.'

"The next day he assisted on an angioplasty on me. He is now my cardiologist."[29]

---

[27]ibid.

[28]Personal email, May 31, 2004.

[29]Manuel Berriozábal, Math Medley, October 26, 2002.

CHAPTER 7

Reawakening: The Association for Women in Mathematics

By the end of the turbulent 1960s, the second wave of the women's movement was beginning. People were increasingly aware of the limitations of individual effort and courage in effecting both one's own advancement and systemic change. Each woman had her own story, but it was time to organize into a whole that would be greater than the sum of its parts.

The Mathematics Action Group (MAG) had been meeting regularly at national mathematics meetings to take action on a variety of issues both within and outside the mathematics community, including supporting politically active mathematicians in other countries. At the end of the MAG meeting during the Joint Mathematics Meetings in Atlantic City in 1971, Joanne Darken suggested that women remain behind to discuss the status of women in mathematics. At least seven[1] women joined her in that first session of what would develop into the Association for Women in Mathematics: Mary Gray, Judy Green, Diane Laison, Gloria Olive, Françoise Schremmer, Annie Selden, and Ruth Silverman. They were convinced that a new organization was needed. Soon they linked up with a group of women mathematicians who had been meeting in the Boston area to start the Association of Women in Mathematics. Soon it was renamed the Association *for* Women in Mathematics. Gary Laison and Lee Lorch quickly became active members as soon as men were accepted.

Mary Gray agreed to be the first president and Alice Schafer, from the Boston group, the second. Mary typed the first few AWM newsletters herself. They were in tiny type, but to those us in the hinterland, they were bold and exciting. I was in my full-time mothering years when I saw a small announcement in the February 1971 *Notices of the AMS* about a newly forming Association of Women in Mathematics. (The preposition was changed shortly thereafter.) Immediately, I sent in my registration. For five years I had not talked with a mathematician. I had read some mathematical

---

[1] Harriet Lord heard the announcement and wanted to stay, but felt sufficiently ill that she had to return to her room at that fateful hour. Previous writings have claimed that there were only six women there including Harriet Lord, but these nine women, including her, are all still alive as I write this 33 years later, and all claim to remember that day. Eight have convincing memories of that meeting. This account is written after email or personal conversations with all nine. One wrote, "I doubt very much there were as many as 8 women there, but I could be wrong."

tomes such as Rickart and Naimark while nursing babies, but the prospect of companionship — no matter how tenuous — was marvelous. Newsletters by and about other women mathematicians, no matter how small the type, were eagerly read cover to cover.

The first public AWM activity was a panel at the 1971 Summer Meeting at Penn State. It was organized by Christine Ayoub, and included Mary Gray, Gloria Hewitt, and Mary Ellen Rudin. About twenty-percent of the audience was female, unprecedented at a mathematics conference as far as those present could remember. "A great deal of attention was focused on cultural conditioning.... Young girls are indoctrinated to set low goals for themselves, e.g. to become a nurse, not a doctor, and in particular, to believe that they cannot, and indeed should not, if they are to preserve their femininity, succeed in mathematics.... It was pointed out that children's literature and high school counselors are real menaces. Several feminists groups have come out with lists of literature they feel is appropriate for children, but no one has a workable proposal for dealing with the counselors."[2] It was pointed out that previously indifferent men often became concerned about these issues when their daughters were choosing careers. The contributions from the panelists were not identical, but disagreements were polite among both panelists and the audience. Afterward, however, several men accosted a panelist and said, "Women belong in bed, not at the board."[3]

In 1970 there were no tenured women at the five mathematics departments considered to be the leading ones in the country.[4] There had been no women officers for decades in either the American Mathematical Society or the Mathematical Association of America. Only rarely were women invited to serve on committees of these organizations, or to speak at conferences, or to be editors of research journals. In 1970 no women had served as president of either organization, and Charlotte Scott had been the only vice president of the AMS in 1905-1906. Clara Eliza Smith had been the second and most recent vice president of the MAA in 1927. Only one woman had delivered an AMS Colloquium Lecture, Anna Pell Wheeler in 1927. Some women were mathematicians, including research mathematicians, but there weren't many, and they weren't receiving the recognition they deserved. Visibility was one of the first goals of the infant AWM. Women simply weren't considered.[5]

Three months after the founding of AWM, in April 1971 the AMS Council appointed a Committee on Women to recommend actions that the Society

---

[2]Mary Gray, "Women in Mathematics," *American Mathematical Monthly*, May, 1972, 79, pp. 475-9, p. 476.

[3]ibid, p. 478.

[4]Mary Gray often said this at the time, and confirmed doing so in an email, March 21, 2005.

[5]Bettye Anne Case, Math Medley, "Developing an Association for Women in Mathematics," December 13, 2003.

should take "to alleviate some of the disadvantages that women mathematicians now experience and document their recommendations and actions by presenting data." Cathleen Morawetz chaired the committee. Its other four members were Mary Gray, Israel Herstein, Charles B. Morrey, Jr., and Jane Cronin Scanlon.[6]

The Committee sent a questionnaire to the roughly 650 women with doctorates in mathematics that they located. From these they received 369 returns, 314 of whom were from women who were U.S. or Canadian born. Among these, 234 received their doctorates before the age of thirty, 225 were married, and 30 divorced. Among those who had married, only 71 did not have children. About 16 or 17 were from religious orders.[7]

The median salary for women with a Ph.D. in mathematics was $12,300, compared to $14,700 for men. Among new Ph.D.'s the median salary for women was $500 less than for men; similar statements could be made for the quartiles. "Until 1971 30% of unemployed mathematicians were women, in contrast with the fact that only 11% of mathematicians are women."[8]

"Approximately 20% were in government or private employment. Those in academia... [included] 10 instructors, 137 assistant professors, 86 associate professors, 54 professors. There is no indication that women are a bad investment because they drop out of their careers. The older age groups had had many or frequent interruptions if they had families; among women receiving their degrees since 1962 interruptions were infrequent and short (six months). The pattern that many of us imagine of women who wish to take five to ten years off to raise a family and then return to a career is not substantiated."[9]

Other questions indicated that most wives are rooted by the geography of their husband's jobs, although increasing numbers have taken jobs involving long distance commuting. The questionnaires were tabulated by graduate students, who also read the many comments in the space provided. "As they became aware of the many special difficulties revealed through the data, and the stated facts of what some women mathematicians have endured in the past, they themselves were discouraged."[10]

To put a human face on their findings, the Committee included a profile of the "median" American woman mathematician.

> She was born in the U.S.A. and received her Ph.D. before
> the age of thirty and within the last five years. She is married and has children. Her husband is also a mathematician and supports her professional efforts enthusiastically.
> Her job prospects are limited because she cannot move
> unless her husband gets a suitable job. However, she has

---

[6] AMS Council minutes of January 24, 1973, p. 6, courtesy of the AMS staff.
[7] "Summary Report of the Committee on Women," p. 5, courtesy of Sergei Gelfand.
[8] ibid, p. 4.
[9] ibid, p. 5.
[10] ibid, p. 6.

roughly achieved what she set out for, feels perfectly competent and is reasonably content about her future. Her median salary is considerably lower than her colleagues', in general, but she is satisfied to be an assistant professor at a four year college or university. There is a one in four chance that her husband would not be employed there, too, because of nepotism rules. The school is almost certainly not one of the prestigious schools. She feels that although she did not fail to obtain a job because of it, there is some prejudice still and she would prefer prospective employers to avoid questions about her domestic, marital or parental life.[11]

The Committee report in 1972 made six recommendations to the Council, two of which were adopted: (1) "To maintain a roster of women with Ph.D.'s in mathematics" that would facilitate the mathematical community's complying with affirmative action and (3) "to cooperate with the Mathematical Association of America to investigate the status of women not in the Ph.D. track." It was understood that the MAA was not committed to such an investigation but it was hoped that the offer of cooperation would encourage them to commit themselves.[12]

The other four recommendations of the Committee, not adopted by the Council, are revealing:" (2) To encourage the use of the Grievance Committee on Academic, Freedom, Tenure and Employment Security of the Society for explicit cases of discrimination in hiring or in the awarding of fellowships or assistantships at the graduate or postdoctoral level.... (4) To use the Society's best efforts to encourage advisors and employers to avoid disparaging sex-oriented remarks. (5) To encourage women to use their maiden names professionally and to support the abolition of questions regarding marital or parental status on employment applications. (6) To maintain this committee for another year, at least, for the implementation of the above."[13]

Mary Gray decided that women needed to be more integral to the central decision-making process of the American Mathematical Society. Shortly after she became president of AWM, she carefully read the AMS bylaws and discovered that the AMS Council meetings were officially open to all members. One of her first acts as first AWM president was to show up in the room where the Council was about to meet and sit down.

She was asked to leave. She replied that according to the bylaws, the AMS Council meetings were open to all members, and she was a duly paid member. The response was that there was a gentleman's agreement that only board members would be present during board meetings.

"I'm not a gentleman," was her now-famous reply. "I'm staying."

---

[11]ibid, p. 3.
[12]Minutes of the Council, January 24, 1973, page 6.
[13]"Summary Report of the Committee on Women," pp. 1-2.

Mary Gray's determination inspired a change in the attitude of many male leaders of the American Mathematical Society, and they complied with the movement she led for the right of AMS members to submit names for Council elections by petition. Having accomplished this, Mary Gray ran by petition in 1976 for the position of vice president of the AMS — and won! She was the first woman to serve in that position since Charlotte Scott in 1905-1906. At one of the meetings of the Council where she was vice president, she wrote, "the president appeared wearing a tie popular at the time. The pattern was neatly embroidered pigs with 'MCP' (male chauvinist pig) under each. As he leaned across the table so that the tie dangled in my face, I asked, 'Would you wear a tie that said, 'I am a white supremacist?' To his negative reply I responded, 'So why the 'MCP'? An incontrovertible answer came back, 'Women are different; we live with them'."[14]

Mary Gray (b. 1938) was born and raised in Hastings, Nebraska, the only child of Neil Claude Wheat and Lillie Alves Wheat. They were both high school graduates who never went to college. "They were supportive," she says of their attitude toward her career aspirations, but they had little personal experience with the life their offspring would lead. Her father had been a policeman, a mechanic, a truck driver, and a manager for a trucking firm. "That's how I learned to drive semi-trailers. I'm not an expert on driving them, but I can do it."

He also taught her Nebraska history and mental arithmetic. His family had come to Nebraska in the mid-nineteenth century, as had one of Mary's other grandparents. The fourth had immigrated from Germany to Nebraska in the 1890s. Nebraska was integral to the family's heritage. Mary's father's brother married her mother's sister and that couple also had one child. They lived nearby and he was one year ahead of his cousin throughout school and college. The extended family was close. It was clear the young people would go to college, but nobody spoke of graduate school. Mary's cousin became an early computer professional.

Her father died of a second heart attack in her senior year of high school, after which her mother worked in the Hastings College cafeteria.[15] Mary went to Hastings College, a school of about 800 students in those days, and graduated at the top of her class. During her second year Jim Standley joined the mathematics faculty, and she took her advanced math courses from him. He encouraged her to go to graduate school, a new idea to her. They remained friends until his death in the 21st century. There was one other woman in her advanced math classes, and Mary remembers no questions ever being raised about women studying mathematics until she was in graduate school. Upon graduation from Hastings, she was granted a Fulbright fellowship and spent a year in Germany.

---

[14]Mary Gray, "The Association for Women in Mathematics — A Personal View," *The Mathematical Intelligencer*, 13:14, 6-11, p. 7.

[15]Mary Gray, telephone interview on May 8, 2004, and personal emails.

She then began graduate studies at the University of Kansas, where she first confronted negative comments about women doing mathematics. Shortly before she was granted her doctorate, the dean of the graduate school was asked by a newspaper reporter why there weren't more women in his mathematics program. "Women can't do mathematics," was his public reply.

As soon as she received her diploma a few days later, she went to his office and plopped it down on his desk. "Some women *can* do mathematics," she told him. Hers was the only doctorate in mathematics that the University of Kansas had granted to any woman since 1926. That recipient, Wealthy Babcock, was teaching there as the only woman on the math faculty. Mary took one course from her.

Meanwhile, she was active in an off-campus endeavor that was destined to play a crucial role in shaping her future. Those were the days when supermarkets hired boys to help customers deliver their purchases to their car. There was a boarding school for Native Americans near the city, and the supermarkets refused to hire its boys. "Of course, they didn't hire *any* girls."

The graduate students organized and appealed to the managers to stop their discrimination, but to no avail. After an appropriate warning, the graduate students descended upon one store, filled the carts with frozen food, wheeled them to the check-out counters, and left. Unable to return the frozen foods quickly enough to the freezers, that supermarket lost money and its ability to serve customers. Immediately, all three supermarkets in Lawrence capitulated to the graduate students' demands that they hire Native American boys in their delivery staff.

"The first action I tried worked," she observed in 2004. "They don't always work, but they work frequently enough so that the satisfaction that people's lives have been made easier or better makes you want to try again."[16] The impact of her early success is evident in her sustained efforts over the decades.

Meanwhile, during her first year at the University of Kansas she met Alfred Gray, who was finishing up a four-year bachelor-master's degree program. He then went to UCLA, but the romance continued long distance. After they both received doctorates in mathematics in 1964, they were married. He obtained a faculty position at the University of California at Berkeley and she went with him. She was upset by the nepotism rule that prevented her from even being considered for a faculty position at Berkeley, but there was plenty to do. The Free Speech Movement was in full swing, and Berkeley hired her to teach one math course during the summer. The second year she began a full-time faculty position at the California State University at Hayward.

---

[16]ibid.

In 1968 Alfred received a faculty appointment at the University of Maryland in College Park and Mary at American University in Washington. They bought a house between the two campuses, where commuting was not difficult for either. By now she was glad to be in the nation's capital, where she could influence major decisions. They had already decided not to have children, and she hasn't regretted that decision. She has generated two large "families" of students for which she is the professional parent, and with whom she maintains a caring closeness.

One such "family" has been her dissertation students. She taught herself statistics and mathematics education, taught these subjects along with mathematics, and supervised theses in statistics and mathematics education as well as mathematics. Twenty-eight doctoral students have completed their Ph.D. dissertations under her supervision, most in mathematics education and about six in mathematics. She has supervised no Ph.D. dissertations in statistics, but has had a number of statistics master's degree students. Her twenty-eight doctoral graduates include nine African Americans, five of whom are women. In general, a majority of her doctoral graduates are women.

Less than three years after her arrival at American University, she became the first president of the Association for Women in Mathematics, typing its early newsletters herself. Before long she was national chair of Committee W of the American Association of University Professors. ("W," of course, is for "Women.") She decided that women mathematicians needed someone who read more than the bylaws of the AMS. Although she was soon department chair at American University, she also attended law school. In 1979 she graduated from law school and passed the bar. Using her legal credentials and her position as chair of Committee W, she played a role in achieving the U.S. Supreme Court decision that brought equal retirement benefits for women, including those college faculty covered by TIAA-CREF, arguing that breaking groups down into subgroups is arbitrary and that each individual is a member of the larger group, and her or his future is unknown.

It is impossible to summarize her many accomplishments briefly. Florence Fasanelli wrote, "...she might easily be found in Bosnia, Chile, Israel, or Rwanda. She might be found testifying before congressional committees on Capitol Hill or appearing as an expert witness in California courtrooms[17] ...She has been a member of the U.S.A. Board of Amnesty International since 1985,... has been treasurer of the Montgomery County section of the American Civil Liberties Union; treasurer and chair of the Women's Equity Action League; and vice-chair of the American-Middle East Education

---

[17]Florence Fasanelli, "Mary Gray," in *Notable Women in Mathematics*, edited by Charlene Morrow and Teri Perl, Greenwood Press, Westwood, CT, 1998, p. 71.

Foundation..."[18] She later held leadership positions in the American Association for the Advancement of Science. For the past eight years she has been chair of the American-Middle East Education Foundation.[19]

Soon the Grays began to live an international life. He would spend many semesters in Spain and Italy and one each in Belgium and Switzerland. Sometimes she would join him, sometimes not. Back in the United States he was an advocate for international students, "and they needed one."[20] Alfie and others also worked on behalf of mathematicians in other countries, especially one in Tunisia who has been under house arrest for more than fifteen years — but who before their efforts had been in prison. He also advocated for the civil liberties of various Latin American mathematicians. In 1998, while spending a semester in Spain, he had a fatal heart attack.

Years ago the Grays purchased a flat in London, originally to avoid Washington summers, but later to facilitate their cross-Atlantic ventures. She has had a "serious involvement" in the Middle East since 1980, frequently visiting Jerusalem and the West Bank and Gaza. She has worked hard to find funding for computer equipment, especially in Palestine and Syria. She has arranged for forty-three students to come to the United States to earn master's degrees in computer science or statistics, mostly from Palestine. Over a quarter have been women, and she has maintained a personal relationship with each of the forty-three (her second "family"). She spent July 2003 in Iraq, supervising a study of its 3400 secondary schools to see what they needed in equipment, personnel, and teacher training. When I asked her to appear on Math Medley in 1999, she chose the title, "Using Statistics to Make the World Better" and told of supervising a study of Rwanda prisoners and analyzing the data in an effort to bring better understanding to the challenges of that country.

Her multifaceted life as professor, administrator, lawyer, and activist awes those who know her. She even pulls the dandelions from her ample front lawn by hand to avoid pesticides! Lenore Blum, third president of AWM, referred to Mary Gray in her speech celebrating the AWM's twentieth anniversary (available on the AWM website) as "The Mother of Us All." She "tries to" get six hours of sleep a night, but sometimes gets less, "never more."[21] She told me that she never reads her own writing after it is published; there is no point being discouraged by something you wish you had said differently because you can't change it after it's published. She's an opera fan, and enjoys the best opera companies in the world during her travels.

When I asked about the role of religion in her life, she told me a story. A ten-year-old boy, the son of a "colorful" close friend of hers, telephoned her from England to ask her to be his godmother. He had been sent to a British boarding school where he was told he would go to hell if he weren't baptized.

---

[18]ibid, p. 74

[19]Mary Gray, email dated August 13, 2004.

[20]Mary Gray, telephone interview on May 8, 2004.

[21]ibid.

Mary Gray with her godson Andres Donaldson at the International Statistical Institute meeting in Istanbul. Photo courtesy of Mary Gray.

"My friend was very clever to have *him* call me. If *she* had asked me to be his godmother, I would have said, 'No way!' But if a ten-year-old asks you to keep him from going to hell, how could anyone say 'no'?"

The ceremony waited for her to cross the Atlantic. They retreated to a twelfth century church — her godson Andres, his brother and sister, the priest, and the six adults who had agreed to be godparents. The priest noticed her American accent, and expressed doubts that she belonged to the Church of England. She admitted she didn't. He mused aloud that godparents were supposed to be members of the Church of England. Then he brightened.

"Oh, well. You *are* a Christian?"

"I was raised a Methodist." The priest reflected that she had come all the way from Washington for this moment and decided to proceed with the ceremony. She obviously continues to take pleasure in her relationship with her godson, who is now a student at Cambridge University.

In 1972 Mary Gray wrote a list of goals for the Association for Women in Mathematics that were greeted with shock and amazement. She advocated, "1) Equal consideration for admission to graduate school and support while there, 2) Equal consideration for faculty appointments at all levels..., 3) Equal pay for equal work, 4) Equal consideration in assignment of duties, for promotion and for tenure, 5) Equal consideration for administrative appointments at all levels in universities, industry, and government, [and] 6) Equal consideration for government grants, positions on review and advisory panels and positions in professional organizations." She continued, "Because of past injustices, special efforts will have to be made for some time to find women to consider. AWM is ready to help. Now is the time for discrimination to end." Lenore Blum, the third AWM president, commented in her speech at the twentieth anniversary of the AWM, "What seems quite amazing now is that these were considered radical demands!"[22]

The Association for Women in Mathematics seized upon them with energy. Women alone could organize panels at national meetings. Transcripts of these panels reprinted in the newsletters educated us all about the depth and dimension of the problems. Harold Stark's talk at the Missoula Summer Meeting in 1973 gives a human picture to the situation many women faced, even those with supportive males around them. It is easy to see why women with male relatives hostile to their mathematical aspirations would be driven away from the pathway to their dreams. Stark's piece is short enough to be worth reproducing in its entirety.

THE LIFE OF A MATHEMATICAL COUPLE
by Harold Stark[23]

First, let me tell you a little about us. We were married in 1964, shortly after Betty received a B.A. from U.C.L.A. and I received a Ph.D. from Berkeley. We went to Michigan where I was an instructor and Betty a graduate student. Our one child was born in 1969 and Betty received a Ph.D. in 1971. (Contrary to the opinion of one chairman, Betty did not have a glandular change when Pearl was born and drop out of mathematics.) We are now in the Boston area. I have a tenured position at M.I.T. and Betty has a non-tenured position at Northeastern.

---

[22]Lenore Blum, "Mary Gray: The Mother of Us All," in the "History of the AWM" posted on the AWM website, www.awm-math.org.

[23]*AWM Newsletter*, July-August 1975, 5:5, p. 4, reprinted with permission.

The household chores are a nuisance, since neither of us has an excuse to palm them off on the other. Some chores are handled by one or the other of us (e.g., I do the shopping and laundry, Betty does the cooking), some chores are farmed out (we have a company of cleaning men) and some chores have been proclaimed unnecessary (e.g. ironing and window washing). Mathematical work with an awake child present is very difficult although now that Pearl is 5-1/2, it is at least possible for one of us if the other is present. We have had a babysitter since Pearl was born; we pay more than the minimum wage and have had no trouble getting or keeping good babysitters. Next year, Pearl will go to a day care center located in her elementary school. She has been going twice a week this year and loves it.

Our major problem is the attitudes of colleagues and their spouses (and, of course, relatives). Betty has borne the brunt of this. One wife informed Betty at a party in Michigan that she had seen Betty on the campus and Betty had looked just like a student (I don't believe it was meant as a compliment). There are all sorts of pressures on the woman to quit. Some imply that women aren't any good, so why bother? I would place the familiar (at least to us), "There aren't any women good enough to be in our department" in this category. Others are related to children. A typical comment before Pearl was born was, "Just wait until you have a child, then you won't be able to continue." After Pearl was born, the comments were of two types: "Just wait until she walks and talks, then you won't be able to continue" and "Why did you have a child anyway, if you wanted to work?" Also prevalent before HEW were gems like, "I don't hire women because they quit after they have families." One chairman explained this by citing an example from twenty years earlier. The same chairman informed Betty that he also wouldn't hire women because every time their children have colds, the women wouldn't come in.

There have been pressures on me to do what is best for me professionally and ignore Betty. These pressures were at their worst at the end of our second year in Michigan when I took a job in Dearborn so that Betty could continue in graduate school. One chairman could not believe I would not go to the best place available because of my wife. He told me a story of a man who had been let go because he helped his wife with the housework! The

M.I.T.-Harvard-Brandeis group causes us more problems than the Northeastern group. One professor here informed Betty that no woman is good enough to be in his department. Another time, at a colloquium party for a visiting group theorist (Betty's field) which I did not attend, several people did not believe that Betty could be there without me. "What, a Northeastern professor here?" "Oh, she's married to Stark." "Well, where is he?"

These are the major problems relating to our life as a couple. Both of us also have the usual problems of teachers. These have nothing to do with us as a couple, except that perhaps each of us understands better what is happening to the other.

The next newsletter had a spoof signed only "by Everywoman, Ph.D." about how to behave after you have been hired as the first female in the department. The situations sounded familiar even to those of us who were not first. When you are being asked questions as if you were a secretary, say, "I don't know. You'll have to ask a secretary." When men insist upon carrying your cafeteria tray, you can try to whisk it away saying, "Thanks, but I can manage." To "May I help you on with your coat?," you can try, "Thank you, may I help you on with yours?"

Less common than these was the sympathetic, "How can you bear to go home and cook dinner after working all day?" Everywoman suggests, "My husband is cooking dinner tonight." (And leave him there to pick up his teeth and count his blessings.) Or possibly, "Good Lord, yes, don't you find it miserable too?"[24]

Everywoman reappeared in the February 1976 issue, this time with more commentary than advice. At her first faculty committee meeting, the eight men sat around the table consecutively, with the two women facing them and an empty seat between the women and the men on each side. A graduate student in one of her classes asked her if she was married. When she said she was, he responded, "That's too bad; you're a pretty neat chick!"[25]

When Mary Gray handed over the AWM presidency to Alice Schafer in 1973, Alice asked Mary what the next priorities were. Mary said that money was needed for the next steps, and to receive grants, AWM needed to be incorporated. Alice dutifully initiated the incorporation of the Association for Women in Mathematics, but was shocked when the lawyer's bill was $500. She sent out an appeal to collect money for this outrageous sum. The lawyer said that the next step would be to obtain tax-exempt status for the organization; for that he would charge another $300. She said, "I'll do it myself."

---

[24] *Newsletter, AWM*, September-October, 1975, 5:6, pp. 7-8.
[25] ibid, February, 1976, pages 10-11.

"You can't." That was the challenge Alice Schafer needed. She had done enough already that people said she couldn't do. She succeeded in obtaining tax-exempt status for AWM herself.

Alice T. Schafer (b. 1915) was raised in Virginia by an aunt, and they were both supported by another aunt; her parents died before she can remember. Her aunts encouraged her to enjoy being the smart little girl that she was. She won a scholarship to Westhampton College, a "coordinated" college of the University of Richmond. "Coordinated" meant that the men's and women's colleges were separate, but they collaborated, and sometimes women could go to the men's classes; the reverse never happened. There was a large lake in the middle of the campus. The women lived and went to classes on one side of the lake and the men on the other.

When she arrived, the dean said to her, "You are going to be a mathematics major, and take mathematics courses on the boys' side of the lake." She was told that no girl had yet attended the advanced mathematics classes, but she, Alice, was going to do it and pave the way for the other girls. She didn't feel she had a choice; she was going to be a mathematics major. The one woman mathematics instructor, who taught only the very elementary courses ("mostly arithmetic") on the women's side of the lake was very encouraging. So were two humanities professors who had grown up in Germany. "They greatly encouraged me, but they didn't want me to go into their fields. They thought it was time for a woman to study mathematics."

She was, therefore, the first girl to enter the annual campus mathematics contest. She won first place! She was surprised. The papers were judged in closed session, and not returned. The department chair told her, "I was surprised. I didn't think you would win." "They were fair. They may not have been supportive, but they were fair." At the age of 86, however, she still remembered the sting of the department chair's comment 65 years earlier.[26]

Alice then went to the University of Chicago, where she earned a doctorate in mathematics. She married Richard Schafer and eventually they had two sons. She followed him to the University of Michigan, where women "couldn't" be on the mathematics faculty. However, it was very difficult to find qualified mathematics faculty in those days, and she had a doctorate from the University of Chicago. Cornered, the department chair offered her a position. Subsequently, the head of the physics department saw her walking down the hall with a mathematics text.

He looked at the text and then at her and commented, "Hildebrandt must have been desperate."

"He was," she replied simply.

When Richard Schafer went to the Institute for Advanced Study at Princeton, Alice found a position at the New Jersey College for Women (now Douglass College). He then went to the University of Pennsylvania

---

[26]Alice Schafer, Math Medley interview, December 1, 2001.

Alice Schafer during her first visit to China in 1980. Her second trip was with the MAA, and during her fourth she led an AWM China tour. During her fifth trip to China, she took and placed banners saying, "Mathematics Empowers Women," at the United Nations Beijing Conference on Women, as suggested by Frances Rosamond. Photo courtesy of Alice Schafer.

while she taught at Swarthmore College. He spent most of his career on the mathematics faculty of M.I.T., and she at Wellesley College. When they "retired" to Virginia, she obtained a position at Marymount University, where she became department chair and was still working full-time at the age of eighty. They now live in a continuing care retirement community in Massachusetts, near most of the members of their family.

She was crucial in organizing women mathematicians of the Boston area in the early 1970s, perhaps the most active local manifestation of the national AWM. When she became president, she found a "permanent" office for the national organization in the psychiatric ward of the Wellesley College infirmary.

Until Alice became president, it had been customary for AWM meetings to focus on women's problems at their meetings. She decided it was time to have a mathematical research speaker at an AWM meeting. She invited Cathleen Morawetz, then professor of mathematics at New York University and later to become the first woman director of the Courant Institute, a mathematical research center. As the day of the meeting approached, a friendly man told her that a group of men were intending to break up the AWM meeting. She told him, "I can handle it. If I can handle a class of twenty-five high school boys, I can surely handle a group of research mathematicians." ("What," I asked her. "You taught at a boys' high school?" "No, I taught at a public high school while I was saving the money to go to the University of Chicago. But no girls took advanced mathematics, so I taught classes that were all boys. They were a handful, but I could handle them. So I figured I could handle a few mathematicians.")[27]

Despite her bold response to the warning, she was inwardly shaken when she arrived at the meeting to find that the two or three front rows were filled with hostile-looking men. This was more than she had expected! She covered her trepidation and introduced Cathleen Morawetz, who delivered an impressive speech. "She was a far better mathematician than most of those men." After her talk, the entire two or three rows walked out silently.

The AWM newsletters of that time tell of departments asking women to apply for jobs to please Affirmative Action regulations, but not getting even an acknowledgement of the application. Women were being used, at considerable cost to them because preparing an application takes time, without being seriously considered for openings. The conversation had begun, but it seemed that it was not being taken seriously. One could almost wonder if any progress was being made.

In 1975 Mary Gray reflected upon what the AWM had accomplished during its first years. When the AWM was first organized there had been no women on the Council of the AMS within the memory of "very senior" mathematicians. Since 1971, nine had been elected. It was now possible to nominate by petition, and Mary Gray herself was planning to run by petition for vice president; indeed, the following year she would become the first female vice president since Charlotte Scott in 1905-1906. The Council meetings had been opened, both literally and figuratively.[28] Gradually, other women's names began to appear on the regular ballot for AMS board members, and some of them were elected. In 1986 Julia Robinson would become the first female president of the American Mathematical Society.

---

[27]ibid.

[28]Mary Gray, *AWM Newsletter*, September-October, 1975, 5:6, pp. 6-7.

Throughout the 1970s it was still not easy for the Association for Women in Mathematics to organize sessions at AMS meetings, as symbolized by the confrontation Alice had faced. The AMS leadership was not any more cooperative than it had to be, except for Hope Daly, a woman on the staff who was in charge of organizing the meetings. The early organizers learned to work directly with Hope and not ask permission from her supervisors. Bettye Anne Case was one of those early organizers.

"We were invisible!" she commented recently. "Whenever we weren't in the room, the men forgot that women existed."[29] She remembers attending her first AWM meeting. She happened to meet Alice Schafer in a rest room.

"Do you have a doctorate in mathematics?"

"Yes."

"Then you *must* come to a meeting we are having right now of the Association for Women in Mathematics." When Alice said you must do something, most people did.

Bettye Anne Case coordinated meetings for AWM at the national meetings for about twenty years, eventually becoming Meetings Coordinator in a newly created position. Her own career path was unusual. After nine years on the faculty of Tallahassee Community College, she was recruited for a position at Florida State University in Tallahassee, where she is now the Olga Larson Professor of Mathematics and director of the graduate program in actuarial and financial mathematics. She has published research in complex variables, mathematics education, and the history of mathematics, and recently co-edited a book on women in mathematics *Complexities: Women in Mathematics*, published by the Princeton University Press that includes a number of the biographical articles from the early AWM newsletters.

When I asked Bettye Anne why she has been so devoted to the AWM, she spoke of the need to facilitate others' making change within the mathematical community. She and I remember the Atlanta Meeting of January 1978 (my first winter Meeting) where Karen Uhlenbeck,[30] the second woman mathematician in the National Academy of Sciences, introduced a motion at the AMS business meeting that it should meet only in states that had ratified the ERA. With Bettye Anne's help, the business meeting had unprecedented attendance. I remember the hushed moment when Karen Uhlenbeck was recognized; the motion was already on the agenda. Her motion passed, and the effectiveness of collective action within the AMS was clear.

Bettye Anne Case and Hope Daly connived to sneak in as many AWM speakers as they could. I was one of those speakers in March, 1978, because

[29]Interview on Math Medley, December 13, 2003.

[30]A biography of Uhlenbeck based on an extensive interview by Claudia Henrion is in *Women in Mathematics: The Addition of Difference*, Indiana University Press, Bloomington, 1997, pp. 24-46, and a short biography by Lyn Taylor is in *Notable Women in Mathematics: A Biographical Dictionary*, edited by Charlene Morrow and Teri Perl, Greenwood Press, Westport, CT, 1998, pp. 261-266.

my research about Charlotte Scott had attracted some attention from AWM leaders. Actually, there wasn't much competition.

This was the first time I had ever given a talk away from my "home" institution. It was at a New York City meeting at the Hotel Biltmore. I had never wallowed in such lavishness before. My middle-class habits of thrift and modesty were challenged. So much gold! So much ostentation! As I searched for the meeting room where I was the invited speaker, I passed two

Bettye Anne Case (above right) and Anne M. Leggett (below) were surprised to receive awards for Outstanding Service to the Association from then-AWM president Jill Mesirov at the twentieth anniversary of the Association for Women in Mathematics on January 17, 1991. Photo from the articles "AWM Twentieth Anniversary Celebration," in the March-April issue of the *AWN Newsletter* (pp. 8-9), p. 9, and "AWM in the 1990's: A Recent History of the Association for Women in Mathematics" by Jean E. Taylor and Sylvia M. Wiegand in the January 1999 *Notices of the AMS* 46:1 (pp. 27-38). Photo courtesy of the Association for Women in Mathematics and the American Mathematical Society.

signs announcing my talk. Those were the early days of "Xerox" machines; I was excited to see my name on a mass-reproduced piece of paper.

A couple of weeks after the conference, I received a stern letter signed by some imposing name I recognized in the AMS. He asserted I had not paid my registration fee for the AMS meeting at the Biltmore, but I clearly had been there, since my name had been observed on signs in the hall as a speaker. The bill was enclosed. It was an awesome sum for a assistant professor with two small children. That bill was an effective technique for keeping one potential AWM leader from crashing AMS meetings again. Back to isolated study for me!

Almost a decade after the beginning of AWM, Mary Gray and I met at a national meeting. "Pat Kenschaft!" she exclaimed. "I've been wanting to meet you." What a sense of welcome! The great Mary Gray had heard of me! I expressed my surprise that she knew my name. "I think I know the name of every woman mathematician in the country," was the reply. "There are only about a thousand." Mary Gray believed that radical change was possible, and her determination was a major factor in making it happen.

Of course many people, both women and men, were vital for the change. Fortunately, wonderful biographies based on interviews have already been written about the third and fourth AWM presidents, Lenore Blum and Judith Roitman.[31]

Anne McDonald is another person who, along with Bettye Anne Case, has played an enormous role for decades. She has edited the AWM newsletter (which now might be more aptly called a "journal") steadily since 1977. When I asked her to describe why and how she had remained such a reliable devotee to a difficult, time-consuming, non-paying job, she wrote a most interesting email, which is worth quoting at length.

> I first attended an AWM meeting when I was an instructor at M.I.T. Judy Roitman attended logic seminars there when she was on the faculty at Wellesley, and we became friends. I went to my first AMS meeting in 1975, when my instructorship was ending, and stayed up way late typing headers for petitions on Mary Gray's typewriter at her house, which she had offered to some of us young AWMers as a free place to crash.
>
> Judy thought I should be on the Executive Committee, and when she ended her term as editor to become co-vice-president, she talked me into serving as newsletter

---

[31] Claudia Henrion, *Women in Mathematics: The Addition of Difference*, Indiana University Press, Bloomington, 1997, includes fascinating chapters based on extensive interviews with, Lenore Blum on pages 144-164 and Judith Roitman on pages 166-187. For a more purely factual account, *Notable Women in Mathematics: A Biographical Dictionary*, Greenwood Press, Westport, CT, 1998, includes a piece by Teri Perl on Lenore Blum on pages 11-16 and another one by June Mark on Judith Roitman on pages 90-95.

editor. I've always like writing and editing, and I wanted
to serve AWM but never to be president or vice-president
(now called either president-elect or past president), so
becoming editor seemed like a good way to do my duty.
Some of my friends thought I was nuts to take on the
position before I had tenure, and the "congratulations"
memo that went around the department at the University
of Texas could just as easily been interpreted as a memo
of warning to my colleagues. But the two years went by
pretty quickly. Although my original intent had been to
serve two years only, when Judy became president, she
asked me if I would stay on, and my arm wasn't too hard
to twist.

When I was applying for my next job, I put my position as newsletter editor in my resume, as part of my
service to the profession. Some folks warned me that this
could make it more difficult to get a job in what was
already a very bad job market, but I told them that if
putting that on my resume was enough to kill my chances
for a job, I didn't want to spend my life in that kind
of department anyway. As time went along, the Executive Committee kept asking me to re-up, and I would say,
"yes," for one reason or another.

It ebbs and flows, but I've spent at least 40 hours a
month on AWM related work for many years. I've worked
with lots of presidents. Scheduling my life around six issues a year is sometimes a pain. There have been times I
have been real close to quitting. Then AWM does something nice for me, or a president sends me a lovely note of
thanks as she leaves office, or.... And I've been lucky that
my service work, although not as appreciated as I think
service work would be in an ideal academic setting, has
been valued at Loyola. Loyola funds travel for officers of
national professional organizations, not just for presenting
research talks. Being an editor of the journal of a national
professional organization helped my case for tenure, and
helps my annual evaluations. And I would never have been
involved in the process of editing/writing the book Bettye
Anne and I have put together, had I not done the newsletter for so long. Although the process took far longer than
either of us dreamed it would, I'm real happy with the
resulting book.[32]

---

[32] *Complexities: Women in Mathematics*, Princeton University Press, Princeton, NJ,
2005 includes articles from the AWM newsletter and much more.

I've also enjoyed the hands-on process of using the computer to produce the newsletter. [She then includes two paragraphs longer than those above about the details of production on increasingly complex software and hardware. "I learned a lot about the guts of PCs." Then she summarizes the benefits of her dedicated decades.]

Of course, what I value most about my service as editor has been the opportunity to help AWM in its work of advancing the position of women and other underrepresented groups in the profession.... On the personal level, I value the friendships I have made and the knowledge I have gained. On the professional level, my research has changed from mathematical logic to gender issues in mathematics and the history and sociology of mathematics. Last but far from least: I could never have done this for so long if my husband Gerry were not so completely supportive of my work for AWM, which has had such an impact on how we order our lives.[33]

The AWM newsletters document the frustrations, efforts, and progress of women mathematicians over the past few decades. Gradually the structural obstacles to women participating fully in the mathematical communities diminished. With courage and hard work of women and men, both within and outside mathematics, female Americans have become more adequately represented in mathematics. Eliminating structural obstacles does not guarantee equal access because invisible individual human emotions and decisions determine social forces that cannot be written down. But the 1970s were a time of great change for women in mathematics, and the six "radical" goals that Mary Gray wrote down in 1972 are largely accepted as reasonable, if not completely accomplished.

---

[33]Anne Leggett McDonald, email on July 17, 2004.

CHAPTER 8

Skits Tell What's Happening Around 1990

The Mathematical Association of America had seemed friendlier toward women than the American Mathematical Society in the early 1970s, and women's efforts had concentrated on the AMS, especially since it could be a path toward research. However, in 1987 the MAA decided it needed a Committee on Participation of Women. I well remember the moment when the great Ken Ross (whose name I knew not only from his years of being MAA secretary but also for his support of Gloria Hewitt as reported in Chapter 2) telephoned me and asked if I would chair the committee. How could I hesitate?

One of the novel experiences at that first meeting was having men present at a feminist meeting. I remember my own inner reaction that the men, David Ballew, Donald Bushaw, and Paul Campbell, seemed to care about equity for women as much as we women, Deborah Tepper Haimo, Rhonda Hughes, Marjorie Stein and I, did. My internal dialogue was revealing. "Pat, you are feeling the way you hope blacks don't feel when you are at meetings promoting racial equity. Why shouldn't the men care as much as you? After all, you are already here, with a secure position in the mathematical community. Both you and the men are working primarily for others. Why should that surprise you?" As I critiqued the prejudice in my own soul, I wondered how much such feelings thwart the progress toward equity that so many of us crave.

The seven of us put on a great panel at that first summer meeting that was arranged by telephone and letters. A few dozen people came. Most were already recognized as activists in "the movement." Outwardly, we were satisfied, but inwardly and among ourselves, we questioned whether it was worth it. At each national meeting, we sponsored a panel or talk that was reasonably successful, but unsatisfying because of the small size of the audience.

By the summer meeting of 1989 in Boulder, Colorado, it was becoming clear that we needed a new vehicle to share the news. We enjoyed being together, and we agreed there was much to say. Sue Geller was a new ex officio member since she was chair of the Joint Committee of the Mathematical Sciences (which had evolved from the AMS Committee on Women established in 1971). She told how she had been watching the ducks on a campus duck pond when a mathematician joined her. Although she tried to move the conversation to research, he insisted upon talking about teaching. When another man joined them, he immediately asked the newcomer what his research field was. Another woman told how a mathematician at lunch addressed all his questions to her husband, apparently unable to comprehend that she was the mathematician attending the conference and her husband was the non-mathematician guest.[1]

Amid the chuckles, Gloria Gilmer quipped, "These stories would make great skits." The mood was lighthearted and everyone laughed uproariously at the prospect.

When the laughter died down, I felt a light bulb go on. "Let's do it!" I said. The laughter resumed.

"No, I mean it. Skits would be a good way to get our ideas across."

The group stared at me in disbelief. Skits at a *mathematics* conference?

After we talked about it for a while, the group decided that it was worth a try. What else were we experiencing?

Sue told the story of going on a Rocky Mountain trip the previous day. While the bus was loading for the return trip, she and another participant were sitting at window seats with the two seats between them unoccupied. An eminent mathematician and his friend came in, sat in the two aisle seats, and continued their conversation about research across the aisle. Then the conversation changed to large calculus sections. The man at the other window chimed in and seemed to be included. Sue tried to join too, but was insistently ignored. The following day someone introduced her to the eminent mathematician, and asked if they had met.

"No, I don't think I have had that pleasure," was his reply.

"Actually, we sat next to each other coming home from yesterday's field trip," was her rejoinder.

I recounted how irked I had felt in the cafeteria line that noon when I met a man who I thought was my friend. Alas, as we turtled through the line, he would say only, "My, you're looking good!" in spite of my efforts to make more significant conversation. The others laughed uproariously in recognition.

Another said the most annoying thing that had happened to her was trying to enjoy Perci Diaconis's delightful lecture and having the man next to her continually making comments to enlighten her as if she couldn't understand it, despite her best efforts to "shhh" him.[2] Jerry Porter observed that this can happen to men too at mathematical lectures, but he thought it would be a good situation to dramatize so that offenders might think about how annoying it is.

We had a good program! Sue Geller offered to write the scripts. I had had experience directing plays and agreed to be director. I would also narrate, as chair of the committee. Not to put all our eggs in one basket,

---

[1] *Winning Women Into Mathematics*, edited by Patricia Kenschaft and Sandra Keith, MAA, Washington, 1991, p. 3.

[2] ibid, pp. 69-72.

Gloria Gilmer would speak first on "Unity in Diversity," so the skits would follow a more formal presentation. It was too late to register our program formally for January, but we were able to get a room. We posted signs and hoped that some people would come.

Who would be the actors? Sue Geller and Jerry Porter immediately volunteered, but there were those who had cold feet about making fools of themselves in front of an audience. At the beginning of the January 1990 conference in Louisville, Sue Geller and I summoned our courage, and roamed together through the exhibits trying to recruit actors. Some people were shocked at our request, and many said they were too shy. Nevertheless, we were incredibly successful. Tom Banchoff, Marcelle Bessman, David Boliver, Stephan Burr, Larry Corwin, Nathan Corwin (age nine, who enjoyed bouncing on a "bus," as the real bus had bounced in the Rockies), Pete DeLong, David Lantz, Cynthia Miller, Bill Perry, and Alice Schafer joined Sue and Jerry in the cast.

Part of the first cast of skits. (left to right), Sue Geller, Nathan Corwin, Pat Kenschaft, Cynthia Miller, Larry Corwin, Alice Schafer, David Boliver, Frances Rosamond, and Stephan Burr. Photo courtesy of Pat Kenschaft.

In response to our signs, over 200 people jammed into the room. Their attention was riveted on the skits, and the laughter of recognition was gratifying. At the end of the conference one of the exhibitors told us that the skits had been the major topic of informal conversation of mathematicians roaming the exhibits. Just what we had hoped! We left the conference feeling triumphant.

Meanwhile, we had a committee meeting where we reflected on the skits and contemplated what we should do next. Without hesitation we decided to do it again, but the skits themselves seemed not enough. Everyone wanted an opportunity to respond. Discussion groups following the skits seemed obvious; the chairs in most conference rooms could be moved into discussion-sized circles. One man questioned whether we were prepared to lead discussions on such a delicate topic. Another, who happened to be from Ohio State where the 1990 summer meeting was scheduled, offered to acquire the services of someone on that campus qualified to facilitate group discussions and to prepare other leaders to do so.

Gay Hadley from the Ohio State University Office of Human Relations led the well-attended training session. Both male and female mathematicians felt more eager to lead discussions about gender issues than to depict them on the stage. "Throw it back to the group," was her repeated advice. "Can you men tell us how we can correct you and leave you intact?" Later she suggested, "Is there something desirable about being able to count on having someone tell you what they really think?" Together we decided to request that each group include at least one-third women and one-third men (which seemed possible judging by our initial audience) and no two people from the same institution. She provided us with a list of questions for men and another for women that would provoke thinking and discussion.

That spring our balloon was burst just a little when we were told that some AWM leaders thought skits were too undignified and might undermine respect for women mathematicians. We discussed how important it is to be dignified, and decided that getting people to think and talk about what they were doing was worth the risk to our dignity. In Columbus we reenacted the skits to a smaller audience at the smaller conference, and in our committee meeting we shared "micro-inequities" we had experienced since January that seemed like promising material for future skits.

It was apparent that there were many possibilities from the entire mathematical community, not just at meetings, and that the following January we should dramatize situations that were happening throughout our professional lives. Sue Geller and I had received many suggestions as a result of the first set. She again agreed to write them up so actors could just read them. Someone — was it Larry Corwin? — dubbed her the "skitwright."

Getting ready for the skits in January 1991 was greatly complicated by the beginning of the first Iraq war. People tended to be glued to the TVs in the hotel halls. Outside our San Francisco hotel windows we could see and hear people screaming in protest and setting fires. Nevertheless, about four hundred people showed up for skits about micro-inequities in the math community, this time scheduled in a ballroom. In my opening remarks I observed, "The question of how to promote peace between groups of people is still open."

The first skit was about the frustration of a woman professor calling a man with a secretary and saying, "This is Dr. Jones calling for Dr. Smith," only to be repeatedly told, "Dr. Smith is here and waiting. Please put Dr. Jones on the line." Secretaries can have trouble understanding the meaning of "I *am* Dr. Jones," with a consequent considerable waste of time for women professors.

The next two skits were about not being noticed. One was about a woman repeatedly making a suggestion that was not heard until a man made it somewhat later; most women mathematicians report this happening to them much too often. Another was about a meeting to plan the department's seminars for the semester. The women's persistent offer to give a session was simply ignored, despite pleas for more offers. When a colleague congratulated her months later for a fine contributed paper at a regional AMS meeting, she responded that it was the same one she had offered to give for the department the previous semester. "You offered?" was the surprised reply.

The fourth 1991 skit was the first time that a miscreant acted herself committing a micro-inequity. I was the guilty party. I had been handing out the newsletter of the program I directed for elementary school teachers, but I overlooked the two men at the table. Each had to ask for one individually, although as I talked, I was handing them out to the women. A woman asked, "Hey, Pat, do only women get them without asking?" The whole group delighted in shouting, "Sex discrimination!" In my introduction to the first set of skits, I had emphasized that we all commit micro-inequities; the chickens had come home to roost.

The fifth skit was about a panel presentation of a male graduate advisor at Major State University of Some State (Sue's style lightened the message whenever possible) who was appealing for answers as to why "the little gals" who start the mathematics graduate program don't last. A Latino peer said that in his department the retention rate is the same for both sexes; he speaks at least once a semester to each graduate student to help them handle problems and make sure they know the unwritten rules. He said he had found that the problems of women and minorities were similar to those of white men, but they often didn't have the resources to handle them; he tried to find needed resources. The speaker declared that in a department as large as his, he couldn't "babysit the gals." The Latino suggested other possibilities, and always the speaker interrupted with a "yes, but...". Finally, a woman in the audience, first expressing appreciation for the speaker's concern, said that his language might be a problem. He always referred to the male graduate students as "men," but the females as "gals" or "little gals."

"What's wrong with that?"

"It's belittling. It indicates that you take females less seriously than males. In fact, your body language was different when you used the two words. When you spoke of men, you stood squarely and looked serious.

When you spoke of gals, you looked somewhat lower, as if looking at a child, did not square your shoulders, and had an indulgent smile on your face. You may think that words do not make a difference, but they do. They are very powerful, as is body language. Considering that you have this innate and unknowing way of dealing with the various students and you are one of the most concerned members of your department, as indicated by the effort you made today and your presence here, I suspect that your department is quite inimical to females, both students and faculty." After a long dead silence, the panelist suggested that it was time for the next presentation.

The next skit showed two former co-students, now both dissertation advisors. When the woman told the man that her student Chris had just accepted a job at a university where one of his former students was employed and asked for insights about the working conditions there, her friend immediately referred to Chris as "she." "Actually, Chris is male."

The final story in this group was of an entire math class in which there is only one woman. She is the one who consistently gets the answers to the hardest problems and presents them to the class. Although the institution in which this happened has a reputation of being one of the most supportive to women in the country, the professor finally says, "I'm disgusted at you men… letting the little woman beat you!"

After this provocation, I invited the audience to stay for informal discussions. At Gay Hadley's suggestion, we had a man and a woman co-leading each group. I had made colored squares, two of each color, that the pair would wave above the audience. Members of the audience would gather around each pair, and rearrange the movable chairs into a circle. We told the audience to arrange themselves in roughly equal groups with no two from the same institution in the same group.

The proposal worked pretty much as planned. We had six groups, each with fifteen to twenty people roughly equally divided between men and women and with great diversity in age. The discussions by all accounts were friendly, exciting, and revealing.

Every one of the six groups had a similar overriding experience. All of the women said, "Yes, that's the life I lead! That's my world." All of the men were baffled. "Where? At what institution? I haven't seen that!" The perceptions seemed to be independent of age, from the bold undergraduates who joined their elders to the most experienced retired professors. There appeared to be no difference in age groups. Everyone was polite. The women didn't say, "How could you be so blind?" The men didn't say, "Are you sure you aren't making this up?" However, in listening to the immediate oral reports of all the leaders (and more leisurely follow-up reports written from others), I heard of no exceptions.

Men of good will were eager to learn, but just hadn't noticed. As Margaret Mead once said, "If fish were anthropologists, they would never notice water." Later that year Anita Hill's testimony in Clarence Thomas' hearings, as he became a member of the Supreme Court, generated nationwide discussion on similar topics. One example I knew was a man who published professional papers focused on women's issues, but who learned only at that time that aspects of his wife's and sisters' lives that they had never gotten around to telling him before.

Sue and I decided that by January 1992 it was time for her to make the introductions. She repeated my comment that the question of how to promote peace between groups of people was still open and observed "little progress has been made on it since last year." In contrast with the "Anita Hill/Clarence Thomas fiasco, a case in which everyone involved lost... we prefer to teach with a light, but memorable touch." She told how we hope people will recognize themselves and try to change, and that again all the events were true and had occurred within the math community in the past year. She added "only the names have been changed to protect the guilty."

She confessed that the first skit that year was a variant of the first skit presented the previous year, but had been reported to us in its current form by more than a dozen women. The woman is at home, not in an office. The report came from women of all ages, from young mothers to older women; marital status and living arrangements didn't seem to matter. Since the problem was so omnipresent and the skit brief, it seems worth reproducing in its entirety.

> Woman: Hello
> Caller: May I speak to Dr. Johnson, please?
> Woman: Speaking
> Caller: Yes, hello, may I speak to Dr. Johnson, please?
> Woman: This is Dr. Johnson.
> Caller: No, I want the real Dr. Johnson.
> Woman: This is a real Dr. Johnson.
> Caller: But I want the actual person, not just the home.
> Woman: This is the actual person.
> Caller: Oh, good, please put him on.

That kind of interaction is not terribly important in itself, but multiplied many ways in many contexts takes time. It also chips away at one's sense of acceptance.

The next two skits depicted situations reported by students. The first two skit sets had been entirely about faculty, and by now students were providing us with situations and wanting to be included. The first skit involved a group of graduate students wondering about how many students Dr. Jones has now. Someone said he had heard he had six. They counted up only five. Finally, the only woman in the group pointed out that she too was one of his students. They had omitted a person sitting right in front of them!

Several students reported a classroom situation where all the male students look confident and happy as the professor uses phrases such as "Clearly" and "By now it should be obvious even to the dullest of you that...". He leaves quickly at the end of class, and the overwhelmed female student decides to appeal to her classmates for help. All those who respond to her questions say they didn't understand either. The others leave without comment. Nobody claims to understand, although all looked cheerful and confident during the lecture except the woman.

In her introduction to the next skit, Sue commented that we all are sometimes too preoccupied to really listen to others. However, sometimes it seems as if there might be other issues. In this skit an organizer recruits a man and a woman to help give math content talks at nearby high schools. They are together at the time of the recruiting. When he complains to her weeks later about the extra work and she agrees that she too is finding it challenging, he looks startled. "You're going too?"

The next borders on a mini-inequity, Sue observes. The full professors in one department are discussing who should be the next chair. Two adamantly decline, and one of these suggests the only woman. "What about Jane, guys?"

"She can't. She's a woman."

There is a dead silence during which a few nod in agreement and the rest look horrified and stunned. Finally, Jane breaks the silence with, "Gee, Ed, you finally noticed. Congratulations. It took you only ten years to figure out that I'm female." The group laughs and looks relieved that Jane did not make an issue of it, but her candidacy is not taken seriously.

Sue confessed to the audience that the final incident depicted her and my frailties and those of a male. "Our main male companion in foot-in-mouth disease knows that we are publicly exposing our wrongdoings. We ask you not even to speculate about who he may be. He is one of many male mathematicians who are truly interested in making the mathematical community a sensitive, humane, and peaceful one. He endeavors not to hurt anyone and to care for each person he meets."

Sue and I were preparing to leave the summer conference with deadlines back home. While Sue finished her breakfast in the campus cafeteria, I decided to get a final drink despite our hurry to leave. As my drink ran into its glass, a friend asked to join us.

"I'd like to talk with you, but Emily and I are leaving soon to go home." (We consistently changed names to protect the guilty and this time we didn't say which of us was which.)

"Okay, but I'd like to join you even for a few minutes."

This man wanted to tell us that research shows that men tend to dominate conversations. This was not news to us, but he told us, and told us, and told us, and gave us examples. Sue kept trying to get a word in edgewise, and I conspicuously kept looking at my watch. Sue got my message, but this good man did not. At one point, I said, "Emily, stop interrupting

Fred." I was feeling hurried, frustrated, and wanted him to run down so we could leave.

Another man came to join us, but we insisted that we were about to leave. Both men protested, but we left them to each other's company. As we were putting our trays away, Sue observed. "You know, I wasn't interrupting Fred. He was interrupting me."

It took me a few moments to realize the truth, but I apologized (as did my character on stage). Emily's last line is, "This would be a great skit for January."

Again we had discussions after the skits, even though this year, in response to several suggestions, we also paused for about ten minutes between skits so that people could talk about them with their neighbors in the audience. As before, we admonished the groups to discuss how to diminish micro-inequities against women in the mathematical community and *not*

  micro-inequities toward minorities, Southerners, or short people, or
  micro-inequities outside the mathematical community, or
  personal histories that cause micro-inequities, or
  other problems that women and/or others suffer.

The summer of 1992 the International Congress on Mathematics Education (ICME), which meets every four years, held its conference in the city of Quebec. Frances Rosamond and David Boliver, by now both experienced members of the Committee on the Participation of Women, undertook the massive project of organizing and presenting previously performed skits with and for an international audience. They recruited the actors on site during the conference. Fran remembers they included at least two women from France. John Poland of Carlton University in Ottawa was a great help, and Peter Taylor from Queens University in Ontario also participated.

Publicity was not easy, since they made the decision too late to be in the official program. Fran remembered 22 years later that her announcements of the skit performances were not always welcomed at other sessions. Nevertheless, a gratifyingly large audience came. David remembered in 2004 that conversations afterward indicated that the situation in the United States was significantly better than in many countries. "Several of them shared stories which convinced us that true macro-inequities still existed in many countries rather than micro-inequities."[3] It was his impression that the situation was not much different in Europe than in the United States, but in some countries it was much worse. (As indicated in what follows, macro-inequities had not disappeared from the United States either.)

In January 1993 I started the introduction to the fourth set of skits by commenting that the number of skit plots submitted to Sue and me was unprecedented. There were over fifty people who took the effort to inform us about their experience. I congratulated Sue for having a cartoon about her skits appear in the September 11, 1991, issue of the *Wall Street Journal*.

---

[3]David E. Boliver, personal email on September 28, 2004

She was truly remarkable in turning vague or intensely personal reports into usable scripts. She had just finished a comic strip commissioned by *Glamour* magazine and scheduled to appear in the April 1993 issue. Then I turned the leadership over to her for the evening.

Sue observed that the deluge of new suggestions indicated we have a long way to go and not everyone is changing. However, we thought we had noticed a cultural shift, and it was certain that more conversations were taking place at math conferences about male-female relationships. As groups of us had reflected on the process, we thought we noticed five stages.

1. Hostile incomprehension: "What the [bleep] are you talking about?"
2. Denial (in an outraged voice): "I don't do that!"
3. Resignation, or here we go again (in a long-suffering voice with rolled eyes): (sigh) "Yes?"
4. Acceptance (embarrassed): "Oh, yes, that's right."
5. Participation (warmly): To quote a recently received email, "Here's a micro-inequity that I very thoughtfully committed for inclusion in this year's skits."

The first set of five skits focused on forms of address, each illustrating one of the aforementioned five stages. The first depicted a woman consistently being called "young lady" by her department chair. When she gets the courage to ask him to call her by her first name, as he does the other full professors, he demands to know what is wrong with his current mode of address.

"Okay you asked. I find the term demeaning. To me, it puts a distance between us, you as high and mighty, me as your underling. But I'm am not only your colleague, but also a full professor. I want you to treat me as such and to refer to me as such."

He protests he doesn't mean it to be demeaning, and she observes he doesn't call any of the men "young man." The conversation gets increasingly heated until he says, "I need only be polite to you and can call you anything I wish. It's none of your business what I call you. Good day." Hostile incomprehension, indeed.

The next scenario shows a man introducing a man and a woman, he with his title, and she without any title. When she observes later that she would like the treatment to be parallel, the man who misspoke responds, "I what? No, I didn't do that. Besides, what difference does it make?"

The next shows a student saying, "Hi, Miss Smith," and asking about the whereabouts of Dr. Jones. When "Miss Smith" reminds him he should use the same form of address for both since they have the same degrees and the same job title, he looks pained and says, "Yes, Ma'am."

In the next skit, a student interrupts himself to change "Miss Jackson," to "Dr. Jackson," with a sheepish grin.

The fifth of these five skits shows one man correcting another.

After this set of skits, we paused for discussion, which was animated.

Next we depicted our first macro-inequity, reported to us by a man. A group of men was conniving to exclude women, although they recognized the dean's choice for Associate Dean was less qualified than a female applicant.

The second was an even worse macro-inequity. A woman is asked to apply for a specific opening by a chair saying, "This is Steve from Nice U. We have an opening in your field and I thought of you. I'd like to work with you. How about applying?" She obliges and puts in the considerable time needed to submit an application.

About a month later she receives a letter from the same man. "We have a position open in your field. To date, no qualified mathematicians have applied. I am asking you to please suggest names of suitable researchers that we might contact. I thank you in advance for your help."

In her commentary, Sue said, "Please do not take this skit as permission not to ask women to apply. We welcome being asked when we have the requisite background, but not just to fill in numbers so it looks like you tried to hire a woman. So please do not ask us if you know we are not qualified or not what you are looking for. It is not without cost to us, since it takes time and energy to apply, and rejections hurt." This issue, which had taken so much space in the AWM newsletters two decades earlier, was still very much alive.

A third macro-inequity, told to us by a shocked man, depicted an all-male committee deciding which papers to accept. Everyone agrees that one paper by a woman is very good, but nobody can vouch for whether the work is really hers or how well she would present it. Unwilling to take a risk on an unknown, one member offered to write a lukewarm review so it could be turned down. How often do such deliberations keep out newcomers, female and male?

A new feature of the January 1993 skits was that there were *four* actors who played themselves in a skit depicting a micro-inequity they had committed that year. David Boliver, David Cruz-Uribe, Jim Smith (from San Francisco State University — there are seven James Smiths in the 2004 Combined Membership List!), and I had all been caught in the act, had confessed, and had volunteered to do public penance by showing the world how easy it is to be thoughtless. We ourselves had erred.

David Boliver played himself at a professional conference. David is fond of TV quiz shows and especially enjoyed a particular beautiful woman who he thought was great at flipping letters. When introducing the person who would be changing transparencies at a professional conference, he said, "Instead of hiring a professional model, we have our own Ann Stehney." The resulting audience groan prompted him to report himself to the skit authorities.

David Cruz-Uribe, who would receive his Ph.D. the following spring from the University of California at Berkeley, caught himself in a prototypical faculty micro-inequity. He realized after the fact that he had not recognized the suggestion of a woman student until a male student supported her by saying "Sally is right." *After* the male student explained what Sally had twice said, he realized that her method for solving the problem was faster and better than the solution he had presented, but he didn't pay attention until a male student demanded he do so. Being an already experienced skit actor, he promptly offered to play himself in the next skit performance.

Jim Smith's micro-inequity had actually happened fifteen years earlier, but he had recently turned himself in to the Sue-and-Pat team, prompted by a still-active guilty conscience. We had heard of similar incidents this year, so we cheerfully allowed him to expiate his guilt by showing the world how *not* to act. He meets a married couple, both of whom are looking for jobs. The husband tells him somewhat ruefully that his wife has landed a job at a community college. In his eagerness to comfort the husband, Jim heard himself saying, "Well, Richard, don't feel too left out. After all, she's a lot prettier than you are."

Illustrating yet again that not only men are guilty of sexist remarks, I played myself presenting the Committee's new book *Winning Women into Mathematics* to the MAA Board of Governors. "I urge you to send a copy to your congressmen and to your nieces."

One man responds, "There are congresswomen too, Pat."

Another chimes in, "What about our nephews?"

We did not dramatize all fifty of the submitted scenarios that year, but we did offer a hefty bunch, including a skit about how serious conversations turn to more frivolous topics when a woman tries to enter them, another about how a Stage 5 man returned personal conversation back to mathematics after others' attempts to divert it when a woman joined them, and one involving an email to a woman saying, "You are smart enough to know better." One skit was about a nine-year-old's not knowing whether to call his mother or father to the phone when the caller asks for "Dr. Reed." Another depicted graduate students engaging in egregiously sexist remarks; later when the department chair pleads for less sexism among graduate students, they are sure that he cannot be addressing them. Whew! There was still plenty of room for improvement in the mathematical community. Friends in other fields, academic and otherwise, assured us that ours reflected society at large.

In the audience discussion during this set of skits, someone stated that research has shown that girls are active participants in math classes until preadolescence. Nathan Corwin, then age twelve, raised his hand and stunned the crowd by saying, "I don't know about other schools, but in my sixth grade class it's the girls who do all the talking."

Sue and I would like to acknowledge Nathan for all his help during these four sets of skits. Each year he worked with us in the preparations, willingly running errands, and making the logistics much easier. He cheerfully carried signs across the stage saying such things as "Some time later" that helped move the action and charm the audience, and he was there and willing whenever we had a child's part.

Altogether, there were five completely different sets of skits performed at the January Joint Mathematics Meetings from 1990 to 1994 inclusive, each set culled from events that had actually happened during the past year. By 1994, Carole Lacampagne had succeeded me as chair of the Committee on Participation of Women, and she presided over the final set of skits. Most were still written by Sue Geller, but David Boliver also contributed. The 1994 skits had four themes — perceptions of what women can do, personnel actions, appearance, and "Sometimes they get it." After the skits illustrating each theme, there was a pause in the program so that the audience could digest the ideas and discuss them with their neighbors. The buzz during these discussions was animated.

Skits showing stereotypical perceptions of women's abilities included (1) a scene in the exhibits in which the exhibitor assumes the woman visitor is teaching a liberal arts course and the man abstract algebra, when actually it is the opposite, (2) one where a male insists upon "helping" a female after she exclaims over a computer frustration when she is just as capable as he, and (3) another where an advisor telephoning his graduate students' office asks for males by name until he gets a male student to tell him whether the air conditioner overflow tub is nearly full, completely ignoring the competence of his female graduate student who originally answered the phone.

The skits about personnel decisions included two dramatizing concerns about "reverse discrimination," one in academia and the other in industry. The third shows a male faculty member composing a memo about a meeting to discuss the first woman up for tenure in their department in ten years. Realizing he wants to get this "right," he rejects addressing her as "Mrs." and revises it to "Ms." When the department's only senior woman asks him why he didn't use "Dr." for her title, the malefactor is crestfallen. "But I tried. I worked hard on picking Ms. I even showed the memo to two people and they didn't notice." The senior woman points out that some people have already asked her if the younger woman doesn't have a doctorate, and he sheepishly agrees to send out a corrective memo.

The group about appearance begins with a pair of students, both with the same dissertation advisor, meeting a really "big" mathematician in their field but at different times. The woman, who meets him first, has an animated, helpful, and totally appropriate conversation with the eminent mathematician. A few years later, her male colleague introduces himself as one of their advisor's graduate students. The response seemed worth reporting to the skit-makers. "I met another of his students a few years ago. She was a very attractive young woman." The narrator then asked if raising questions about such comments is an example of "political correctness" run rampant when we have better things to worry about.

Less debatable is the situation in the subsequent skit. The chair of a search group is asked to review who the candidates were, so the search committee can remember which talk corresponded to which portfolio application. The chair reviews the six candidates, identifying the three men by several sentences about the subject of their presentation and the three women by some brief physical description.

Finally, we see a dinner at a research conference with a newly minted doctoral student at one end of a long table and an eminent leader in her field at the other. When she mentions to a nearby colleague that she would like to meet him, her colleague walks to the end of the table, puts his hand around the shoulder of his colleague, and says in a stage voice so all can hear, "There's a gorgeous girl over there who wants to be introduced to you." The young woman abruptly leaves the room looking embarrassed, but not before she notices the discomfort of the senior mathematician. Fortunately, the narrator informs us that they were introduced later more appropriately and have continued an email conversation about their research.

After the break to discuss the role of appearances, the final skit of the evening (and the last of those produced in these five years by the Committee on Participation of Women) depicted a mathematician accepting correction graciously about the way he refers to nineteenth century women. Although the research he presents was largely by a woman, Alicia Stott, he refers to her as a "housewife," while he calls her male colleagues "mathematicians." A female listener to his talk chases down his reference and discovers that the males were a schoolmaster, a lawyer, and a rug dealer, respectively; they were no more professional "mathematicians" than Stott. He agreed that his point was that in the nineteenth century many amateurs were doing mathematics, and agrees to speak more appropriately in the future.

By now, both the skits and the discussions afterward were well established. We had a significant coterie of willing actors and actresses. Among those who participated over the years (in addition to the initial actors listed at the beginning of the chapter) were Sarah Marie Belcastro, Howard Bell, Bettye Anne Case, Fred Chichester, Amy Cohen, David Cruz-Uribe, Marjorie Enneking, Peter Flusser, Virginia Flusser, David Foley, Mary Ellen Foley, Leon Henkin, Mary Hesselgrave, Jack Hodges, Alice Kelly, Karen King, Carole Lacampagne, Sandra Leonard, Patrick McCray, Mickey McDonald, Wanda Paterson, Charles Peltier, David Pengelley, Jessica Polito, Emily Puckette, Jack Quine, Barbara Rice, Catherine Roberts, Frances Rosamond, Barry Schiller, John Schumaker, Jim Smith, Ann Stehney, Rebekka Struik, Ellen Torrance, Alan Tucker, Rebekah Valdivia, Steve Weintraub, and Dorothy Williams.

In October 1991 the MAA distributed a "skit kit" written by the Committee on Participation of Women so that other groups could lift our ideas, our procedures, our discussion outlines, and even our skit scripts, although we encouraged (and still encourage) others to collect and dramatize micro-inequities reported within their own communities. The *Chronicle of Higher Education* published my letter announcing it, and requests came for copies from outside the mathematical communities. Skits about micro-inequities have since been produced in a variety of contexts, not just higher education. Some took ours, and many took merely the idea and produced their own. A complete set of the scripts is now available at Sue Geller's website: http://www.math.tamu.edu/~geller.

In 1999 Frances Rosamond published an article, "Our Voices: Using Skits on Equity and Diversity for Initiating Institutional and Personal Change"[4] in an international publication. The skits themselves have been disseminated and performed internationally. We like to think it is now an established way to share concerns about the ways that groups see themselves being treated.

But in late 1989 and January 1990, skits were a novel and daunting undertaking, comparable to entering the math community as an "outsider." After the January 1990 skits, Sue Geller and I sat around very pleased with ourselves but continually repeating that neither of us could have done it alone. It had to be two of us, not because our talents were complementary (although for this purpose they were), but because neither of us would have had the emotional fortitude to have sailed into *these* unknown waters alone — although both of us were by then highly experienced at solo sailing.

At this writing, we have roomed together fourteen times, sometimes for a week at a time. It may be interesting to revisit the relationship that made the first micro-inequity skits possible. We had talked casually as many mathematicians do at conferences before the International Congress of 1986, but that was when we really *met*. It was at the AWM party on the University of California at Berkeley campus, when someone lit up a cigarette. I have myasthenia gravis, a defect of the nicotinic receptors, and if I am exposed enough to nicotine, my muscles will collapse and I will fall to the ground, unable to get up under my own steam for several hours. Thus, one person lighting up at a party means I *must* leave. My husband was having a good time, and wanted to stay. Sue offered to walk me back to our dorm, a considerable hike across the campus. It was dark and isolated.

The experience of walking without a man across a dark, isolated space generated conversation about Sue's growing up in Newark, New Jersey, the daughter of a local merchant. Her family moved to a suburb blocks from Newark when she was in grade school, but she continued to spend time at the store, both working in it and playing outside. Her father's store was destroyed in the Newark riots of 1967, but as she was growing up, she learned not only lots of practical math very young in order to help her father, but also basic street survival skills. I had grown up less than fifteen miles away in Nutley, but in a safe neighborhood with parents who supported my ambitions in every possible way. Sue felt capable of protecting me, even in my weakened myasthenic state.

We talked for a long time in the dorm after we had arrived safely. It was better than a party, by far, for both of us. Sue had early discovered that her

---

[4]Frances Rosamond, "Our Voices: Using Skits on Equity and Diversity for Initiating Institutional and Personal Change," *Social Justice and Mathematics Education: Gender, Class, Ethnicity and the Politics of Schooling*, edited by C. Keitel, International Organization of Women in Mathematics Education, Freie Universitat, Berlin, 1999.

Sue Geller is seen here with a companion near Cairnes in Australia after she gave a talk at a symposium in Sydney. Sue loves zoos. She and the author have visited many zoos the day before math conferences. Photo courtesy of Sue Geller.

quick mind was the path to freedom. Her father provided her lots of applied math problems in childhood. As a child and young adult, she knew hunger. As a child, she was excruciatingly thin and very short. As a young adult, the choice was sometimes between books or food, and she didn't always choose food. One day she put her head down in class, an unusual occurrence. The professor looked and saw what she was staring at — a notice of eviction for non-payment of dorm fees. He took the note, told her they'd talk after class, and to please join the class discussion. He was a good professor and she a leading student; there was ample respect between them. So after class she confessed to him not only her dire need for immediate money but also her worry about whether she could afford to return to the Case Institute of

Technology the following semester. He called someone, explained the need, gave her fare to go downtown, and told her whom she was to meet. When she reached the executive, he had a check ready for her for the total amount she owed that semester and bus fare back. His only conditions were that she never reveal the name of the company nor his name and that she pass along such kindness as she was able. Due to his kindness and others, she finished college and has not been hungry since. She is no longer skinny.

I was much relieved at the end of that long evening together when Sue suggested we room together the following January. My husband, Fred Chichester, had other things to do than care for me, and I needed someone to protect my weakened body who was as strong and caring as Fred and Sue.

The following January in San Antonio, Sue learned what a challenge she had taken on. Fortunately, it was a group of us who ate together in one of San Antonio's charming outside restaurants next to the canal. It was a delightful evening socially, and because I was sitting down, I didn't notice what was happening to my body. There were people smoking at other tables, and I ignored them. When I tried to get up, I had no muscular strength left. One of the men slung my left arm around his shoulders and Sue did similarly with my right. Together they dragged my limp body back to my bed.

After that Sue became an adept sleuth of safe places for me to eat. We ordered up many meals to our smoke-free room, and she would pack our hotel refrigerators with food before each conference so I could eat most breakfasts and lunches without foraying out to dangerous territory. It was in some sense an odd pairing. Sue was at a research institution; I was at a state college. She had an international reputation for her research in K-theory, a field of abstract algebra; with four courses to teach each semester, I soon concluded I had to find other ways than research in which to serve the mathematics community. She never married; I had two children. We had significant religious differences too, but our political views were similar, and we both have a driving concern for making this world a fairer place, whether the issue is gender, handicap, economics, or "other."

Math conferences became less frightening for me. When Ken Ross invited me to chair the CPW the following spring, I felt emboldened to accept. By the time the skits were gestating in the summer of 1989, Sue and I had a close relationship that not only empowered both of us but also enabled us to work jointly to overcome the external obstacles that confront pioneers.

My own biases could interpret the gratifying development from the invisibility of women in the early 1970s to the enthusiasm with which the skits were greeted by many men twenty years later as evidence that men can change when they are educated. However, I am reminded of other possibilities when I remember the time when, as chair of the MAA Committee on the Participation of Women, I was rejoicing to the Board of Governors of the Mathematical Association of America that two consecutive women had been elected president of the MAA — Lida Barrett, 1990-1992 and Deborah

The leadership of the Mathematical Association of America in 1990. (left to right), Lida K. Barrett, president; Deborah Temper Haimo, president-elect; Marcia Sward, executive director; and Rhoda Goldstein, associate director for finance and administration.

Temper Haimo, 1992-1994. I gushed, "What does that tell you about the male members of the MAA?"

With uncharacteristic impulsiveness, the MAA's executive director, Marcia Sward, exclaimed, "They don't vote." I have rarely seen anyone look so guilty in public as Marcia did after that little slip! Her comment suggests, however, what can happen if one group organizes and the establishment doesn't resist.

As we produced and discussed skits about micro-inequities year after year, it was inevitable that the question of macro-inequities would recur. We all knew that they continued. We women who were leading the skit production believed that the micros set the stage for the macros, allowing men to not notice, or to deny, truly outrageous behavior of their colleagues. The men weren't so sure. For them the dichotomy between micros, which everyone committed, and macros, which were unthinkable for all of us who cared about fairness, was huge.

What were some of the macros? In the early 1990s I was told three stories by women who by then were in senior positions at highly respected universities. All were dynamic leaders, known far beyond their own universities. Nobody would consider them to be easily victimized, and therefore nobody would guess what they had endured in the past. One can only wonder how similar events might have deterred other, perhaps less resilient, young women from pursuing professional careers, and not just in mathematics.

The first woman told about going to her dissertation advisor's office for help, at which point he physically assaulted her. She fought back, the attack escalated, and he began throwing her around the room. Although his colleagues heard the noise, they did not intervene and instead urged her to drop out of the program "for your own protection." Unwilling to give up her career, she persisted, defending herself as well as she could while the assaults continued. She eventually received her doctorate and went on to a highly successful academic career.

Another told me that when she entered her dissertation advisor's office, he would grab her breast. "It got to be ridiculous," she told me. "I would slip drafts under his door, page by page. I was afraid to open the door. I would connive to talk with him in any possible public place." She too finished her degree under the man who repeatedly physically assaulted her.

A third safely earned a doctorate and landed a tenure-track job at a prestigious university. One day when she was sitting at her desk, a colleague entered her office and closed the door. She didn't think much of it, until he lunged across her desk and reached for her breast. She had grown up in a tough neighborhood where survival depended on defense skills. She was programmed to take a swat at an aggressor. Quickly her fist removed one of his front teeth. He happened to be a close friend of the chair and, although her publications record and teaching were superior to that of many of her colleagues, she was denied tenure.

One good man was especially persistent in his requests that the Committee on Participation of Women address macro-inequities. As reported earlier, we did dramatize some distressing discussions reported by men without women present. I thought we were making headway, but he wasn't satisfied. He was surely correct that we were not addressing the very worst problems in the mathematics community. Finally, I decided he and I must have a conversation that wasn't just casual in the hallway. Together we found ourselves an empty room in the institution where the meetings were then located and closed the door.

He began by insisting that the Committee was side-stepping some really serious situations. I agreed, but said I didn't see how they could be addressed at the national level, at least not without local initiation. Finally, I dropped the challenge.

"But one of the worst offenders that I have heard of is in your department. Why aren't the good men doing anything about him?"

He looked utterly shocked. "Who is that?"

"You mean you really don't know?" I was very skeptical. They had been colleagues for decades.

"Well, there was a demonstration by women against X last year...". It was said very slowly, softly, reluctantly....

"So! You *do* know!" I allowed myself a small feeling of triumph.

"No. I never thought the charges were true."

"*What?!!!* You thought a group of women would organize a demonstration on campus to protest the behavior of one man, and there was *nothing* to their charges?" As I contemplated the amount of effort and courage such a demonstration would require, I felt thunderstruck at the blindness of this usually very wise man.

He looked ashamed. He realized that his loyalty to his friend had deceived him. We talked for a while about what should be done, and he acknowledged that there is no obvious response to men who commit macro-inequities, especially when the men are an integral part of a professional community. Personally, I suspect that the omnipresent micro-inequities set a context in which good men can convince themselves that *only* micro-inequities are happening, even when a group of women organize a demonstration against one of their colleagues.

Alas, micro-inequities continue to be rampant in the early twenty-first century. Dramatization is one way to help good people become better; it certainly promotes conversation. Laughter can be an effective medicine.

CHAPTER 9

Women in Mathematics Now (2004)

What about the present? What is the situation for women now? This is even more dangerous territory than trying to choose revealing stories about the past.

Tentatively, I believe that significant progress has been made in the past decade. While the micro-inequities reported in the skits still happen, there seem to be fewer of them. Certainly there are far more men at stage five. I hear people of both sexes saying cheerfully, "Uh-oh! Sexism?" Sometimes there is a rueful nod and the conversation moves quickly on, and other times a significant discussion ensues about whether the incident in question was really sexism and more generally what constitutes sexism. Such conversations hardly ever happened in 1990, especially not with people of both sexes participating.

A friend told me recently of a radio announcement she hears repeatedly now that would have been unthinkable in 1990. A child's voice says, "Daddy, why did God make the sky blue?"

"To match your beautiful eyes, my dear."

"Not even close!," the child replies, and then she preceeds to give a scientific description of why the sky appears blue. The voiceover then tells the audience how important it is to teach girls mathematics and science when they are young.

There are, of course, still serious problems for any young mathematician, and some extras that apply only to women. I know of one young mathematician who after several miscarriages managed to give birth to two children in the twenty-first century with lots of medical assistance. It wasn't easy. There were times when friends and family feared for her health, and the possibilities for the unborn were truly alarming. However, she managed to give birth twice. Both she and her husband were ecstatic.

During their ordeal he had been supporting the family in a job that was not particularly satisfying, and shortly after the second birth, both husband and wife were pleased to land similar promising jobs with the same employer. He was eager to enjoy his children for a change and she to get out of the house at last. So he took a part-time position, and she worked full-time. Like Harold Stark's wife, as reported in Chapter 7, she has received plenty of criticism, although not from mathematicians. The one that hurt the most is, "If you don't stay home with your children, you didn't want them." Didn't want them! After all the physical, emotional, and career risks she had taken to have them?!! But, along with being a devoted mother, she is also a mathematician.

The research of David and Myra Sadker about gender issues in K-12 classrooms spans several recent decades. As a married couple in the early 1970s, they noticed that although they were taking the same graduate courses from the same professors, they were having a very different classroom experience. David was recognized quickly when he raised his hand, so he did so frequently. When he contributed an idea, it was credited to him repeatedly. When Myra raised her hand, it was often ignored, so she tried less often. Much worse, when she contributed an idea, it was generally ignored until a male classmate repeated it (without attribution) some time later, after which it was credited to the male classmate.

The Sadkers did careful research, including making videotapes of classroom patterns throughout the United States, and they documented that Myra's experiences in graduate school were ubiquitous throughout American education, starting in kindergarten. They wrote books and articles about their findings, which were well publicized in the popular press. They were invited to popular talk shows such as the Oprah Winfrey Show, and the popular culture tried to address the issues that troubled the Sadkers. Such behavior is not easy to change, but there seems to be some progress. Their videos document ingrained inequities, not just in the behavior of teachers, but also in the perceptions of audiences that don't see the inequities until they are pointed out.

More measurably, admissions policies have changed in higher education. Almost half the students in American medical schools and law schools now are women. Engineering schools have risen from five percent to fifteen percent women. Computer science, while starting on a remarkably equitable footing, has slipped and is now far more sexist than it was two decades ago. One factor may have been that computer science migrated from being perceived as a child of mathematics to a child of engineering, but another is the great influx of mostly male foreign graduate students, many of whom remain in the United States after graduation.

"After one barrier falls, there is another barrier," says David Sadker. He points out that the salary gap between men and women in law and medicine is greater than the salary gap in other professions. "Women concentrate in the lower-paying fields," he observes. In medicine these are pediatrics, ob-gyn, and internal medicine. The higher paying fields, such as surgery and orthopedics, require longer residencies, and these coincide with the rapid ticking of a woman's biological clock. Women lawyers are concentrated in nonprofit and government work, instead of the higher-paying corporate fields.[1] Similarly, women in mathematics are concentrated in community

---

[1]David Sadker on Math Medley, "Are Our Schools Failing at Fairness Still?" June 19, 2004.

colleges and bachelor's-granting institutions, in contrast to the high-prestige, and somewhat higher paying, universities and research think-tanks.

David (b. 1942) and **Myra** (1943-1995) **Sadker** met when they were earning MAT's (master's degree in education) at Harvard,[2] were married in 1965,[3] and pioneered research and publicity about gender bias and sexual harassment. They published many dozens of research papers on these subjects, and reports of their work have appeared in the most widely read popular periodicals, including *USA Today, Parade Magazine*, the *New York Times*, and the *London Times*. Their book *Failing at Fairness: How Our Schools Cheat Girls*, the first popular book on the subject, was widely read, and their introductory teacher education text *Teachers, Schools, and Society* has gone through seven editions.[4]

David and Myra Sadker with their two daughters, Robin Sadker (left), who is now a physician, and Jacqueline Sadker, who is now an attorney. Photo courtesy of David Sadker.

The Sadkers were both professors of education at American University, and Myra was Dean of the School of Education. Myra Sadker died at the age of 52 while undergoing treatment for breast cancer.

---

[2]David Sadker, personal email, June 27, 2004.
[3]David Sadker, personal email, June 21, 2004.
[4]www.american.edu/sadker/bio.htm and personal email on July 6, 2004.

Mathematicians, school children, and all others are greatly affected by the government that makes the policies under which we live. As this is written, only 59 of the 435 seats in Congress, or slightly less than 14 percent, are held by women, and only 14 of the 100 senators are women. Women constitute about 16 percent of corporate officers and about 12 percent of the board seats in 500 of the country's largest companies.[5] In contrast 36 percent of the parliament of Norway is women, and in the summer of 2004 they will vote on proposed legislation that would require the boards of every publicly traded company to include at least 40 percent women by 2005.[6] Generous parental leave and easily available, safe child care are two common European practices that may have resulted from having more women in decision-making positions. Both these issues are major ones for current women in mathematics, as we shall see below.

In late 2003, the Association for Women in Mathematics surveyed its members to help determine both the future direction of AWM and the more general issues that face women in mathematics today. Although the responses to the question about unresolved issues is most applicable to this book, the list of AWM 2003 services is interesting. Thirty-plus years after the founding of the AWM, the organization asked its members to evaluate the effectiveness of its networking opportunities, mentor network, newsletter and other publications, online discussion forum, workshops for graduates and postdocs, travel grants, award programs, online advertising, website, career resources, student chapters, and lectures. Most responses were positive for these and for the Sonia Kovalevsky high school days, which provide an opportunity for dozens of young women in high school to spend a day exploring live mathematical concepts and meeting women with successful careers in mathematics-related fields. The Association for Women in Mathematics is making a difference.

There was an open-ended question on the questionnaire about the issues affecting women in mathematics that should be addressed more aggressively. The number one answer — with forty percent of the respondents mentioning it — was "flexibility in the tenure process to address the 'fight' between the tenure clock and the biological clock and to allow a better balance between career and family."[7] This problem is, of course, not specific to mathematics. In response to women throughout academia, the American Association of University Professors has changed its position on tenure:

> The AAUP now recommends that, upon request, a faculty member be entitled to stop the clock or extend the probationary period, with or without taking a full or partial leave of absence, if the faculty member (whether male or female) is a primary or coequal caregiver of newborn or

---

[5]Marie C. Wilson, "Closing the Leadership Gap," *Ms. Magazine*, XIV:2, Summer 2004, p. 14.

[6]ibid.

[7]Carolyn S. Gordon, president of AWM, personal email on May 18, 2004.

newly adopted children. Thus, a faculty member would
be entitled to stop the tenure clock while continuing to
perform faculty duties at full salary. Institutions should
also take care to see that faculty members are not penal-
ized in any way for requesting and receiving extensions of
the probationary period.[8]

Such leave is not uncontroversial, even among feminists. Mary Gray,
founding president of the Association for Women in Mathematics and former
national chair of Committee W of the AAUP, writes, "I don't think most
women (OK, there are exceptions) can take a year off a couple of times
and really get back to the place they would otherwise have been in the
profession. Encouraging dropping out is not, in my view, a good idea. On
the other hand, better child care, with government support, is a good idea
and greatly needed — even the Pope came out in favor a week or so ago."
Perhaps "dropping out" needs to be better defined. Some women would
regard dropping out of teaching as facilitating a mother's *not* dropping out
of research (there being time for only one of these during a baby's first year),
and that research requires continuity more than teaching.

The next most commonly mentioned issues on the 2003 AWM survey
were the need for mid-level career support, support for women not on traditional paths or in traditional settings, and more travel grants. Other concerns were the "two-body problem" (the late twentieth century jargon for
the efforts to maintain a relationship while both partners pursue careers by
seeking good jobs), "discrimination against women at the graduate level,"
the dumbing down of math programs, especially for women and minorities,
and the plight of "pioneers" (solo tenured women at small colleges). Respondents to the survey urged the AWM to increase many of its current activities,
including featuring speakers at conferences, publicizing jobs, networking opportunities, and collecting and disseminating statistics. There were also requests for more support for conferences, including finances for impoverished
students, roommate matching services, and child care provisions.[9] A good
sign was that there were many comments about the omnipresent children at
the January 2004 Joint Mathematics Meeting in Phoenix.[10]

One need only look at the statistics to see that there is much room for
improvement. In a 2004 article the president and president-elect of AWM
pointed out that in 2002, 31 percent of the new doctorates in mathematics
went to women, but only 24 percent of those from Group I institutions.[11]
Group I comprises the forty-eight highest ranked mathematics departments
in the country. However, only 11 percent of the tenure-track untenured

---

[8]www.aaup.org/statements/REPORTS/re01fam.htm.

[9]Carolyn S. Gordon, president of AWM, personal email on May 18, 2004.

[10]ibid.

[11]Carolyn S. Gordon and Barbara Keyfitz, "Women in Academia: Are We Asking
the Right Questions?," *Notices of the AMS*, 51:7, pp. 784-786. They were citing the 2002
Annual Survey of the Mathematical Sciences.

mathematics faculty in Group I institutions are women, and only 7 percent of those already tenured.[12] There is, admittedly, some time-delay in equity moving up the ranks, but the proportion of women among Americans receiving doctorates in mathematics has been at 20 percent throughout most of the past two decades.[13]

Why the discrepancy? Gordon and Keyfitz call for "a careful reexamination of the methods by which we make the most important decisions in hiring and granting tenure and of the support given to the untenured faculty...". "If one looks around most departments, including the best, one sees that even in judging male faculty at the time of tenure, promotion committees have not invariably made decisions that were in the department's best interest." They refer to a recent study by Donna Nelson and Diana Rogers[14] that calls for a reexamination of universities' "culture, attitudes, and policies." The Nelson-Rogers study quotes a Princeton chemist, George McLendon, saying, "Academic institutions are intrinsically monastic institutions that were created in the 13th century. They might need a little fine-turning."[15] Gordon and Keyfitz then quote Derek Bok's study showing that in the two decades following the passage of Title IX in 1972, universities were opened up to women in mathematics, science, engineering, law, medicine, and business, but the increase in women professionals in the latter three fields has been dramatically more than the former three. "Apparently, the marketplace in the professions has been friendlier to women than has the professoriate. In the competition for talent, universities have generally been losing ground to better-paying careers. It would be doubly unfortunate if universities, faced with a shrinking pool, are making that pool even smaller through poor recruitment or retention practices."[16]

As she contemplates taking the helm of AWM, Barbara Keyfitz is keenly aware of the discrepancies at the top in mathematics. "Thirty years after Title IX, the number of senior women in mathematics and engineering is still small. Even in the junior ranks, women are a smaller proportion than those getting Ph.D.'s. The proportion of women among Americans getting Ph.D.'s in mathematics has been close to thirty percent for twenty years, but this is not reflected in faculty positions, especially in tenured full professors. This is not just in mathematics, but also in science, even the 'soft sciences,' where women are in the majority."[17]

When pushed to guess why the situation is still so inequitable, she says slowly that it is "not just legacy and prejudice, or even the old boys' network.

---

[12]ibid.

[13]"1989 Annual AMS-MAA Survey," *Notices of the AMS*, November 1989, 36:9, p. 1159 for the years 1973-1989.

[14]"A National Study of Diversity in Science and Engineering Faculties at Research Universities, Final Report," www.now.org/issues/diverse/diversity_report.pdf.

[15]Carolyn S. Gordon and Barbara Keyfitz, "Women in Academia: Are We Asking the Right Questions?," *Notices of the AMS*, 51:7, pp. 784-786.

[16]ibid.

[17]Barbara Keyfitz, telephone conversation on June 1, 2004.

We all tend to look for people like ourselves when hiring." She tells of a man who said to her recently that there was "no way" they could hire a woman in his department without lowering standards. "What do you mean?," she asked. He said that top women are in great demand, and his department could not hope to recruit one of them. And the next level are a risk. "What happens when they have a baby?" She adds that such men don't seem to wonder what happens if a man becomes an alcoholic or has a mid-life crisis.[18] The nineteenth century image of separate "spheres" for motherhood and careers lingers.

Lillian Moller Gilbreth (1878-1971) is the only engineer on a United States stamp; since there is not yet a mathematician on a stamp (despite the best efforts of Eileen Poiani), she represents "us," both female and male, to the American mailing public. The engineer on the United States forty-cent stamp gave birth *twelve* times. She received her doctorate when pregnant with her eighth child, the second having already died of diphtheria. Her husband died when the oldest was nineteen, and she put the surviving eleven children through Ivy League and Seven Sisters colleges with her own earnings as an engineer. (Frank Bunker Gilbreth is another example of a good man. He supported his wife's earning a doctorate although he had never gone to college, and he prepared her in practical ways to take over his consulting business when, as he correctly anticipated, a heart attack would render him suddenly unable to support the family.) When she no longer needed so much money, she took an academic job at Purdue University and started the Society of Women Engineers. Her eleven children were all remarkably successful, although they were raised by a single mother with a thriving business. They persuaded her to retire when she turned ninety. Fortunately, there are several readable books about her life written by two of her children, Ernestine Gilbreth Carey and Frank Gilbreth, Jr.[19]

Alas, even such an emphatic counterexample has not dispelled the myth that motherhood and technical careers don't mix. What can be done? "I'm not convinced that the traditional way of evaluating risk is correct," says Barbara Keyfitz. She thinks mathematicians and others have to reconsider more of the risks when they are evaluating candidates for a job or promotion. "Even if you look just at morbidity and mortality figures, hiring women is taking less of chance than hiring men." Women are significantly more likely to survive in decent health to the age of sixty-five. "The amount of time for a baby is a few years, a small fraction of your career." She concedes that "once-in-a-century mathematicians" are "mostly male and mostly started young." But if you look at *all* of the members of *any* sizable department, even the best, some members have become "dead-wood," not contributing

---

[18]ibid.

[19]Jan Lancaster, "O, Pioneer!" *Brown Alumni Monthly*, February 1996, pp. 30-34. *Time Out for Happiness* is the book about her life most highly recommended by her grandson David C. Gilbreth, although *Cheaper by the Dozen* is better known.

Lillian Gilbreth (right), the only engineer, mathematician, or physicist on a U.S. stamp, with her husband Frank Gilbreth (left) and their eleven children, (l-r) Frank, Bill, Fred, Dan, Jack, Bob, Jane, Lill, Martha, Ern, and Anne in 1923. Photo courtesy of David C. Gilbreth, Lillian's grandson.

to the intellectual life of the department.[20] How can a committee of humans predict which candidates will fulfill their promise and which will be diverted or atrophy? She suspects the complete answer does not exist, but hopes that mathematicians will stop crediting motherhood with more distractive powers than it deserves.

Barbara Keyfitz (b. 1944) spent her first fifteen years in Ottawa, Canada. Her father graduated from college in 1934, during the depths of the Depression. He was fortunate to be hired as a clerk in the Canadian census with the security of a civil servant. He continued to pursue his dream of becoming a college professor, and in the early 1950s received a doctorate. At that time college professors received a very low salary compared to civil servants, but in 1959 professors' salaries had risen enough so that he could accept a faculty position at the University of Toronto in mathematical demography.

---

[20]Barbara Keyfitz, telephone interview on June 1, 2004.

Barbara finished her high school education in Toronto, and did her undergraduate work at the University of Toronto. "At that time Canada was not ready for women in graduate school." However, Chandler Davis suggested she pursue a doctorate in mathematics in the States. His wife, Natalie Zemon Davis, would later become a professor of history at Princeton University. The Davises lived in different countries for 23 years, but when Keyfitz was an undergraduate, both were at the University of Toronto. Keyfitz still feels mortified when she remembers her response to being introduced by Professor Davis to his wife with, "She's in the history department." "Oh," the undergraduate Keyfitz said, "Is she a secretary there?"

Barbara Keyfitz with her two children, who are now adults.
Photo courtesy of Barbara Keyfitz.

At Davis's urging, Keyfitz went to the Courant Institute of Mathematics at New York University, where she earned an M.S. and a Ph.D. Her research area is nonlinear partial differential equations, and her first two positions were in the engineering departments at Columbia and Princeton universities. "It was a terrible career choice at the time, because I disappeared from mathematical circles. However, in the long run, as the mathematical community has become more inclusive of applied mathematics, it has been helpful to have that applied background."

Eventually, she joined a mathematics department at Arizona State University. She later became the John and Rebecca Moores Professor of Mathematics at the University of Houston. As this is written, she is excitedly moving to Toronto, where she will be the first woman director of a federally funded mathematics research institute in the United States or Canada.

There are five such institutes in the United States and three in Canada. (She points out that the Courant Institute at NYU is a group of mathematical departments, and its director is like a dean of a college.)

To take this job, she will be leaving her husband Marty Golubitsky in Houston, and participating in that modern phenomenon, a two-city marriage. She and Marty have a grown son and daughter, so their care is no longer an issue. "He *can't* go," she said in response to my question as to why he didn't move too. "He has five graduate students here and is PI [Principal Investigator] of a grant in its first year." She then adds that he will be the president of SIAM during the same two years that she will be president of the Association for Women in Mathematics. "So we will meet at least four times a year at meetings of the CBMS!"[21] The Conference Board of the Mathematical Sciences is an organization of the presidents of the mathematical societies that meets to discuss, and perhaps take action, on issues of common concern to all the mathematical communities.

Carolyn Gordon, current president of AWM as this is written, talks about the variation in atmosphere among universities. In "some schools there is a very competitive atmosphere, especially in the early years of course work, and in other schools the atmosphere is very cooperative where students study together, work together, and encourage each other. I think for both men and women the supportive atmosphere works better, although there are people who are motivated by competition." This supportive atmosphere can be especially valuable for "women who have in the past been discouraged from going into mathematics or who have been exposed to the stereotyping that says women are not as good at mathematics.... It has nothing to do with the quality of the program or the level of work that is being done, but simply the atmosphere.... Once one gets into research, then someone who was motivated by competition will probably not be sustained. Once they get into thesis research... they are not about to get gratification in a short amount of time. You might work on a problem for a couple of years before you actually have your results. It takes tenaciousness. You have to be able to put up with discouragement. Sometimes you have to realize that a problem simply isn't going to have a solution. Having worked on it for several months, you have to shift gears — and you have to do that without getting so discouraged that you don't want to continue. So in that sense the supportive atmosphere is much more conducive to research than the competitive atmosphere...."[22]

In the past this desire for a supportive atmosphere was considered feminine, and women were more likely to acknowledge their need for it, but men are increasingly able and willing to acknowledge that they too thrive better among friends. When the atmosphere of a university becomes more cooperative everyone benefits, but it seems to require more change from men

---

[21]Barbara Keyfitz, telephone interview on June 1, 2004.

[22]Carolyn Gordon, Math Medley, "Women in Mathematics Now," January 31, 2004.

than women. A change that women themselves could possibly implement involves their handling of "stereotype vulnerability."

"Claude Steele at Stanford and Steve Spencer at Hope College have done some fascinating studies on the vulnerability of people in groups that are stereotyped about their vulnerability to the stereotyping and its effect on their work. For example, they gave a task where two groups that consisted of half white and half African American students were all given the same test. But the experimental group was asked to write their race at the top of the exam. Just writing that down gave the implication that maybe the task was... something blacks didn't do so well. The results were quite dramatic. In the control group, the blacks and whites did equally well, but in the experimental group, where they had written down their race, the whites did equally well as the control group, but the blacks dropped way down.

"They did similar experiments with similar results with women. They said there are two possible explanations. One is that the stereotypes are internalized so that the person is viewing themselves according to the stereotype. Or it could be that they are resisting the stereotype, but that creates enough tension in taking an exam that it again pulls them down."[23]

When I asked her what could be done about stereotype vulnerability, she responded, "I think one of the most effective ways of combating internalized stereotypes is to provide role models and mentors. And a mentor does not have to be a person with the same gender or race, but someone who reaches out to them and encourages them to continue. Role models are extremely important.

"There is a delightful story that one of our recent Ph.D.s at Dartmouth told me. When she was taking undergraduate math courses at Smith College, she was telling another student, who I will call Lisa, about a problem she was working on with a male student named Joe at another college. Lisa looked rather quizzical, so my student asked if she had understood the problem. 'Oh, yes,' said Lisa. 'It's just that I forgot that men do mathematics too.' Seeing lots of other women doing mathematics helps erase stereotypes."

She told a less cheerful, but also funny, story about a woman who was the first in her department to achieve tenure. "An opening came up for the new chair of the undergraduate program. There was general agreement that she was probably the best person for the position, but she was told, 'While we agree you are the best qualified, the problem is you insist on being female'."

Carolyn Gordon now teaches in the mathematics department of Dartmouth College, which hardly more than a generation ago was a staunchly male bastion. Now, however, the students are half women, and four of the approximately twenty members of the mathematics faculty are women, "which, unfortunately, is fairly high in comparison with equivalent colleges

[23]ibid; see also www.mathsci.appstate.edu/~sjg/class/1010/wc/stats/stereotype.html.

and universities." She adds that "...the atmosphere here is very encouraging for women."

Carolyn Gordon (b. 1950) earned her bachelor's and master's degrees at Purdue University. After receiving a doctorate from Washington University in differential geometry, she spent a post-doc year in Israel and then taught at Lehigh University in Pennsylvania for a few years. Then she went back to Washington University in St. Louis, this time as part of the faculty, where she met her husband, David Webb. He now is also tenured in the mathematics faculty of Dartmouth College, evidence of a major change within academia in the past thirty years. Until the early 1970s the nepotism rules at most institutions of higher education prevented the hiring of two members of a family, as noted in Chapter 4. The effect was to keep most aspiring women mathematicians from getting a conveniently located full-time job. Gordon and Webb are possibly best known for their joint paper, "You Can't Always Hear the Shape of a Drum?"[24]

Carolyn Gordon. Photo courtesy of the American Mathematical Society.

"I adopted my daughter after I already had tenure, and found that the academic life along with parenting was perfect in my case — lots of flexibility.... I've actually taken my daughter to many conferences with

[24]www.ams.org/new-in-math/hap-drum/hap-drum.html

me since she was two or three. I've often had her participate when I'm presenting a lecture. I've managed to have her help when I'm giving some demonstration."[25]

She observes with joy the change in national mathematics meetings over the twenty-five years that she has been attending them. There are not only many more women, but also a remarkable number of babies, especially at the January 2004 meeting. "There were strollers everywhere you looked. A lot of them were being pushed by men, which was very encouraging as well. It was wonderful to see the number of young women in mathematics with babies. And the other thing that struck me was the comfort they had bringing their children to the Joint Mathematics Meeting. When I started out my career twenty-five years ago, I was very private about my personal life. I'm not sure I would have been so comfortable at that time bringing a baby to a national meeting, so it's wonderful to see that number of babies and the comfort with which they were being carried around."[26]

Two younger but established women mathematicians, whose educational years began after the second wave of the women's movement, agreed to talk with me about their perception of women in mathematics now. Both are currently on the board of the Association for Women in Mathematics.

When I asked Catherine Roberts what was the greatest challenge for women in mathematics now, she didn't hesitate. "Many women are having problems with the two-body problem. When should you reveal that both of you are looking for jobs together? Some people have been forced to compromise by having commuter marriages or taking 'compromise positions' such as an assistant in their husband's laboratory or that of another cooperative established person."

She speaks passionately of the differing time tables of prospective employers. There were three times that either she or her husband had an alluring job offer, and the other had good prospects in that neighborhood, but the deadline for responding to the firm offer was too much earlier in the other's search. Once she had an offer for "my *dream* job — I won't say where," but the response had to be within one week. She begged, but there was no flexibility; if she turned them down, the employer wanted to offer the job to the next in line. Two months later her husband was told he was a finalist for the job for which he was applying in the same geographical region, and invited in for an interview. "He didn't go, so we don't know whether he would have been offered the job."[27]

What to do about this? In many cases there seems to be no resolution, because the wish of the employer to move on to the next best candidate is understandable. However, Roberts thinks that within the same institution, deans might insist on a similar timetable for different departments. In the

---

[25]Carolyn Gordon, Math Medley, "Women in Mathematics Now," January 31, 2004.
[26]ibid.
[27]Catherine Roberts, telephone interview on June 10, 2004.

aforementioned paragraph, she and her husband were seeking jobs in the mathematics and chemistry departments at the same institution. It would seem possible to coordinate sibling departments so that extending offers would be less than two months apart.[28]

When asked if there are fewer micro-inequities in 2004 than when she first came to national meetings in 1991, she responded, "Absolutely."[29]

Catherine Roberts (b. 1965) has made her marriage a priority. Twice she and her husband have changed jobs in order to be able to stay together in academic positions. Each time they've been on the job market, each has turned down preferable jobs because of their desire to find jobs where they could continue to live together while they worked.

Catherine Roberts is shown here with the Grand Canyon in the background. Her research has involved developing a mathematical model of recreational white-water rafting traffic patterns in the Grand Canyon, funded by the National Park Service. She is also editor of the journal *Natural Resource Modeling*. Photo courtesy of Catherine Roberts.

She has recently achieved tenure for the second time in her career. She notices that if she hadn't moved around, she would now be a full professor and perhaps a department chair. However, she does enjoy her position at the College of the Holy Cross in Worcester, Massachusetts. Her husband is at Worcester Polytechnic Institute, "just down the road." Holy Cross is another institution that was all male until the past few decades. Now there

---

[28]ibid.

[29]Catherine Roberts, personal email, June 13, 2004.

are seven women and nine men in the mathematics department — just one
person shy of parity!

"The department is so. . . nice! . . . the college is extremely family-friendly."
Without her asking, the department chair scheduled all her classes between
10:00 AM and 2:00 PM so she would be free when her school-aged children
were home.

She postponed having children until she had completed her doctorate.
"I got pregnant the day that we both signed contracts so we knew we could
get jobs together. And, yes, you can publish that." This resulted in her first
baby being born in February, after she taught earlier on the same day. She
was the second women hired by that department, and the first woman had no
children, so this was "the department's first baby. There was no maternity
leave policy, but everyone was very accommodating and very nice." She
took a week off, and then there was a week-long spring break. When her
son was three weeks old, she resumed teaching.

The logistical problems of child care have been a "big headache." She
had just paid the last child care bill as I talked to her; it felt like a great
triumph. Nevertheless, she breastfed her firstborn for eighteen months and
her second son for fourteen months. Living close to the campus and having
child care at home, she was able to dash home between classes for feedings.
Her sons were six and eight in 2004.

She went to her first national meeting in 1991 (and soon became an
actor in the micro-inequity skits). At that time, as she remembers, the
ladies room was almost empty. That is no longer true. When she sees it
full, she is delighted. "It's a funny gauge, but it is really noticeable!"[30]

Helen Moore (b. 1966) also notices significant changes in the treatment toward women during her career, and she feels there are fewer micro-
inequities. She remembers people in the past saying things like, "Oh, she's
just a co-author and probably didn't contribute anything." The community
is now generally much more supportive of women and minorities.

Earlier in her career, she made the opposite choice from Roberts with
regard to the family vs. career balance. "It seemed like a huge sacrifice,"
she said about the prospect of winding her career around someone else's.
She would like to have a life partner and a child, but this is not something
anyone accomplishes at an appointed time — either by hard work or by
clicking one's fingers. Upon completing her Ph.D., she accepted a tenure-
track job at a liberal arts college that supported her research and travel, but
was in a geographically isolated small town. She later left that position for
the chance to teach and do research at Stanford University for several years.

She is now Associate Director of the American Institute of Mathematics (AIM) in Palo Alto, California. She loves this work. She spends some
of her time doing research in the mathematical modeling of leukemia and
HIV, and some of her time helping arrange for mathematicians to come to

---

[30]Catherine Roberts, telephone interview, June 10, 2004.

Helen Moore warming up for one of her favorite activities, an Ultimate
Frisbee tournament. Photo courtesy of Helen Moore.

the Institute for workshops about their own varied research interests. She
also attends conferences for women and minorities in mathematics, collects
names, interests, and addresses, and emails people when research opportunities arise in their field. "A lot of good will is out there, but there is a lack
of knowledge. My goal is to connect the people who want to help with the
people they can help."[31] She doesn't know of any other position like this in
mathematics.

When asked what she sees as the biggest hurdles for women mathematicians now, she responds, "responsibilities outside the career — motherhood
and running a household. Expectations are higher for women."[32] A recent
report by Stanford University of its faculty concluded that women felt that
the demands of their career were too high, but men much less so.[33] The
committee hypothesized that women feel more torn between their career and
their outside life. Changing these patterns requires changing the atmosphere
of the entire culture.

---

[31] Helen Moore, telephone conversation on June 10, 2004.
[32] ibid.
[33] www.stanford.edu/dept/provost/womenfacultyreport/PACWF.pdf, page 8.

A recent book, *The Door and the Dream*,[34] about the women who made it to the National Academy of Sciences, reports that many of these women tried to reduce their work load. They tried to avoid teaching and advising altogether, typically either by taking a research position or by working in a spouse's lab. Moore advocates making more reasonable demands on all academics, perhaps redefining success somewhat. "The current academic structure was put together at an unusual time in history when an academic had a full-time partner running the household."

This is true; American academic traditions were established in the late nineteenth and early twentieth century. Before the mid-nineteenth century women and men had similar obligations. The concept of a "family wage" for men — so that they could support a family without their wives' being distracted from homemaking by earning money outside the home — was one of the major issues of the unions, which began in the late nineteenth century and whose power peaked in the mid-twentieth century. As we saw in the account of Barbara Keyfitz's father on page 178, the "family wage" reached (the largely non-unionized) academia only in the second half of the twentieth century. When unions then lost power, United States income taxes on the very wealthy were cut and money was concentrated in the hands of the super-rich, shifting the primary tax burden to the middle class.

This loss coincided with the second wave of the women's movement, and some women, typically including the most articulate, were glad for the expectation that they would be working outside the home. This grateful group included most women mathematicians. However, as Moore observed, academic work patterns solidified while most academics had a supportive partner maintaining the home. Doing two full-time jobs is difficult for people with less energy than Lillian Gilbreth. Many find it impossible, but others struggle along, maintaining adequate careers but becoming deeply tired and having little time for self-nurturing and for the citizenship activities that are so necessary for maintaining a healthy democracy.

Another issue raised by Helen Moore (with her wide sweep of perspective) is the "lack of regulation or poor legislation regarding child care." Susan Holmes, now an associate professor of statistics at Stanford University, told her that having babies and small children while a student in France turned out to be a great idea. "All French towns have very solid child-care facilities. I lived in a village of 1,000 people for which we created our own childcare facility with a lot of help from the government."[35] Safe and competent child care is amply available in France, protected by government regulation. Holmes adds, "At Stanford, we lose most of our women to industry because they feel they can have families and a career there." Moore observes, "When I talk to women in Europe, they say, 'I just had my children whenever I wanted to'." In the United States public child care is scant

---

[34]Elga Wasserman, *The Door and the Dream: Conversations with Eminent Women in Science*, Joseph Henry Press, 2000.

[35]Susan Holmes, email on August 4, 2004.

because "if anything goes wrong, there is litigation, so people are afraid to provide child care."[36] This, compounded with the low salaries of child care providers, results in a serious scarcity in the United States compared to many European countries.

Moore notes that the tenure clock is also an issue. She points out that some places now have a policy in place addressing this, typically by adding one extra year to the tenure deadline for each newborn (born or adopted), up to two children.

Moore is in favor of allowing more time on certain examinations — not unlimited time but more time per problem than is currently allotted for high-stake graduate examinations. Some research indicates gender differences can be eliminated by changing testing conditions in this manner.[37] Awareness of this research mandates a rethinking of the examinations that are used to determine who is allowed to write a Ph.D. thesis. Are students who are able to think more deeply being weeded out in favor of those who think more quickly?

Moore also supports the use of double-blind refereeing for mathematical journals. This was tried briefly by the AMS when Moore was a child in the mid-1970s and Mary Gray was on the Council. It was quickly dropped "because nobody was making an issue of it any more."[38] Gray remembers, "The establishment comment was, 'How can you tell if it is any good if you don't know who wrote it?' It is a problem not only for women, but for those from less prestigious institutions (which, of course, includes proportionately more women)."[39] As I remember, the editors said it was too hard to get referees if the authors' names were omitted. They also argued that reviewers could probably identify the author because of the references, but if this were mostly true, it would seem that pleasing those who wanted double-blind refereeing would have been easy.

Like Gordon, Moore mentioned the effects of stereotype vulnerability, and Claude Steele's research demonstrating the effect that expectations can have on student test scores.[40] She also emphasized the implications of the Sadkers' research indicating that not only does differential treatment of the sexes occur in American classrooms, but when groups of teachers are shown videotapes of classes, they do not notice the routine gender discrimination until it is specifically pointed out to them. This happens in spite of the fact that the teachers know the Sadkers' agenda. Rerunning the tape is routinely needed to get willing teachers to perceive what they saw but did not observe

---

[36]Helen Moore, telephone conversation on June 10, 2004.

[37]David Goldstein, Diane Haldane, and Carolyn Mitchell, "Sex Differences in Visual-Spatial Ability: The Role of Performance Factors," *Memory & Cognition*, 1990, 18:15, pp. 546-550, p. 549.

[38]Mary Gray, personal email, June 12, 2004.

[39]ibid.

[40]www.pbs.org/wgbh/pages/frontline/shows/sats/interviews/steele.html

in the first showing — even though they knew they should be looking for gender discrimination.

Helen Moore's overall observation is that many people want to help, but lack information to act. She advocates a resource database in which women and minorities mathematicians could enter their own information. Then others who want a speaker or job candidate could search by research field or geographic area. Already SIAM (the Society for Industrial and Applied Mathematics) and the American Physical Society have such data bases. Almost all federally financed workshops must include a reasonable number of women and minorities, and such a database would help them locate such people. It is her job to help groups funded by AIM to locate such people, but some mathematical institutes and funding sources do not provide such a service.[41]

Carolyn Gordon, 2003-2005 president of the Association for Women in Mathematics, said in early 2004, "Overt discrimination is much less than it was in the past, and the professional societies are very cognizant of the need to encourage women to go into mathematics and to give more recognition to women in mathematics. They've been very supportive of the programs of the Association for Women in Mathematics and have had programs themselves that encourage women.... Discrimination is much more subtle and mostly unintentional." When asked what her goals are for the next few decades, she responded, "Of course, I would hope to see complete equity, where the number of men and women mathematicians are roughly equal and women feel completely comfortable integrating their personal and professional lives. We already are seeing women receiving more and more recognition, and we hope that will continue. Maybe we will see the first woman to receive the Fields Medal."[42]

---

[41]Helen Moore, telephone conversation on June 10, 2004.
[42]Carolyn Gordon, Math Medley, "Women in Mathematics Now," January 31, 2004.

CHAPTER 10

Minorities in Mathematics Now (2004)

Writing about minorities in mathematics at the present time is even more risky for a white woman than writing about women now. However, the topic is an obvious one, and it can be approached both statistically and anecdotally. As with the status of women in mathematics, it would appear that there has been considerable improvement, at least for the most fortunate, but it is even more obvious that equity is still far away. Even more than with gender, it seems clear that a drastic economic and educational transformation of our culture must precede equity in mathematical communities. However, in contrast to just a few decades ago, both African Americans and Latinos are much in evidence at national mathematics conferences. It appears that even in the Southeast Section of the Mathematical Association of America, African Americans are welcomed and participating, even as leaders.

The good news is the derivative. From 1993 through 1997, 75 Latinos earned doctorates in mathematics; from 1998 through 2002, 84 did, an increase of 12 percent. In 1993-1997, 37 blacks earned doctorates in mathematics; in the subsequent five-year period 75 did, an increase of 103 percent. Comparable figures for Native Americans are five and eleven, an apparent increase of 120 percent.[1] Both of the first two groups include immigrants, and since they are not further disaggregated, it is not possible to be sure what is happening to people born in the United States and those coming here as young children.

The counting problems with Native Americans seem even worse. Robert Megginson, a Native American mathematician at the University of Michigan who has been Deputy Director of the Mathematical Sciences Research Institute in Berkeley and a candidate for president of the MAA, points out that varying criteria are used to define "Native American." Failure to differentiate sometimes between being Native American and having Native American ancestry, particularly when reporting the ethnicity of others, can lead to great overcounts of Native Americans in certain populations. In particular, the actual number of Native American Ph.D. mathematicians may be

---

[1]Herbert A. Medina, "Doctorate Degrees in Mathematics Earned by Blacks, Hispanics/Latinos, and Native Americans: A Look at the Numbers," *Notices of the AMS*, August, 2004, 51:7, pp, 772-775, p. 773.

in the neighborhood of fifteen, a fraction of the much larger numbers often reported.[2]

The bad news, in general, is that the numbers are so small. Over the ten-year period of 1993-2002 only 2.6 percent of the doctoral degrees in mathematics granted in this country to citizens or permanent residents went to Latinos, who constituted 11.9 percent of the U.S. population in the 2000 census. Only 1.9 percent of the doctoral degrees in mathematics went to blacks, although the 2000 census claimed they were 12.2 percent of the U.S. population. Native Americans with 0.7 percent of the population reportedly received 0.3 percent of the doctorate degrees in mathematics.[3]

Recent numbers are very slightly more comforting. According to the annual survey of the mathematical sciences, of the 441 recipients of doctorates in mathematics from American institutions in 2004 who were U.S. citizens, 12 were black (2.7 percent) and 13 were Latino (2.9 percent).[4] Comparable figures in 2003 were 16 blacks (3.3 percent) and 12 Latinos (2.5 percent) among 489 U.S. citizens.[5] In 2004 the numbers were 12 blacks (2.9 percent) and 8 Latinos (1.9 percent) among 418 U.S. citizens.[6] The numbers *may* be increasing but they are clearly too small to indicate a convincing trend.

Chapter 6 ("Latinos Mathematicians") includes mostly recent stories, since few are available from previous eras in the United States. The immigration of Latinos has accelerated in recent decades. However, remembering the survey of William Vélez in 1978 that indicated there were only seven Mexican-Americans on the full-time faculty of doctoral-granting mathematics departments in the U.S. Southwest (reported in Chapter 6), I did a similar survey in the summer of 2004.

There are now eight Mexican Americans (by Tapia's definition given in Chapter 6) tenured or on tenure track in mathematics departments in all the 22 institutions of California, Arizona, New Mexico, and Texas that grant doctorates in mathematics. There are also three Mexican American statisticians, and since Vélez' 1978 survey included Richard Griego, who was a statistician teaching in a mathematics department, one might reasonably include statisticians in a comparable counting. I have located 26 other Latinos who were born in Mexico, Spain, the Caribbean, Central America or South America, but who did not come to the U.S. until graduate school or later, and now are also tenured or on tenure track in these institutions. Since almost fifteen percent of the United States population is now Latino (three

---

[2]Robert Megginson, personal email, January 12, 2005.

[3]Medina, p. 773.

[4]Ellen E. Kirkman, James W. Maxwell, and Colleen Rose, "2004 Annual Survey of the Mathematical Sciences," *Notices of the AMS*, 52:2, February, 2005, p. 243.

[5]Ellen E. Kirkman, James W. Maxwell, and Colleen Rose, "2003 Annual Survey of the Mathematical Sciences," *Notices of the AMS*, 51:2, February, 2004, p. 219.

[6]Ellen E. Kirkman, James W. Maxwell, and Colleen Rose, "2002 Annual Survey of the Mathematical Sciences," *Notices of the AMS*, 50:2, February, 2003, p. 239.

times the percentage of 1980) and they are concentrated in the Southwest, these numbers are appallingly low.

The Mexican Americans now tenured or on tenure track in the departments of the Southwest granting doctorates in mathematics include three from the 1978 survey: Efraim Armendariz, professor and department chair at the University of Texas at Austin; Richard Tapia, director of the Center for Excellence and Equity in Education and the Noah Harding Professor of Computational and Applied Mathematics at Rice University; and William Vélez, distinguished professor at the University of Arizona. The others are Carlos Castillo-Chavez professor at Arizona State University; Edward Dean, associate professor at the University of Houston; Dante DeBlassie, associate professor at Texas A&M; James Epperson, associate professor at the University of Texas at Arlington; and Oscar Gonzalez, assistant professor at the University of Texas at Austin. John C. Baez, professor at the University of California at Riverside, is sometimes considered in this group, but since his mother is of Dutch-Irish American descent and neither she nor her son speak Spanish (and the father has no accent), this designation is debatable. Rudy Guerra and Javier Rojo are professors of statistics at Rice University, and Francisco Samaniego is now professor of statistics at the University of California at Davis; he is the statistician that Vélez missed in 1978. There are twelve names in this paragraph, hardly more than the eight (including Samaniego) in 1978, although the percentage of Latinos in the U.S. population has tripled.

There are also five other Latinos — by a broader definition — each at the University of New Mexico and the University of Texas at Austin, four at New Mexico State University, three at Texas A&M University, and two each at UCLA and the University of Arizona. One is on each of the mathematics faculties of the University of Texas at Arlington, the Naval Postgraduate School, and the University of California at Davis, Berkeley, and Santa Cruz. There appear to be no Latinos by any definition in ten universities in the Southwest that grant doctorates in mathematics, including the University of North Texas, Texas Technical University, the University of Texas at Dallas, Baylor University, Southern Methodist University, New Mexico Technical University, Cal Tech, Stanford University, Claremont Graduate School, or the University of California at San Diego. Altogether there are 38 Latino mathematicians in the doctoral-granting institutions of the Southwest.

It is interesting to contemplate these lists while remembering William Vélez' comments about the University of California system reported in Chapter 6. There are no Mexican-American mathematics faculty in doctoral-granting mathematics departments in the California system unless John Baez, who doesn't speak Spanish, is counted. Francisco Samaniego is in the statistics department of UC Davis. In the larger list (including these two) there are a total of eight Latinos in California, compared to thirteen in New

Mexico and Arizona, which have a combined population of less than a quarter of California. The remaining 17 are in Texas, which has a population somewhat more than half that of California's.

The situation with African American mathematicians is more encouraging. William Massey, the first black mathematician to become tenured at Princeton, has been active in generating new black mathematicians. "Rather than waiting around to see if I would be getting new colleagues, I have been busy creating them."[7] He recognizes, of course, that the potential colleagues have to make an enormous effort themselves; he is clear about the need for both personal responsibility and social support for an individual's success.

Massey was one of the black mathematicians of New Jersey that I interviewed in 1986, when he had a relatively new doctorate in mathematics. He said then, "I would like young blacks not to be ashamed of being interested in mathematics and science. If a black is in sports or entertainment, everyone thinks it is great. If you excel in math or science, they ask, 'What good is that for our people?' But I think they are expressing their own insecurity."

When I asked him in 2004 if he would stand by his 1986 statement, he replied, "Unfortunately, one can listen to the recent complaints Bill Cosby has made of some black students not appreciating the value of an education to see not too much has changed." However, he does emphasize, "New things have happened."

William Massey (b. 1956) was born in Jefferson City, Missouri, and grew up in St. Louis. There he was able to participate in a program for gifted students. He observes that one of his friends in that program, James Ellis, is now editor of *Business Week*. He knew then that he was interested in patterns. He also learned that blacks could be intellectual leaders; most of the white parents in St. Louis either paid to have their children go to private school or moved to the suburbs, so the children in his "gifted" program were primarily black.

When he was about to begin tenth grade, his parents were able to move to University Heights, a suburb of St. Louis. They were both teachers with master's degrees; his mother taught home economics and his father taught history. He has one sibling, an older brother.

At University City Senior High School he had a superb physics teacher, John Wiegers. On the basis of his high school course, he was able to place out of first year physics at Princeton University. The summer after his senior year at Princeton, 1977, he worked at Bell Labs and did research that resulted in his first publication. He now has published about fifty research papers.

Bell Labs then paid for him to go to graduate school. Bell Labs had hired its first black scientist, William Lincoln Hawkins, in 1942, five years before Jackie Robinson integrated the baseball major leagues. Hawkins, a chemist,

---

[7]William Massey, telephone interview on July 29, 2004.

devised a plastic coating for copper cables resistant to radiation; the lead that had been used previously was eaten by squirrels and other animals, but the wires covered with Hawkins' plastic lasted much longer. Hawkins died in 1994, and now James West is the senior black scientist. In the late 1960s West started the Bell Labs "Cooperative Research Fellowship Program" for minorities; he led the black scientists in persuading their employer that a fellowship program was needed. It helped that AT&T, the parent company of Bell Labs, was a monopoly and that there had been riots in Newark; a monopoly has a major incentive to appear socially concerned because it remains a monopoly only at the pleasure of the government. Each new doctoral candidate was provided a mentor; Massey's was James McKenna.

After receiving a Ph.D. in mathematics from Stanford University in 1981, Massey became a Member of the Technical Staff at Bell Labs. He comments, "AT&T was a monopoly and Bell Labs was the center of the universe. Why look at any other place?" He describes the 70s, 80s and 90s at Bell Labs as "the Harlem Renaissance for black scientists."[8]

Massey mentored six students himself while at Bell Labs. His first protegee was Arlie Petters, who now has a tenured appointment jointly in mathematics and physics at Duke University, which forty years ago would not even allow blacks and whites to eat in the same facility. Massey's last student, Robert Hampshire, went with him to Princeton and will be his first doctoral graduate there.

Mentoring individuals was not enough. Massey wanted to create a community of black mathematicians. Working closely with physicists and chemists at Bell Labs, he knew that each of those disciplines had an active black research group. The National Society of Black Physicists had had annual meetings since the mid-1970s. The chemists also had been meeting for about twenty years. He thought to himself, "Why not us?"

In 1995 he organized the first CAARMS conference (the Council for African American Researchers in the Mathematical Sciences) in which black mathematicians can share their research with each other. In the ten years since, fifty of the graduate student participants have already earned doctorates in mathematics. These conferences meet in late June in various parts of the country, usually with about eighty participants. Since the second year, there have been poster sessions with typically about twenty presentations by graduate students a year. Thus far Massey has organized all of the CAARMS conferences. "What is gratifying about being involved in CAARMS is that rather than sitting around wondering if anyone is going to pop up somewhere, you can actually look down the pipeline," he observes.[9]

Meanwhile, the AT&T monopoly was broken and Bell Labs became less idyllic. It has only 40 percent of the technical staff in 2004 that it had five years ago. In 1999 the Department of Operations Research and Financial

---

[8]ibid.
[9]ibid.

Engineering was formed at nearby Princeton University. In 2001 Massey joined the faculty of that department as the Edwin S. Wilsey Professor, thereby becoming the second black mathematician to have a tenured position in an Ivy League institution. (The first was C. Dwight Lahr at Dartmouth.) He is also a member of the Applied and Computation Mathematics Program at Princeton and an associate member of the department of mathematics, which means that mathematics students can do their doctoral research under his supervision.

He says he has gained a new insight recently. His career's first twenty years were spent at Bell Labs where good research was going on and was more welcoming of minorities than academia, but if you really want to see more minority Ph.D.s, you have to go where they are created, so he encourages younger mathematicians now to go into academia. However, the great increase in the number of black research mathematicians during his own career means he doesn't feel the sense of isolation that he once did.[10]

Massey sees the relationship of CAARMS to NAM (the National Association of Mathematics), which is the heir of the original 1969 conference of African American mathematics faculty, as analogous to that between the AMS and the MAA. "Sometimes black organizations fall into the trap of having to be everything to everybody." Massey sees advantages in having two organizations for black mathematicians. The June conference of CAARMS, which includes graduate students, is balanced by the NAM MathFest for undergraduates each fall. Also, NAM has a dinner and a program embedded in the January Joint Mathematics Meetings. The Granville-Brown-Haynes lecture is a presentation by a new Ph.D., and the Clayton-Talbot lecture is delivered by a well established African American mathematician.

SIAM has a Diversity Day embedded in its joint meeting. Diversity Day is the brainchild of Margaret Wright, the white chair of the computer science department of New York University; she and Richard Tapia organize Diversity Day in SIAM as part of the SIAM meetings. It is usually Wednesday and includes a series of talks by graduate students about their research. "It's a welcome to the research community."

Scott Williams is another black research mathematician who has spent significant time increasing the visibility of black research mathematicians. He hosts a website[11] that includes biographies of five hundred Mathematicians in the African Diaspora (MAD). About three hundred are African Americans. Most have doctorates, but Williams has also posted some whose research qualifies them for inclusion although they don't have the paper credential. The website also includes some biographies of whites who have been involved in the movement.

Scott Warner Williams (b. 1943) was born in Staten Island, New York, but spent his early years in Greensboro, North Carolina, where his

---

[10]ibid.

[11]http://www.math.buffalo.edu/mad

father was a professor of psychology at North Carolina A&M, "one of the better of the HBCUs [Historically Black Colleges and Universities]." One of his uncles lived with them when Scott was four and played math games with the tot.

When Scott was five, his nuclear family moved away from the uncle because his father took a position as chair of the psychology department at Morgan State in Baltimore. Uncle and nephew wrote letters including math games, and whenever they visited, the math games and puzzles would continue. By the time he was eleven, Scott did not need such play any longer; he was hooked on serious mathematics. That uncle was an artist, although Scott did have another uncle who was a math education professor. He was an only child and an only grandchild. He missed having a sibling, but he received plenty of attention from the previous generation.

Eventually his father became the vice president of Morgan State and then acting president. "He hated administration, as do I." [12]

His mother, Beryl Warner Williams, was "more political." She grew up in Bangor and was the second black to graduate from the University of Maine in any field and the first to get a master's degree. Her younger sister was third and second, respectively. Beryl's master's degree was in mathematics, and she told her son she wanted to get a Ph.D. but she couldn't find any university that would admit her. She taught at Claflin College in Orangeburg, South Carolina, where she met Scott's father.

Morgan State would hire her to teach mathematics only part-time, so she earned a master's degree in English and taught full-time in the English department there. "Stephens [chair of the mathematics department from 1947-1962] wasn't there yet. He would have had no problem hiring a woman." For many years she was a dean at Morgan State.

When he became college age, Williams lived at home and went to Morgan State. He reflects on his mother's career troubles, "When I was there, there were a number of couples at Morgan." In 1962 Clarence Stephens, the third black mathematician to spend a year at the Princeton Institute for Advanced Study, won a National Science Foundation grant that allowed him to provide a summer of advanced study for eight undergraduates, four men and four women including Williams. All four of the men subsequently earned doctorates, three in mathematics, and one in mathematically intense electrical engineering. Two of the women set up their own successful businesses using operations research. The other two could not be traced in the 1980s.

In 1964 Williams was graduated from Morgan State, and in 1969 he was granted a Ph.D. in mathematics by Lehigh University in Bethlehem, Pennsylvania. Then he was offered and accepted a position as research associate at Penn State. During this time Williams was active in the civil rights and

---

[12]Scott Williams, telephone interview, June 18. 2004.

Scott Williams at the time he received the 2004 award from *Science Spectrum* magazine and Career Communications Group, Inc., as one of the top fifty most important blacks in research science. Photo courtesy of Scott Williams.

anti-war movements to the detriment of his mathematical research. However, the University of Buffalo took a chance on hiring him in 1971; Williams suspects it was because of the new attitude toward blacks. He has worked hard to prove worthy of the appointment; by now he has almost forty mathematical publications (not counting the MAD website). A few are in set theory and dynamics, but his major field is topology. In 1985 he became a full professor.

When I asked him why he had started the website, he immediately replied, "It started when I first came to Buffalo in 1971. There was a newspaper headline saying 'University hires one of the five best black mathematicians.' I thought that was insane. I was an assistant professor. I wanted to know who was around."[13]

---

[13]ibid.

However, it was time for him to do mathematical research, so he didn't find out much until 1996 (although I remember him eagerly participating after one of my talks about black mathematicians in the late 1980s). He was inspired by a new "magnificent website about African Americans, but there were only four postings in mathematics — and some weren't mathematicians!" However, it was then possible for individuals to set up websites, so he began. He first posted the dozens of black mathematicians in *Black Mathematicians and Their Works*,[14] along with those in my papers and a preliminary edition of Johnny Houston's forthcoming book based on biographies included in NAM newsletters. Then Williams began to do his own research. The MAD website began in May, 1997. It is at http://www.math.buffalo.edu/mad.

Most of the subjects on the website were glad to be included, but there were some resisters. One was adamant that he did not want to be included on the website, even though he was undeniably a black mathematician and all the information on the MAD website was true and posted elsewhere. After an exchange of acrimonious email, he theatened a lawsuit. Williams handed the letter to the university lawyer, "and they took care of it. The University has been completely supportive." (I too have received a threat of a lawsuit because of my biographical research, but not while writing this book. Since I have not tried to include "all" of any one category, I have used only public information and reports of conversations and emails cheerfully volunteered.)

Williams writes most of the website. "It's fun. I tried to limit it to late nights after 9:00 P.M. and on weekends. You can do research on weekends, but my research doesn't function so well after nine o'clock. Before I had my stroke in 1998, I slept an average of four hours a night. Most nights I slept five hours, but I would stay up all night twice a week, so the average was about four hours — for probably thirty or forty years. I can't stay up all night now. I've always been a high-energy person. It works well as long as I keep my emotions calm.

"After the stroke in March of 1998, I was off my feet for a month or six weeks. I taught the following fall but just one course. I didn't do a whole lot of math that time because I was tired a lot. I taught full-time the following spring but it was hard." Now he's fine, except that his speech slurs when he is tired.

Along with being a mathematician and an activist, Williams was "an ardent blacksmith for eleven years, 1971-1982. I was doing decorative things; I showed at the Smithsonian and Rochester Folk Art Show."[15] For 33

---

[14]Virginia K. Newell, Joella H. Gipson, L. Waldo Rich, and Beauregard Stubblefield, *Black Mathematicians and Their Works*, Dorrance and Company, 1980.

[15]Scott Williams, telephone interview, July 18, 2004.

years he's been an active student of Gurdjieff, a teacher or spiritual Russian/Armenian teacher, who died before Williams was born. He has "three lovely daughters" by his first marriage.[16]

When asked how much he believes the situation of black mathematicians has changed in his lifetime, his reaction is much more emphatic than that of Massey, who was born only thirteen years later but whose early years benefited from the civil rights movement led by Martin Luther King. "It's changed a lot. First of all, at least the possibility of working at any university is now clearly present. It only *started* to happen when I was starting out as a new Ph.D. in 1969. I was hired by Penn State, which was an amazing thing. My parents, who were academic people, didn't think it could happen. When I wanted to do research, they just didn't think it was possible. Things had started to change a few years earlier. A few people were getting positions in the mid-60s. Eugene Madison [b. 1933] was hired by Iowa in 1970. Dwight Lahr [b. 1944] became the first Ivy League tenured person, I believe. He was hired by Dartmouth in 1975 and tenured in 1981.

"There is another underlying change. Somehow people that have great research potential are being sought after. At one time they hired African Americans so they could say they had one. Or they hired people with great potential. In general, I did not produce. I was lucky to get a job at Buffalo when I decided to become a real researcher. At Penn State I was busy doing politics. It was civil rights time and anti-war time. That was to be my mathematical downfall. On the other hand, those endeavors needed people who could think well. It was just bad for my career. I say to youngsters, 'At this point, you don't need to do it and it is bad for your career. Wait until you're tenured or preferably full professor. Then people will pay attention to you.'

"However, Jonathan Farley has done it all. He just became Harvard's Scientist of the Year for 2004, an award given only to Harvard graduates. He deserves that. He has solved famous problems that were unsolved for decades. As a graduate student he got the award for the best graduate student at Oxford. He's done very well, but he's involved in politics. He even ran for Congress on the Green Party ticket."[17]

Jonathan D. Farley (b. 1970) was born in Rochester, New York. Both his parents were on the faculty of nearby SUNY Rockport[18] and are now professors emeriti of that university. His father is a native of Guyana and holds a Ph.D. from the London School of Economics. His mother, a Jamaican, holds a Ph.D. in American history and is a Regent of the State of New York. All four of their sons are Harvard graduates.[19] (Anthony is a professor of law at Boston College; Felipe is a former player in the

---

[16]ibid.

[17]ibid.

[18]ibid.

[19]www.math.buffalo.edu/mad/PEEPS/farley_jonathan.html

Puerto Rican professional basketball league and is now a patent attorney; and Christopher is a senior editor for news at *Time magazine.*[20])

Jonathan was graduated *summa cum laude* from Harvard in 1991 with the second highest grade point average in his class of about 1600 students; he received 29 A's and 3 A-'s. His undergraduate advisor was Garrett Birkhoff. After winning Oxford University's highest mathematics awards, the Senior Mathematical Prize and Johnson University Prize in 1994, he received a D.Phil. in mathematics from Oxford in 1995 under lattice theorist Hilary Priestley. He then spent two years as a post-doctoral fellow at the Mathematical Sciences Research Institute in Berkeley, California. He joined the faculty of Vanderbilt University in 1996, and in 2001-2002 was one of only four Americans to win a Fulbright Distinguished Scholar Award to the United Kingdom. By 2003 he was an associate professor with tenure at Vanderbilt, on leave as a visiting professor of applied mathematics at the Massachusetts Institute of Technology.

He has solved several problems that had been open for decades. In 2003-2004 he solved a problem on "linear extensions of posets" (partially ordered sets) that had been posed by MIT Professor Richard Stanley in 1981. In 2004 he solved a problem attributed to combinatorialist Richard Rad posed in the monograph *Transversal Theory* in 1971, a problem from Richard Stanley's classic text *Enumerative Combinatorics* published in 1986, and two conjectures posed by Robert Quackenbush, executive editor of the journal *Algebra Universalis* from 1985. Previously, Farley had settled another conjecture made by Stanley that had been open for 24 years, and had solved a problem of universal algebra pioneer George Grätzer that had remained unsolved for 34 years.[21]

In the February 18, 2002, issue of the *Guardian* newspaper in Britain, he wrote eloquently about mathematician John Nash and the just-released movie, "A Beautiful Mind," in a piece titled "We Mathematicians Seek a More Elusive Beauty."[22] Farley speaks to students about, "How to Get Straight A's in College." He has written for the hip-hop magazine *The Source* and for the black women's magazine *Essence.* In 2001 *Ebony* magazine named him a "leader of the Future" and he was also profiled in *Upscale* magazine. To an interviewer at the *Black Issues in Higher Education,* he said, "The best thing for me was to get my doctorate here in England.... I'm convinced that no matter what American university I went to, I would not have been recognized."[23]

The city of Cambridge, Massachusetts, officially declared March 19, 2004, to be "Dr. Jonathan David Farley Day."[24] Also in 2004 Farley won the

---

[20]Jonathan Farley, personal email, January 25, 2005.

[21]ibid.

[22]www.math.buffalo.edu/mad/PEEPS/farley_jonathand.getsout.html

[23]Kendra Hamilton, "A Calculating Career," *Black Issues in Higher Education,* January 3, 2002.

[24]http://math.mit.edu/people/faculty/farley.html

Jonathan Farley giving his presentation at the 2004 annual Claytor-Woodard Lecture for the National Association of Mathematicians. Photo courtesy of Jacqueline Giles.

Harvard Foundation's "Distinguished Scientist of the Year" award, a medal presented on behalf of the president of Harvard University for "outstanding achievements and contributions in the field of mathematics."

His work applying lattice theory to counterterrorism has been featured in *The Chronicle of Higher Education, Science News Online*, the *Economist* magazine, the *New York Times, USA Today*, and on Fox News television and Air America Radio. He has also been an invited guest on BBC World News Television and U.S. National Public Radio. In 2005 he is a Visiting Scholar at Harvard University. His current project is establishing an Institute for Mathematical Methods in Counterterrorism.[25]

Another young superachieving black mathematician is Trachette Jackson. She was the third black mathematician to receive a Sloan fellowship. Kate Okikiojlou, now at the University of California at San Diego was the first; her father, a Nigerian, is one of the most distinguished mathematical physicists in the world; her mother is British. Arlie Petters, the first student mentored by William Massey at Bell Labs, was the second.[26]

Trachette Jackson (b. 1972) came from a less academic background than Massey, Williams, and Farley. Her father started college but didn't finish. His career was in the Air Force, so they moved every two years. Her mother, who never went to college, was a homemaker. Trachette has two

[25]email from Jonathan Farley, January 25, 2005.
[26]William Massey, telephone interview, July 19, 2004.

sisters and a brother; she is the second of the four children. Her father retired in Mesa Arizona, so she went to Arizona State, as did one of her younger sisters; the other two started college, but didn't finish.

She has always been very interested in biology, so in her senior year she decided to pursue research modeling the growth of bacteria. The project became her senior honors thesis, and received gratifying recognition. She then realized how much she enjoyed applying mathematics to biology, so that was the beginning of her research career.[27] After receiving her bachelor's degree in 1994 from Arizona State, she went to the University of Washington, where she was granted a master's degree in applied mathematics two years later. In 1998 she was awarded a doctorate from the University of Washington with the dissertation topic, "Mathematical Models in Two-Step Cancer Chemotherapy."

Trachette Jackson
Photo courtesy of Trachette Jackson

She then was a research associate and John Hope Franklin Postdoctoral Fellow at the Center for Mathematics and Computers in the Life Sciences and Medicine at Duke University. In 2000 she joined the mathematics faculty of the University of Michigan, where her husband, Patrick Nelson, is also employed. She became associate professor in 2003. Williams adds in his web bio, "We remark that her invited lecture in 2003 at CAARMS9 at Purdue University was first rate."

---

[27] Trachette Jackson, telephone interview, July 15, 2004.

When I asked her if she had had experiences that a white male would not have in the mathematics community, she exclaimed immediately, "Oh, yes!"[28] She wrote later that the most memorable such experiences were the comments and challenges of other graduate students at the University of Washington. (What a contrast to Gloria Hewitt's experience there 35 years earlier!) For example, on her "very first day during orientation, a fellow incoming student said to me, 'I can't believe that they admitted a nontraditional student this year.' From this point on it was clear that I had to prove myself worthy of being a graduate student in mathematics."[29]

In answer to my question of what she sees as the biggest challenges for African Americans in mathematics, she had two responses. "Finding a department whose atmosphere is comfortable and conducive to our success at both the graduate and tenure-track stage of the academic career. I also think that our own self-confidence, which is a very fragile thing, can be one of the biggest barriers to success."

When I asked her if she had any advice for young African Americans who aspire to be mathematicians, she replied, "If mathematics is your dream... relentlessly pursue it!"[30]

Fern Hunt is an established black woman research mathematician who made the opposite mid-career shift from William Massey. She left academia and went to full-time research in government. When asked about the status of African Americans in mathematics now, she responded, "Almost certainly there have been tremendous changes. There are a cadre of younger mathematicians now that are going to be able to reach the very top ranks of the profession in terms of prestigious academic positions and governance of the societies.... It's only now we see minorities getting prestigious fellowships.... A black woman received a Sloan fellowship two years ago and now another. By that measure, there has been a lot of progress. A number of organizations have been increasingly active. At the top of my list is a semi-organization [CAARMS] led by William Massey at Princeton."[31]

Fern Hunt grew up in New York City, the granddaughter of Jamaican immigrants. Her father did not finish high school, but her mother went to Hunter College for two years. Her only sibling, Erica Hunt, is a published poet and writer. She went through the New York City public schools, where she was especially influenced by Charles Wilson, her science teacher in 8th and 9th grades and the faculty advisor for the school science club throughout her junior high years. Fern went to Bryn Mawr College.

With the help of a fellowship, she entered the Courant Institute, back in New York City. However, a "B" on her qualifying examination resulted in the loss of the fellowship, so she began teaching part-time at City College.

---

[28]ibid.

[29]Trachette Jackson, personal email, July 22, 2004.

[30]ibid.

[31]Fern Hunt, telephone interview, July 20, 2004.

A Martin Luther King scholarship, and she helped pay her tuition, however, she received both an M.S. and a Ph.D. from the Courant Institute, the latter in 1978.

After teaching briefly at the University of Utah, she joined the faculty of Howard University in 1978. Two years earlier Howard University had become the first traditionally black institution to award a doctorate in mathematics. The fact that by 1988 seven such degrees had been awarded implied a pent-up demand.[32] The traditional inadequate support given to the historically black colleges and universities is indicated by the fact that despite its doctoral program, Hunt taught eleven hours a semester.

She spent the 1981-1982 school year at the National Institute of Health in the Laboratory of Mathematical Biology. From 1986 to 1991 she worked part-time at the National Bureau of Standards. She was also a member of the Graduate Records Examination advisory board of the Educational Testing Service from 1988 to 1991.

In 1991 she began working full-time at the National Institute of Standards and Technology (NIST). She did not think it was a permanent change when she began. "It was not easy leaving. I enjoyed my time at Howard." However, at NIST she was able to spend full-time at research on interesting topics. She remained, and in 2000 was awarded one of the three Arthur S. Flemming Awards to a federal employee in a science.

The citation said, "Hunt was recognized for a sustained record of fundamental contributions to probability and stochastic modeling, mathematical biology, computational geometry, nonlinear dynamics, computer graphics and parallel computing. Hunt was also cited for the impact of her work in her extensive close collaborations with scientists and engineers seeking to apply these developments to diverse problems of scientific and technological interest.... She has been a mentor and leading proponent of careers in mathematics for students at the high school, undergraduate, and graduate levels, especially for women and minorities."[33]

Fern Hunt explains, "Some of my work involves collaboration with physicists and chemists, trying to understand the physical and chemical properties of materials and trying to measure these properties. This is important for U.S. commerce and trade. What standards are reasonable? I've done lots of work on new technologies. Computer graphics provide a new way to have virtual standards, not necessarily measuring a material, but instead using a computer graphic that depends on optical measurements."[34]

She gives several talks to students every year, and she also supervises summer students. However, she can do more research than in academia. "The management has been very good at NIST, and it's not an easy job. They have done well at explaining what we do to the wider community and

---

[32] James A. Donaldson, "Black Americans in Mathematics," *A Century of Mathematics in America, Part III*, pp. 449-465, p. 465.

[33] www.math.buffalo.edu/mad/PEEPS/hunt_ferny.html

[34] Fern Hunt, telephone interview, July 20, 2004.

the rest of the government, while still fostering our creativity and independence. It's a very tough balancing act, but they do it well.

"It's a great privilege to be able to do mathematics and be a mathematician, but that needs an infrastructure of political and economic stability and competence and that is eroding. The derivative is positive for black and Latinos in advanced mathematics. However, compared to the potential numbers, there is a serious problem because the schools that should nourish future talent have been taking a real hit the past two decades; the dropout rates have been horrible."[35] Indeed a recently released report identifies 2000 high schools as "drop-out factories" because at least forty percent of their freshmen fail to become twelfth graders within four years. The schools identified serve primarily African American and Latino students.[36]

The New York City public schools "were a problem" when Hunt attended them, "but they are worse now. There were many more hooks then to hold onto and pull yourself up. There were more local corporations who cared about the communities because they had to live with the results. The middle class had not entirely fled the schools. The schools were in many ways reasonable, although I could see deterioration every year." They had tracking, and she was in the top track. "There were limited opportunities for minorities and women, so Charles Wilson ended up teaching in 8th grade. These days he would have been at a university.

"I've thought about it a lot, and I've concluded that race is a social fiction. It's a deep family feud, a socially constructed caste system. The genome project has verified this; the difference within each race is greater than the genome difference between races. From Mother Nature's point of view, race is not an overwhelming factor. Color is an afterthought. Nature has many more important fish to fry.

"However, the situation in K-12 education these days is very serious for everyone in the country. For minorities it is a catastrophe. I think it is going to affect the progress that minorities have made in mathematics. I think it is very important to stem the catastrophe that is about to happen."[37]

So what is the position of minorities in mathematics now? The number of research mathematicians is growing rapidly, but is still small. The impossibility of blacks (and women) being hired in top universities that was standard forty years ago is now a possibility. But economic, political, and social pressures — along with the current emphasis on standardized testing, which can have serious consequences for our public schools — foreshadow changes that could undo the positive progress.

---

[35]ibid.

[36]*Education Week*, July 14, 2004, p. 14. The report is from Johns Hopkins University.

[37]Fern Hunt, telephone interview, July 20. 2004.

CHAPTER 11

Conclusions

People of good will can become discouraged, and too often this leads to their not taking the actions that are open to them. Ghandi once said, "What you do may seem insignificant, but it is vitally important that you do it."

When people say, "You can't fight City Hall" or tell me that some social change cannot happen, I remind them of the advent of the "special education" movement or the changes documented in this book, both of which I have witnessed in one not-yet-finished lifetime. One of the first pieces I put on my website was my account of my mentally retarded brother, diagnosed with an IQ of 50 when he was four and I was seven. In those days a handicapped child was considered a punishment by God for past sins of the mother. My mother decided, after much soul-searching and social support, that she could not believe in a God so cruel as to do this to a child because of her sins. If Bruce's retardation was not her fault, then other handicapped children's parents should not be punished either. She served as publicity chair for the New Jersey Association for Retarded Children (now ARC) for the five years when I grew from age seven to twelve, at the end of which New Jersey passed the first legislation saying that all children, no matter how handicapped, must be educated at public expense. This has had an enormous impact on our culture, and subsequently other cultures, in a manner similar to AWM's impact on EWM, The Association of European Women in Mathematics.

Now many retarded adults live in group homes within the community, many going regularly to standard jobs within our economy. My own brother supports himself living in his own efficiency apartment as the custodian at a small animal hospital. An entire new profession of special education teachers has burgeoned, and districts stretch their school budgets to educate those children who need to be in smaller classes taught by more highly educated and supported teachers. Public buildings install expensive ramps so that physically handicapped people can be included in our public life. It is clear to me that enormous change has happened on behalf of mentally and physically challenged individuals.

I am less sure of the enormity of the change for those of us "at the other end," as my mother referred to me. I wonder if there are still teenage girls who weep in their bed, as I did, and pray, "Oh, God, I'm glad to be a woman and glad to be smart, but why did you give me both?" I remember

wondering if two rights could make a wrong. Now I am unreservedly glad
to be a smart woman who was able to pursue higher mathematics. I hope
today's girls aren't told, as I was, "If you become a mathematician, you will
be the first woman mathematician." Of course, it was a false admonition
even when I was young, but I didn't realize how false it was until I repeatedly
read the name "Emmy Noether" in my graduate texts. I hope that the work
of the AAUW and others has enabled today's girls to know they need not
be excluded from abstract thinking because of their gender.

History and sociology, as mentioned in the introduction, are not nearly
as airtight as mathematics. They do not follow a logical sequence; the role
of particular examples and counterexamples is not clear. Indeed, I am sure
there are unknown, and sometimes pivotal, mathematicians whose stories
I have omitted. Why is Susan B. Anthony (1820-1906) so much better
known than Abby Kelley Foster (1810-1887),[1] who mentored her, who was
the first woman in our country to speak publicly and repeatedly before a
"promiscuous audience" (one containing both men and women), and who
traveled around the United States speaking for decades in opposition to
slavery and subjugation of women? It may be because Anthony opposed the
granting of the vote to black men before women, while Foster argued a half
a loaf was better than none. Feminists were angry at Foster for her apparent
defection, and glorified Anthony. Furthermore, Anthony lived longer into
the time where she was remembered by women who actually got the vote
and were writing about their success. Or maybe it was sheer chance that
Anthony achieved publicity first; some friend of hers wrote about her, and
later writers find it easier to quote earlier sources than to excavate buried
clues.

I do not mean to imply that our society has achieved equality for either women or minorities. A quick glance at the statistics relieves us of any
misconceptions along those lines. Women, with over half the population,
received 33 percent of the doctorates in mathematics granted to U.S. citizens by American institutions in 2004.[2] African Americans, Latinos, and
Native Americans, who together constitute 25 percent of the United States
population, earned only 6.8 percent of the doctorates in mathematics in
2004.[3] We have a long way to go, but society can make progress, and we
seem to be headed, unsteadily, in the direction of equity. The lip service
has become remarkably good, unthinkably improved during my adulthood.
I am encouraged.

Furthermore, the professional gains have occurred in my lifetime with
remarkably little cost in terms of personal choices. Beginning in the 1970s it

[1]Dorothy Sterling, *Ahead of Her Time: Abby Kelley and the Politics of Anti-Slavery*,
W.W. Norton & Company, 1994.

[2]Ellen E. Kirkman, James W. Maxwell, and Colleen Rose, "2004 Annual Survey of
the Mathematical Sciences (First Report)," Notices of the AMS, 52:2, February, 2005,
236-251, p. 237.

[3]ibid.

became easier for a woman to marry or not as she chose. It has again become acceptable for a woman to choose to live alone or to spend her personal life primarily with another woman. Raising children is now possible alone (as an increasing number of celebrity women are doing), with another woman, or with a man. The loosening of societal restrictions means that women are freer to pursue mathematics whatever their personal choices than they were a half century ago.

On the other hand, there are many influences on our future, other than our own society's social climate. Jobs moving abroad influences employment opportunities for all American mathematicians, whatever their gender or ethnicity. Economic crises in our universities affect all intellectuals. The facts that the human population has already exceeded the capacity of the planet if we are to live at a pleasant standard of living (comparable to that of the present Europeans) and that we may already have passed the maximum annual amount of accessible petroleum will have an impact on the entire human family. If these developments cause us to spat among ourselves, the good news of this book may vanish in the "last hired, first fired" syndrome. Worse, it might be that the love of mathematics drowns as we scramble for food and water.

However, the love of mathematics may show us the way. It is useful in helping us learn to share our resources, to use them efficiently, and to invent new ways to live more frugally. Mathematics requires very few natural resources; one can do it with a stick on sand. It brings lots of inexpensive pleasure to many of us.

It seems crucial that we provide the pleasure of mathematics to as many humans as possible, and that the mathematical communities become maximally diverse, reflecting the gender, sexual orientation, age, race, and ethnic composition of the outside community. Such diversity is vital for the health of the mathematical enterprises, the health of humankind, and the health of the larger global community of all living creatures. It won't be easy. We have a long way to go. But as we reflect upon the progress of the past, we see that change is possible. May our group keep growing!

The Careers of 75 African American
Mathematicians of New Jersey in Mid-1985

Of the 75 respondents, four were retired, two were full-time graduate students, and two were on maternity leave with infants less than a month old at the time of the interview. The other 68 were all employed, 40 with careers in education. (However, I suspect that most who did not respond to the survey teach in either middle or high school.) Four were in supervisory capacities, including the mathematics supervisors of both the Camden and Trenton public schools. Fifteen were high school mathematics teachers and four were middle school teachers. There were no mathematics faculty in the Ph.D.-granting departments of New Jersey, although one such person was teaching in New York City. Five, all male, were teaching in departments that conferred bachelor's and/or master's degrees. Eleven more were in either community colleges or college remedial programs, six men and five women. Many reported evidence of racism in New Jersey institutions of higher education, a sad situation apparently not matched in either pre-college institutions or non-academic employers.

What were the others doing? Because there is a serious lack of knowledge about mathematical careers, both within and outside the mathematical communities, a compilation seems in order. Eight respondents were involved in sophisticated computer programming and systems analysis, more challenging than a person educated merely in computer science would be likely to be able to do; three of these were with telephone operations, two with insurance companies, and one each with Dow Jones, a shipping company, and a legal division. Six were technical managers, deciding which job should be assigned to which computer programmer or systems analyst and helping with difficult problems as needed. Two young women were "on rotation," being groomed for top management; at that time one was in marketing and the other with personnel. Three were "systems engineers," explaining to customers and potential customers the technical services available from their employer and facilitating customers obtaining exactly what they needed. Three with doctorates in mathematics were involved with high-level, full-time research and development with private employers. Another investigated sets of real-world data using applied mathematics, comparing his results to the theoretical predictions, and presenting technical reports that included recommendations. One was a statistician in quality control for a large pharmaceutical firm. One was a program budget officer for the U.S. Army. One was a financial analyst, providing monthly analyses and recommendations for the board of directors of a giant corporation describing both its own financial activity and general economic trends that might affect its decisions. A former high school teacher had her own thriving business as a computer consultant and another former high school teacher taught fellow employees within a large corporation about computers and data processing — at a much higher salary than he had received in public school teaching. One was a mathematical examiner for the Educational Testing Service. One was a lawyer who had also started a tutorial program, under the auspices of the local NAACP, that served a hundred black youngsters in a one-to-one program. Another had become a publisher. The most publicly visible, Mildred Barry Gavin, was a dynamic member of the New Jersey legislature, an administrator at Rutgers University, and the author or co-author of six books.